A Co... ...y of
MURDERS

A Comedy of
MURDERS

John Ellwood Nicholson

For my wife Isobel

*Without whose continued support, I would never
have finished this book.*

Acknowledgements

I would like to thank those kind people who helped me through the rigorous process of completing this book, including the ever-lovely Lynne Moore, the Man for all Seasons, Gordon Manfield, and members of the brilliant Ringwood Writers Circle.

LIST OF CHARACTERS

MAIN CHARACTERS

Reginald Grosvenor Smythe (Reggie)

Cressida Smythe (Aunt Cressy)	Reggie's aunt.
Aida	Reggie's Filipina housekeeper.
Miles Elderbeck	Friend.
Mr. Lee su won	Korean neighbour/friend.
Sylvia Makepeace	Re-united lover after 40 years.
Chester (Ches) Makepeace	Reggie and Sylvia's son.
Detective Sergeant Clapp	The first investigating officer.
Detective Inspector Farthing	Took charge of the murder enquiry
Edgar Ormrod	Cressida solicitor.
Grace Pluck	Edgar Ormrod's secretary.
Gertrude Dogberry	Cressida's daughter.
Stella Pinch	Adopted Gertrude Dogberry.
Reverend Marmaduke (Duke) FitzPeter	Ringwood parish priest.
Walter Plinge	Bogus policeman and arch villain.

SECONDARY CHARACTERS

Redknapp (Red) Ormrod	Edgar Ormrod's son.
Dorothy Smerdal	Cressida's housekeeper.
Pandora	Chester Makepeace's lady friend.
Tiffany Golightly	Redknapp Ormrod's girlfriend.
Mrs. fal Kim	Mr. Lee's lady friend.
Felicity Fringe	Gertrude Dogberry's twin sister
Alexander Whacket	Solicitor finalized Cressida's estate.

PROLOGUE

Murder … premeditated cold-blooded murder. There had to be a good reason why a normal person would carry out such a heinous act … there was.

Silently entering the bedroom, the would-be-killer wearing surgical gloves and carrying a small case, crept across the carpeted floor to the side of the bed. Heavy curtains drawn across the windows shut out most of the afternoon sunlight. Half asleep, Miss Cressida Smythe became aware she was not alone.

'Is that you, Dotty?' her voice snappy and irritable. 'Tell Ormrod I want him, you know, Edgar Ormrod that is, not that silly boy of his. Tell him it's urgent.'

There was no answer.

With unsteady hands, the case was placed on a side table. Cottonwool, a syringe, and a small dark-blue bottle were taken out.

Rubbing sleep from her eyes with one hand and covering a yawn with the other, Cressida Smythe propped herself up on her right elbow, her eyes narrowed to crinkled slits. 'Oh, it's you! What are you doing here?'

Beads of cold sweat formed on the intruder's forehead who momentarily froze, eyes wide, then looked away. Opening the

1

bottle, drops of liquid were trickled onto a wad of cottonwool which was immediately pushed over Cressida's nose and mouth, so hard that there was the sound of a crack.

Cressida gave a choked gasp, disbelief in her tortured eyes - a surreal sense that it couldn't be happening. Frantically, she tried to push the hand away, but within seconds - oblivion.

A low groan escaped the assailant's throat, knowing that the killing had to be completed ... the poison had to be injected ... it couldn't wait. Gently lifting Cressida's limp arm with one hand, the syringe hovered in mid-air ... hesitating ... it was now or never.

In the beginning, God created the heavens and the earth.

Later on, he made Reginald Grosvenor Smythe, OBE,
who shall be known as Reggie.

CHAPTER ONE

Reginald Grosvenor Smythe, OBE, gently lifted the lid of a municipal park bin and looked out! The sudden bright light made him blink. Struggling to get to his feet, a mild expletive escaped his lips when his elbow came into sharp contact with a protruding hinge.

Unfortunately, the timing of his unexpected appearance was a touch ill-timed as elderly Miss Abigale Sponge, with her dog, Puddles, were at that very moment taking an early morning stroll in the park. On seeing what she mistakenly took to be the dead rising from a grave, she uttered an ear-splitting shriek, loud enough to waken the dead of Surrey. Puddles, equally shocked, emitted a nerve-shattering howl before performing a spontaneous defecation.

'Good morning to you, dear lady.' Reggie, with the aid of his silver-topped cane, stiffly climbed out of the bin. 'Pray do not be alarmed, madam.' Adjusting his monocle, he brushed pieces of detritus from his clothing. Raising his crumpled Panama hat, he gave an elegant bow. 'You see, dear lady, I have just visited middle earth and can assure you all is well there. So, please proceed on your walk in the land of our fathers, accompanied by your loyal, but loose-bowelled canine companion.'

Clutching her chest, Miss Sponge opened her mouth to scream again … but nothing came.

Stretching to loosen his rigid muscles, Reggie did his best to march off, military style, whilst poor Miss Sponge took several deep breaths before collapsing on a park bench. Feeling faint, she vainly tried to attract the attention of a passing lycra-clad jogger by pointing feebly to the bin uttering, 'I've just seen a m …m … man g … get out of ….' The jogger didn't stop.

A low early morning mist hung over the River Thames as Reggie continued along to towpath, using his key to open the gate to the gardens of the Britannia Towers. Passing the swimming pool and flower beds, he entered the foyer of Nelson Court, taking the lift to his penthouse suite.

Aida, Reggie's housekeeper, met him at the door noticing his unkempt appearance, 'Are you alright, sir?'

'Yes, thank you, Aida.' He handed her his hat and cane. 'I had an unfortunate experience last night. It was rather late and as I walked home through Canberry Gardens, the heavens opened in a torrential thunder storm. I had no raincoat nor umbrella with me, so I took temporary shelter in an empty park bin to wait until the storm passed.'

She raised her eyebrows in disbelief. 'Oh, I see, sir.'

'Unfortunately, I must have dropped off … yes, it was surprisingly comfortable in there, and I must have slept through to … well, just a quarter of an hour ago. The hallway clock showed it as twenty-past seven.

'All night, sir,' Aida quizzed, 'you sleep in bin, not in bed?'

'Yes, but no ordinary bin, Aida. This one belongs to the Royal Borough of Kingston upon Thames. I do have certain standards - you know. And let me assure you it's not a regular habit of mine, but I am now in need of a large single malt. I will then have a shower and I'll be ready for one of your excellent breakfasts. Oh, and I'll leave my suit out so you can take it to the cleaners.'

'Yes sir, I do that for you.'

'And there's a couple of dirty marks on my Panama – do what you can to clean it.'

Aida, who had only been in England from the Philippines for three months, tentatively asked, 'Your panma, sir?'

'My hat, Aida. It's called a Panama hat.'

'Oh, I see sir. There is mail for you – it come early.'

'Thank you. I will attend to it after I've changed.'

Settling in his armchair, a refreshed Reggie used an ebony blade to open an envelope. After reading the enclosed letter, he gave a deep sigh, and then rested his head in his hands. 'Oh no, poor Cressida,' his voice barely above a whisper, 'I could have … I should have, and now it's too late.' Removing his monocle, he wiped an errant tear away.

Her forehead creased in concern, Aida was unsure whether he was speaking to her or to himself. 'Can I help, sir?'

He turned, replacing his monocle as he spoke. 'No thank you, Aida,' he pointed to the letter. 'You see, this is from a firm of solicitors informing me that Miss Cressida Smythe, my Aunt Cressy, has er … well … let me put it this way, she's gone to see her Maker.'

'Has aunt far to see the maker, sir?'

Raising his voice, Reggie said, 'what in the blue-blazes …? Oh, I'm sorry, Aida.' Giving a mirthless chuckle, he added,

'I confused you. What I meant to say was my Aunt Cressy has died.'

'Oh, I sorry sir for dead aunt. In my country we have prayer for dead people – you want I say prayer for dead aunt?'

'A prayer! - well yes, why not?'

She hesitated. 'But I er ... I only know prayer in my language, Tagalog. Is that good?'

'Yes, Aida, it is very good. Being a religious woman, I'm sure she would understand.'

Closing her eyes, Aida knelt and crossed herself murmuring *'in nomine patris'* and said her piece. Reggie stood, head bowed. His thoughts and memories of Aunt Cressy struggled to line up. Every time he tried to align one, it scattered the next.

'Let me explain, Aida. My Aunt Cressy was my late father's sister. She looked after me following the death of my parents. I was only a boy at the time.'

'I understand, sir.'

'But hey,' a faint smile played along the edges of his lips, 'She'd be old - well over eighty by now which is not a bad age before kicking the proverbial bucket and toddling off to lie down in green pastures – you know, Psalm 23 and the valley of the shadow of death ... and all that.'

This only made Aida more confused. Did his aunt die seeing a maker, in blue-blazes or kicking a bucket? Deciding to leave well alone, she asked, 'You want I serve you breakfast now, sir?'

Reggie's face lit up. 'Yes, why not?' He felt a hearty meal would help to buck him up.

'I make same breakfast for you as I make yesterday?'

'Yes please. I particularly like the pancetta bacon as well as the Cumberland sausages, eggs, tomatoes and mushrooms, followed, of course, by toast, butter, Old English marmalade and tea. A jolly good English breakfast.'

Aida was pleased that the death of his aunt, bucket or no bucket, had not put him off his food.

When she wheeled in the breakfast trolley, Reggie smiled. 'Thank you, Aida, it smells delicious. Oh, and one other thing, don't forget a Mr Miles Elderbeck is coming at eleven-thirty, so have a lightish lunch ready for twelve noon.'

'Yes sir, I do that. What food the man like?'

'I've absolutely no idea; I haven't met him before. Maybe salad with smoked salmon or something similar - that should be quite acceptable. Oh, and cheese – most Englishmen like cheese. We'll finish with stilton and mature cheddar.'

'I do all of that, sir.'

This meeting was an area of concern, hoping that the invitation to Mr. Miles Elderbeck wouldn't turn out to be a mistake. Having left an established circle of friends in Africa, a kindred spirit with a similar background would be ideal to ease him into a new social order. Someone who could be trusted and not have to be careful what one says all the time … the kind who won't condemn an occasional over-indulgence. Would he be a chum – an *amîcus certus*?

CHAPTER TWO

At eleven-thirty, a double ring on the doorbell heralded his guest's arrival. Aida showed him into the living room.

'Mr Grosvenor Smythe, I presume.' Miles Elderbeck extended his hand.

'Indeed, I am, and it's Reginald,' he amiably replied, shaking the man's hand whilst eyeing him up, 'though I prefer Reggie.' Older than he'd expected, Elderbeck was a small, smartly dressed man with thinning grey hair, but his pale blue bird-like eyes, peering out from behind thick-framed spectacles, were bright and intelligent.

Aida gave a light cough to get their attention. 'Excuse sirs, I ask your help. How big is knob?'

After a moments silence, Miles smiled, 'That's an interesting question.'

'It say in recipe book to add knob of butter. How big is knob?'

'I think, Aida, it's probably the size of a teaspoonful,' Reggie suggested. 'What do you think, Miles?'

'Since leaving school, old chap, knobs are no longer my speciality, but a spoonful sounds about right.'

'Thank you, sirs.'

'Miles, how about a snifter before lunch. The bar's open by the way.'

'It's a bit early in the day, but now that the rain has more or less stopped and a heat-wave forecast to start tomorrow, a G and T would go down rather nicely, with ice, lemon or lime if possible.'

Aida went through to the kitchen and quickly returned with Miles's drink. He watched her closely.

'A mail-order bride, by any chance?' his eyes twinkling in amusement after she'd left the room.

Emphatically shaking his head, Reggie retorted, 'Good heavens, no. Aida is my Filipina housekeeper, and a jolly good one at that. I've put her and her daughter in the flat next door.'

'Really,' Miles's face creased into an affable smile. 'And pray what services does she provide as a housekeeper? She's quite a looker, and very conveniently located should you ever ... you know.'

'You're way off beam there,' Reggie replied curtly.

'Oh - no offence old chap.'

'That's quite alright, Miles, none taken.'

'Anyway, it was jolly nice of you to invite me for lunch.' Miles gazed round the living room. 'It's quite a place you've got here, so clean and tidy compared to my sorry abode.'

'I can't help it. I blame it on my mother, I was toilet trained at six months.'

Miles gave a snort of laughter. 'And that view looks rather special. The good old Thames – our liquid history. Do you mind if I take a peek?'

Gazing out of the picture window, they could see swans, ducks and Canada geese returning to the water, bickering as if something had happened. 'Ha,' Miles gave a little laugh. 'You know that Zeus performed acts with swans that would debar him from living in this block.'

'I'll have to take your word on that one.'

'By the way,' Miles said. 'How did you find an old reprobate like *moi*?'

'It was Colonel Marsland at Rymers Academy, our *alma mater*. Was he bursar in your day?'

Miles thought for a moment. 'Yes, I do believe you're right. I'd forgotten about him, but if I remember correctly, he replaced the ancient mariner, Sir Stephen Cook.'

'That's correct. When I contacted him with my new address, he kindly told me of another Old Rymerian living nearby – namely, your good-self.'

'That was very decent of him,' Miles nodded. 'I trust that when you were at Rymers, you were well drilled in the skills to embrace all the noble acts and talents needed to rule the Empire.'

'That was certainly the idea. As well as the importance of a cultured sense of humour.'

'Yes, that's right,' Miles's eyes lit up and chuckled. 'Good old Rymers instilled in us that people without a sense of humour will never succeed in life, or even forgive the rest of us for having one.'

Indicating he agreed, Reggie raised his glass. 'Your very good health, Miles. And yes, I was at Rymers from 65 to 76, but at that time, the school hadn't detected that the days of Empire had long gone - the sun had already set.'

Miles shook his head smiling. 'And they probably still haven't noticed,'

Taking a sip of whisky and leaning back in his chair, Reggie sat in a contemplative mood. 'And how about you, Miles?'

'Oh, let me see,' he sighed. 'It was a long time ago. I left Rymers in 1963, two years before you started; you are a youngster after all. The Head at the time, F-Fearless F-Ferguson, had a stutter hence the double F. The sadist imposed mental torture on us all that only algebra had the right to inflict.'

Reggie smiled. 'Double F was still there in my time. A horrible man.'

Miles laughed. 'The old sod never took to me. When I received an offer from Cambridge, his farewell message was that I was not cut out for the rigours of colonial service, and he could not recommend me for a post with the Foreign Office.'

'That was a bit harsh, wasn't it?'

'No, not really. I always thought that public office in the FO is the last refuge of a scoundrel, and the thought of dealing with warring natives in the fever-ridden swamps was never my cup of tea … creepy-crawlies and cockroaches give me the heebie-jeebies.'

'Oh dear,' Reggie said, 'Actually, in my book, cockroaches have been given a bad rap. They don't bite, smell or get into one's booze. Would that all house guests were as well behaved.'

Miles was enjoying himself. 'My other failing was lacking any sporting ability. The FO seemed to think team sports maketh the man - I expect you excelled at those things. The only sport I mastered was backgammon.'

'Oh, well done you,' Reggie teased. 'Without wanting to bore you, Miles, I was orphaned at the age of eight and my guardian - my father's sister, Cressida Smythe, didn't want me hanging around so she packed me off to Rymers. I only stayed with her during school holidays, and that was no fun.'

'Oh, that's too bad, although eight was actually a good age to start at Rymers.'

'Maybe it was but it was jolly rotten at first, you know, being an orphan, but I soon got the hang of things and began to enjoy my time there - nine years all together. Ah,' Reggie's face lit up. 'And I accomplished one of Rymers prerequisites by acquiring a cut-glass English accent – to speak posh like the Royals' he laughed, 'and now I'm stuck with it.'

Miles tittered. 'It's very impressive and goes well with your bearing – and the monocle - quite aristocratic. I'm sure you put it to good use. I know I did my best with my less than successful soniferous cadence. But sizing you up, I'd say you were the archetypical colonial type. A shining example of Rymers *ipsa quidem pretium virtus sibi*'.

'*Absente reō*,' Reggie responded smiling. 'And I did go overseas after my time at Oxford – in fact, I was away most of the time, about forty years all together. I only returned to England on a permanent basis towards the end of last year. I had worked for the Foreign Office in Asia and later Africa. But I was terribly frustrated by the bureaucracy, so decided a more fulfilling and lucrative career beckoned in the private sector.'

'And did it?'

'Oh, yes, definitely more rewarding.'

'Jolly good for you. Tell me more, I find it interesting.'

'Well, if you're sure. Whilst in Africa, I fell in love and married the wonderful Coralie.' He absentmindedly twisted the wedding ring on his finger. 'Tragically, our idyllic thirty-year marriage came to an end with her death a year ago. A heart attack – it came completely out of the blue … no advance warning. Knowing her time had come, she whispered her final words, strangely from Winnie the Pooh - *"if ever we can't be together, keep me in your heart – I'll stay there forever".* Reggie's voice faltered. 'She then peacefully passed away.'

'Deepest commiserations, dear boy. You had clearly struck lucky with your life's partner but such a heartrending ending.'

'Yes, I was distraught – for how long I can't remember. Devastated that the goblet of our life together had been smashed, and that made me return to England, but having done so, I've struggled to adjust to modern society – people treat me like a colonial outcast from another age.'

'I can imagine. You will have noticed there have been a lot of changes in poor old Blighty since you left.'

'Unfortunately, yes, and that's why I'm finding it difficult to settle down, meet people and fit in.'

'Being alone is not the best place to be.'

'You're right. Lonely is not just being alone, it's the feeling that no one cares.'

Sensing that Miles may well be sympathetic to his need of a confidant, Reggie continued. 'Changing the subject somewhat, Miles, and I hope you don't mind but I received a piece of disturbing news this morning. It would be good to share it with someone.'

CHAPTER THREE

'Disturbing news, you say.' Miles hunched forward, thinking it might be interesting,. 'Tell me about it.'

With a flourish, Reggie passed the letter across. 'It's from Ormrod and Ormrod, a firm of solicitors in Ringwood. My guardian, the lady I told you about earlier, Cressida Smythe, has just died.'

'Oh dear.' Miles briefly glanced through the letter. 'Were you close?'

Reggie considered what answer to give. 'No, we weren't. I've not seen the old girl in getting on for forty years. We parted on less than amenable terms.'

'Oh really,' Miles's eyebrows arched in interest. 'Forty years is a long time not to be in contact. Not even birthdays or Christmas?'

'We did that sporadically. I gave her my news once or twice a year, but she hardly ever responded. And now I feel guilty. I should have made more of an effort. You see, in my late teens and early twenties, I was a rebellious young sod, and the poor old girl eventually reached the end of her tether with my behaviour. I deliberately went against her wishes on numerous occasions and, angrily, she'd told me to go away. In fact, I clearly remember she quoted Lady Macbeth. *"Out, damned boy, out I say. Hell is murky".* I was impressed with that, but I didn't blame her. And that was the last time I saw her.' Emptying his glass, Reggie slumped back in his chair. 'I think it was probably that event that drove me to drink, and I didn't have the courtesy to thank her.'

Miles chuckled, 'At least that was a bonus. Was it something to do with your aunt that brought you to Kingston after your years in the colonies?'

No, as I explained earlier, my present unhappy state of mind is the death of my wife – the very basis of my life.'

'Oh, yes, of course. Did her loss prepare you for your new loss?'

'No, not at all. Completely different. And now, here I am, struggling to adjust. Not only that, but I have come back to a country where it pisses down with rain, the Inland Revenue are shafting me left, right and centre, and a decent bottle of Scotch costs a ruddy fortune.'

Smiling at this rebuke, Miles asked what memories he had of his aunt.

Refilling his glass, Reggie's expression slid into a frown. 'She never really liked me – no maternal instincts. Being my closest relation, she must have felt an obligation, no matter how inconvenient. But being at boarding school, I was only with her during school holidays – fourteen weeks a year.'

'Did she look after you well enough then?'

'I'm sure she felt she was, but in those first years, I missed the love and affection I'd had from my parents. I think Cressy was incapable of love. She was cold and uptight all the time.'

'But going to Rymers would have toughened you up – no love or sympathy there either. Did she give you presents on your birthday … and Christmas?'

'Christmas,' Reggie smiled. 'Ah yes, Christmas. Cressy had an amazing gift for assessing her ability to absorb electricity. She had these ancient fairy lights – and I mean ancient - which came out every year to decorate and equally ancient Christmas tree; always tangled in knots that when she straightened them out and plugged them in, the wires fizzed, followed a few seconds later by a spectacular shower of flashes. We had lift-off.'

'Sounds fun,' Miles snorted.

'Ah, there's more,' Reggie refilled his glass. 'The bulbs that actually lit were hot enough to melt skin, and those that didn't was when the fun really began. Getting angry, she continued to struggle until the second when she completed a circuit, and the pent-up power of a thousand volts lit her up like a Belisha beacon.'

'Really?' was Mile's uncertain response.

'Well, I probably exaggerated a tad, but that's how I like to remember it.'

'And why not,' Miles chortled. 'I guess no amount of presents would have provided such entertainment. I assume she must have recovered from being electrocuted like that.'

'Yes, she did … quite amazing. In fact it seemed to give her a bit of gusto – it didn't last for long though.'

'But you must have other memories of your annual fourteen weeks with her.'

'Yes, it's funny the sort of things I remember. She thought the Germans a cruel race as their operas lasted for six hours and they have no word for fluffy. She thought Trafalgar came the day after Waterloo, confusing history with the London underground system, and at bedtime, she positively reeked of Horlicks. She once ate a raffia coaster thinking it was a high fibre biscuit. There, that's what I remember of her, so let's leave it at that, shall we? Or shall I tell you what she thought of the French?'

'Okay, okay.' Miles held up both hands in submission. 'Maybe another time.' It was clear talking about Cressida Smythe had exposed a raw nerve.

A light tap on the door brought Aida into the room. 'Lunch, I serve it for you now, sirs,'

'Thank you, Aida,' Reggie stood. 'Come along Miles. I'll tell you everything after our meal. It's a long story.'

CHAPTER FOUR

After bidding farewell to Miles, Reggie knew that he'd have to go to Ringwood and see Ormrod & Ormrod. He had no choice but to go as a sense of duty – and duty had always been important to him. Not wanting to drive himself, Miles had suggested he should hire a chauffeur and check the local directory.

Swaying slightly, Reggie refilled his glass for the umpteenth time, and went to look out of the window. The rain had stopped. Below him, the Thames looked grey but, there again, unbowed and eternal. Bolstered by the extensive intake of whisky, the sight of this historic river brought on a *'Sceptered Isle'* moment. Over the years, he'd enjoyed Shakespeare's elegant prose and Churchill's powerful speeches. Thus inspired, he steadied himself before thrusting out his chest. *'Over the ages, your glorious waterway has done service to the race that peoples your banks.'* He paused to take another sip. *'What greatness has not flowed into the unknown earth. The dreams of man, the seed of commonwealth, the germs of empire.*

He almost dropped his glass in shock as gentle applause came from behind him. Aida had quietly entered to prepare his dinner. Taking a second to recover, he bowed in her direction.

'Ah, Aida, I didn't know you were there. I was ... er, quoting Churchill ... er ...'

'I like it,' she smiled. 'Very English – it good.'

'Well, that's very gracious of you.' He bowed again, like an aged thespian.

'Mr Churchill beat Hitler and won war. I read it.'

'Indeed, he did.'

Then scowling, she added, 'In Philippine war, we had evil Japanese soldiers. They very bad people, my grandmother raped by many soldiers.'

'Oh Aida, I'm so sorry to hear that.'

'But American General MacArthur free us from them, so it okay now.'

'I'm pleased to hear it.'

Her eyes lit up suddenly. 'Tonight sir, I prepare very English dinner for you from recipe book. It called roast beef, york shire pudding and roasted potatoes. Is that what Mr Churchill eat?'

'Indeed, he did, Aida, every day.'

At seven o'clock, Reggie finished his Churchillian dinner – Aida's culinary skills continued to impress. Taking Ormrod & Ormrod's letter from his pocket, he decided he would call them in the morning. Refilled glass in hand, he gazed blankly up at the ceiling. Unwelcome memories flooded back. Memories he'd deliberately pushed to the recesses of his mind, but now had come back to disturb him. He was only eight years old when he'd been reprimanded by his class teacher for pulling Deborah Anderson's pigtails. Walking home after school, he'd seen a police car outside his house. Naively, he had linked the two events and was going to be punished. He hid behind a neighbour's garage. They soon found him and took him home. His parents had been killed in a car crash.

He remembered crying for what seemed ages, and then oddly, became angry. Didn't they care? Didn't they know he'd miss them? At that age, he had found it difficult to understand what death was but knew they weren't coming back. There were places you went when you died, up or down. Aunt Cressy told him they had gone to heaven which he thought was up beyond the sky. Unhappiness in childhood was worse than unhappiness one encountered in later life – it was so complete, without end.

Only hazy recollections of the funeral remained. It had rained verging on sleet and December gales had blown stinging, cold rain into his face, masking his tears. What happened after that was a blur of time and emotions. How long after the funeral was it before Cressida sent him to boarding school, he couldn't bring to mind?

Sighing forlornly, he refilled his glass and had just sat down when the doorbell rang. Who in the blue-blazes is it at this time? It was nearly nine o'clock. Switching on the lobby CCTV, there was nobody there. 'Bloody hooligans,' he yelled at the screen, and was about to return to his chair when it rang again. There was still nobody to be seen. It then dawned on him that the noise of the bell was, in fact, the bell of his own flat. Maybe it was Aida – but no, she had a key. He opened the door.

What confronted him left him momentarily speechless. A person of minute proportions was in front of him, doubled up in a deep bow.

'What in God's name?' Reggie exclaimed. 'Get up man.'

Straightening, the man was under five feet tall with the thin features found in those of Asian origin. Smartly dressed in a boy-sized suit and tie, he had a minimal nose, and the shell glasses he wore looked like those of an underwater pearl diver. Reggie's six-foot frame, though slightly stooped, towered over this undersized person.

Using the back of his hand, Reggie brusquely gestured him towards the stairwell.

The man, a strained smile on his face, didn't move. As the grin faded, he handed Reggie a business card. 'Thank you, sir,' he bleated in a high-pitched voice, '*Ee su won.*'

'Ee what!' Reggie mimicked.

The little man stood his ground and pointed to the card.

Sighing heavily, Reggie thought he had better look at it before phoning security. Adjusting his monocle, he read, 'Mr Lee su won – Consultant. Oh, you're Mr Lee ... not Ee.'

'That's what I say, *Ee.*'

'It's Lee with an L you ... ah.' From his time working in Asia and with Japanese businessmen in Africa, he knew many Asians found certain parts of the English language difficult to pronounce, particularly words with the letters 'L' and 'R'.

'Yes sir,' the man gave a penetrating laugh. 'I your neighbour. I *wiv* here.'

'No, you don't *wiv* here,' Reggie bellowed.

'*Fwat* twenty-*fwee*,' he pointed down the stairwell. 'I *wiv* here. I come to say *hewwo.*'

Reggie groaned inwardly, a string of expletives muzzled in his throat. The caretaker had told him the flat below him had recently been sold, so this little man with a screeching voice

– a bit like Minnie Mouse on helium - was the new owner. Reggie took a deep breath, his good breeding telling him to be civil. 'So, you are Mr Lee su won, and it says here you are a consultant. On what, if I may be so bold, do you consult?'

The man looked blank.

Reggie's irritation returned. 'Don't you know? Mr Lee, please go away.' With that he gently closed the door. Keeping his ear close to the door panel, he heard childlike footsteps going down the stairs.

CHAPTER FIVE

Aida busied herself in the kitchen quietly emptying the dishwasher. In fact, she did everything quietly. During the last few months, Reggie had come to rely on her; a slight woman in her thirties, with short dark hair and deep brown, soothing eyes. When interviewing her, he'd been impressed by her manner and bearing, conveying, as it did, capability as well as intelligence.

For form's sake, Reggie decided to wait until she had gone before pouring his midday, sunshine pick-me-up. He smiled to himself remembering that when Aunt Cressy gave him an article to read about the evils of drink, he'd decided to give up reading ... that was until he remembered there was no Latin word for abstemious.

Reassuringly, his first medical examination after returning to England included a thorough physical check-up. He was given a clean bill of health. His liver and kidney functions and other organs all performed well within acceptable levels. It was comforting to know that his liberal consumption of whisky over the years was quite obviously a health drink – a tonic.

Soundlessly, Aida entered the living room and gave a delicate cough. 'Would you please inform me your liking for dinner tonight, sir?' She had one of those gentle, serene voices, tinged with a Filipino accent.

Since the loss of his wife and his return from Africa, food and grog had become Reggie's principal pleasures. He waved his hand airily. 'Ah, dinner, yes, let me see. Surprise me.'

'I know,' she gave an anxious smile. 'I have very nice fish. Mr Lee, he give it for you.'

'Mr Lee!' he exclaimed, studying her for a moment, wondering if she could possibly be right. 'You mean the little man from downstairs. Have you met him?'

'Oh yes,' she gave a nervous giggle. 'He nice man.'

'Is he really?' Reggie wasn't sure what to think.

'Yes, he good man, he say he meet you and you very important person. He admire you and give big fish for you.'

'Well, I'll be damned. In that case, Aida, I had better have the fish ... fried, of course, in batter with those delicious chunky chips you make.'

Her smooth, composed face creased into a grin. 'I happy to do that, sir.'

'By the way, Aida, do you know why Mr Lee is living here, and what's his nationality?'

'He from South Korea. His son is manager of factory near London. They make shoes for children, and Mr Lee come to this place to be near family.'

'Does he work here?'

'Oh no,' she grinned, and Reggie was struck by the way her face lit up. 'He not work. He old man like you.'

Well, that's at least honest, Reggie acknowledged with a wry smile. In her eyes, he must look like an antique. At lunch yesterday, Miles had joked that in the chocolate box of life, his top layer had already gone, and sadly, the walnut-whip on the bottom layer had also disappeared. Putting those maudlin thoughts to one side, he picked up Mr Lee's card and showed it to Aida. 'It says here he's a consultant.'

She furrowed her brow. 'No, I not know. Maybe it say that to get visa. He chauffeur.'

'A chauffeur! Are you sure?'

'Oh yes, sir, he told me he had chauffeur business in Pusan, his home in Korea. He had many ... er, how you say the English word, *leemothings*.'

'Limousines?'

'Yes.' Slowly, she practiced saying *limousine*. 'He had *leemosines*, big cars for chauffeurs.'

'Isn't he too small for that sort of work?'

She surprised him with a laugh. He realised it was the first time he had seen her actually laugh since she had worked for him. Poor woman, putting up with a miserable old sod like him.

'He very small man,' she continued to chuckle. 'He has own er ... things to put on car pedals to make him bigger.'

This piece of information was suddenly of great interest to Reggie. Mr Lee - could he drive him to Ringwood? He thought for a moment. 'Aida, I have to go to Ringwood for one or two days, it's about one hundred miles from here. Do you think Mr Lee would drive me there – like a chauffeur?'

She looked pleased. 'I sure so. I tell him come and see you tonight when I make dinner.'

'One other thing, Aida, he wears those very thick lens spectacles – he's not blind by any chance.'

'Oh no sir, they special for chauffeur work.'

'Well then, I'll see you both this evening.'

A strange coincidence or was his fortune about to change? Mr Lee, a chauffeur. To celebrate, he poured his second of the day ... or was it the third or ...? Addressing the now empty room, he proclaimed. 'Where there's whisky, there's hope.' He saluted his reflection in the windowpane, holding up the glass to capture the light in the golden liquid. 'There surely could be no higher achievement in life than the making of fine whisky.' He savoured the smooth, venerable liquor. 'And there's no greater pleasure than drinking it.'

Chapter Six

When Mr Lee agreed to take the wheel and drive Reggie to Ringwood, it was time to make an appointment with the solicitor. Over the years, Reggie had crossed swords with many members of the legal profession, and reluctantly accepted that they were a necessary life form ... like dung beetles and earthworms.

Checking the calendar, he decided that the most suitable date to meet Ormrod & Ormrod would be in two days' time. It should only take one day to get there, sort out any issues, and return the same evening.

The solicitor's phone rang for about ten seconds before a rather timorous female voice announced, 'Good morning, Ormrod and Ormrod.' There was a hint of a Dorset burr in her voice, but it was the deepness of her register that struck him the most.

'And good morning to you, madam,' Reggie articulated distinctly. 'Kindly inform me as to whom I am speaking.'

Giving a light cough, the lady repeated even more diffidently, 'Good morning, Ormrod and Ormrod.'

'I did hear you clearly the first time, Madam,' the polish and delivery of Reggie's diction may have intimidated her. 'I would like to know with whom I am speaking.' He put it slowly as though he was talking to someone who had part of their brain removed.

'Oh, 'she gave a nervous giggle. 'I'm the receptionist, Mrs Pluck, but I only ...'

'Thank you, Mrs Pluck. My name is Reginald Grosvenor Smythe, OBE. Kindly put me through to Mr Ormrod. That is Mr Edgar Ormrod.'

There was moment's silence. 'He's er, in a ...'

'Immediately if you would, Mrs Pluck.'

'I'll put you on hold for ...'

'Mrs Pluck, put me through now.' It was a demand, not a request. Reggie had found over the years that his cut glass English accent, delivered firmly with a degree of panache, made life unquestionably smoother. He knew it was an act which he disgracefully abused, but it proved extremely useful, especially when a table was required at an exclusive London restaurant.

He only had to wait a second before the cowed Mrs Pluck put him through. There, it worked again. He didn't like taking advantage, but he hated being placed on hold, whilst vexatious music was blasted down the earpiece risking the laceration of one's eardrums.

'Yes?' came the response.

'And am I addressing Mr Edgar Ormrod?'

'Erm yes, who is that?'

'I informed your Mrs Pluck that I am Reginald Grosvenor Smythe, OBE, closest relative of Miss Cressida Smythe. You did write to me, but the letter took two weeks to arrive as you used an old address.'

'Oh! Oh, yes. Mr Grosvenor Smythe ... just a moment.' There was the sound of papers being shuffled. 'Ah, I have the details here. As you know, Miss Smythe sadly had a recent negative patient outcome.'

'What in God's name might that be?' Reggie bellowed.

Slightly unnerved, Ormrod replied in a throat-grating whisper, 'She died.'

'Then why, by Odin's blackened tooth, didn't you say that in the first place?'

Ormrod grunted something unintelligible before mumbling ... 'It's just that some people erm, you know ...'

'No, I don't know,' Reggie barked. 'May I humbly suggest, Ormrod, that we precede from here using the Queen's English which we can both understand? Now tell me, on what date did my aunt die?'

More shuffling of papers. 'Er, here we are. Miss Smythe's negative ... she died on July 3rd.'

'Right. And the funeral?'

'There's been a bit of a holdup there, I'm afraid.'

'And the holdup is?'

'It's a bit difficult – you know,' Ormrod muttered. 'But there has to be a post-mortem.'

'A post-mortem!' exclaimed Reggie. 'On an old lady. Why is that?'

'I was surprised myself. I don't have the details as yet but unofficially; I was told that Miss Smythe's doctor thought one was required.'

'Did he indeed. And when, pray, will you be notified of the result? I take it you are an executor.'

'Yes, one of two, actually. The third named executor had a negative erm... he passed away just three days ago.'

'And by that I take it you mean he died.'

'Erm, yes.'

'And the other executor?' Reggie was beginning to feel slightly perturbed.

There followed an awkward silence before Ormrod spoke again. 'I've been trying to contact her since, you know, since Miss Smythe's ... er demise, but so far, she seems to be missing.'

'What the devil do you mean by "seems to be missing". Either she is missing, or she isn't.' Reggie was somewhat disturbed by Ormrod's imprecise ramblings. 'This all sounds a little queer to me, if you'll pardon the expression. May I presume that you are in possession of her will?'

'Yes, we do have it.'

'So, Ormrod, it's clear we must have a meeting. I will travel from my present location in the Royal Borough of Kingston upon Thames to Ringwood in two days' time on the 17th of July, and I will call at your office at one-thirty p.m. I trust that will be convenient to you, and that the missing executor will have been safely located.' Reggie hung up giving Ormrod no chance to argue.

Later that day, Reggie took Mr Lee to his lockup garage to prepare his treasured Rolls Royce for the journey, a 6.7 litre Blue Phantom. As they walked side-by-side, it felt to Reggie that he was accompanying a small boy and was tempted to act in a paternal manner by holding his hand. He resisted.

As they opened the garage door, Mr Lee gave a strangled, oriental gasp, 'Ooooh.' It was a strange noise like the bleating of a new-born lamb. 'It *vewy, vewy* nice *weemosine, a Wolls Woyce.*'

'Thank you, Mr Lee. Is it too big for you?'

'Oh no,' he insisted, and proceeded to fit rather bizarre extensions to the vehicle's pedals. This done, Mr Lee placed a padded cushion on the driver's seat, adjusted all the mirrors, checked the lights and instead of the inbuilt satnav, fitted a mobile phone with a dashboard bracket. Using the images on the screen, Mr Lee then took Reggie for a short spin on the notorious Kingston one-way system, did a circuit of the town and then back along Richmond Road to the lockup. This was all carried out with consummate ease. It was clear to Reggie that Mr Lee was, in fact, a highly skilled driver ... in fact, a chauffeur *extraordinaire*.

CHAPTER SEVEN

An early morning mist rose off the Thames with summer laziness, turning the sky to a bright blue of near alpine clarity. Flocks of house sparrows chattered and darted amongst the trees, while swallows flashed in and out of their nests.

Dressed elegantly in his summer plumage, Reggie took a deep breath of freshly laundered air. Oh to be in England now that summer's here. Feeling upbeat, he only hoped that going to Ringwood would not prove to be a mistake. Thankfully, the rain of the past four weeks had emigrated to continental Europe – and quite right too, he thought.

He was soon joined by Mr Lee who, much to Reggie's amusement, was wearing a neatly pressed white chauffeur's uniform, with gold coloured braid around the epaulettes and peaked cap. The convex lenses of his glasses reflected bronze in the morning light. Beaming, he bowed deeply. 'I *weddy*, sir.'

'And so, you are *weddy*,' chuckled Reggie. 'My Asian Little Lord Fauntleroy.'

Looking blank, Mr Lee didn't query what Reggie said. Since his arrival in the UK, he'd struggled to understand many of the strange English sayings, but took more notice of how the words were delivered rather than their actual meaning. In this case, Reggie's expression was kindly so he reckoned it must have been something nice.

Reggie gave him Ormrod & Ormrod's address and postcode. 'Can you work these blessed satnav gadgets?'

'Yes, of course.' Using his nimble fingers, he quickly entered the information and selected the route. 'We go this *addwess* in *Wingwood*. Are you a *guest-es in Wingwood*?'

'*Guestes*?' Reggie queried. 'Oh, you mean a guest. No, I'm going on business.'

'Ah, business,' he nodded, 'not *guest-es*. In Korea we have saying – when *guest-es awwive*, children *cwy*. You have same saying in your *countwy*?'

'No, we don't.' Oh dear, Reggie was dreading the thought that Mr Lee would want to conduct a form of tortured conversation during the two-hour journey.

'It mean, that when *guest-es awwive*, it honour to give them food, so none for children-es. They *cwy*.'

'How extremely interesting,' Reggie sighed. 'Can we go now, please?'

'Okay.' He adjusted his mobile. 'I *wook* at *woad* picture. That okay?'

'Excellent, Mr Lee. You look at the road pictures and switch off the sound. We have a saying in this country that *silence is golden*.' Reggie wondered if he would take the hint.

'Ah, that good saying.' Mr Lee happily chimed back. Reggie held his breath. 'A shut mouth will catch no *fries*.'

Or even flies, for that matter, Reggie hoped.

Setting off, Mr Lee did keep his mouth closed, concentrating on his driving proficiency to manoeuvre the car through busy, morning traffic, over Kingston Bridge to the Middlesex side of the river. Below, the Thames continued on its stately course east. As they passed Hampton Court Palace, Reggie recalled it was King Henry VIII's favourite residence, where he wined, dined, frolicked and cavorted with ladies of questionable virtue ... not forgetting, of course, a string of ill-fated queens.

Traffic became heavy, and they crawled slowly along until they came to a large road sign for The South West. Was his decision to go to Ringwood a mistake? When questioned years ago by Coralie, he had told her that not even a team of wild Caucasian horses could drag him to that place. He had too many painful memories - memories suppressed since childhood relating to his parents' untimely death, and all that had followed. Aunt Cressy had bought him a trunk-full of scratchy clothes and said boarding school would make a man of him. At the age of eight, he had only just got used to being a boy.

Once on the M3, the traffic eased and they made steady progress through areas of countryside with clumps of dense pine trees stretching away on either side of the motorway, and fields of golden cereal shimmering in the hazy distance. After an hour-and-a-half of steady progress, they joined the M27 at an elaborate junction. Fifteen minutes later, the motorway turned into the A31 at Cadnam.

From there on, the dual carriageway to Ringwood seemed strange to Reggie and certainly much busier than when he'd lived there. He struggled to recognise his whereabouts, but the numerous road signs confirmed they were heading in the right direction. He remembered the places they were passing; Lyndhurst and, of course, the New Forest. As they approached Ringwood, the road sloped down, its prominent church tower with its Union flag clearly visible.

'We turn off here.' Speaking for the first time since leaving Kingston, Mr Lee pointed to the direction shown on his satnav.

'Thank you, Mr Lee. You have driven very well.'

Slowing down from his perfectly maintained seventy miles per hour, they took the slip road into Ringwood. Glancing at his mobile, Mr Lee squeaked. 'We first turn *weft*, then *wight*. Ah, it *wook* difficult,' he furrowed his brow. 'Then I think it is *weft* on *wittle* road to market. You know the *pwace?*'

Reggie's eyes narrowed in memory. 'Yes, a little.' The central carpark seemed larger than he remembered. The cattle market and garden centre had gone, replaced by the Furlong Shopping Centre. They entered the market square down Mr Lee's *wittle* road. Feeling like a ghost haunting his own past, it was extraordinary how much had changed in forty years, yet how little had altered in the town centre. A light breeze blew litter about the street and flowers in colourful hanging baskets danced in the dappled midday sunlight. The shops lining the square had different names and businesses than he recalled. As they drove slowly towards West Street, Reggie hadn't appreciated that Ringwood was an attractive little town. The imposing Parish Church overlooked the market square, as it had from Victorian times. Oddly, the road which used to lead out of Ringwood to the south wasn't there anymore.

Bringing himself back to the present, they were temporarily held up by a lady driver trying to reverse a large vehicle into a space which looked as if it could only have been designed for a shopping trolley. Sitting patiently in the rear of the Rolls, he couldn't help but smile as he glimpsed the vicar scurrying up the church path, presumably late for his appointment with God. Poor God - in Sweden, God has been declared gender neutral.

How the world had changed. In his day, people walked to church but now freshly painted white lines guided worshippers to park their automobiles in orderly Christian rows.

Aunt Cressy had taken him to that same church every Sunday during school holidays. Summer and winter, she had always dressed in the same outfit, like an extra in *Brief Encounter,* wrapped in an ankle length coat, one hand holding onto her hat, regardless of whether it was blowing a gale or serenely calm. During prayers, he'd only ever pleaded for help with algebra and fielding practice – and, of course, chips with every meal.

Eventually, the cumbersome vehicle was parked, but too close to the next car for the lady to get out. Mr Lee laughed. '*Siwwy* woman, man do it better.'

Reggie thought of telling him that was un-PC, but the explanation would be too laborious. Anyway, he was probably right.

As they exited the square into West Street, Mr Lee squeaked, 'We have *weached* our destination.' He pulled into a convenient space at the side of the road. 'It over there, sir.' He pointed to a brick-built office building, set amidst a row of traditional two and three storied brick and rendered, properties with shallow, red-tiled roofs. At the far end was the thatch of the Old Cottage Restaurant where Aunt Cressy had taken him on special occasions – unlike at home and school, he enjoyed the food there very much.

Easing himself out of the air-conditioned Rolls, Reggie stretched his stiffened limbs, placing a hand around the back of his neck to massage muscles sore from the long journey. According to the church clock, it was a quarter to one. The blazing sun shone blindingly on the rows of car windows parked in the square. 'It's hot today, Mr Lee. We have time before my meeting, and I spy an Italian restaurant further down West Street. You and I will go and get a bite to eat.'

'Thank you, sir,' replied the obedient Mr Lee. 'I *wock* the car.'

'Yes, but before that,' Reggie took a pennant out of the front glove compartment. 'Kindly attach this to the front wing.'

'Oooh,' Mr Lee bowed as he planted the flag into a ready-made opening. Ambassador?'

'No.' Reggie smiled. 'The Ancient Order of Scottish Distillers. Looks good, doesn't it? It should keep any pesky officials at bay. Then after lunch, I'll be in that office for maybe a couple of hours before going back to Kingston.'

Mr Lee nodded his understanding.

'I suggest after lunch, you keep a careful watch on the car, and you can also spend some time looking round the town.'

'Yes, it *wook* a *vewy* nice town.'

Entering the restaurant, they were shown to a table for two in the window. 'I *wike* noodle,' Mr Lee informed the Italian waiter, whose grasp of English proved to be limited - Korean English clearly beyond him. He gave a bewildered shrug.

Reggie whispered to the man. 'Give him spaghetti, and tell him they're Italian noodles.'

CHAPTER EIGHT

Ormrod and Ormrod's office was on the building's first floor, along a dimly lit, windowless corridor. Reggie pinched his nose as he passed a door marked 'W C' – the repellent pong of Satan's lavatory hung in the air. Swiftly moving on, he went through the door marked *Edgar Vantage Ormrod LLB*. The small reception area was practically filled by a middle-aged woman perched behind a desk, knitting a long, unseasonal scarf. She had a tiny nose with highly flared nostrils, and grey-blonde hair swept back from her brow. Carefully putting the knitting down, she folded her arms, supporting an enormous bosom.

'Good day to you, madam,' Reggie boomed, moving his eyes from her amazing frontage to look directly into pale blue eyes that narrowed warily under his gaze. 'Do I have the pleasure of addressing Mrs Pluck?'

'Yes sir.' It was the same deep pitched voice from their telephone conversation.

'Well, Mrs Pluck, I'm Reginald Grosvenor Smythe and I have a meeting arranged with Mr Edgar Ormrod for one thirty this afternoon.'

Apprehensively, she reached for her phone. 'I'll see if he's in.'

'Aren't you sure?'

'Oh er ... yes.' Squeezing herself around the desk, she knocked on the connecting door. Her lower half, Reggie observed, was unfortunately out of harmony with such an outstanding upper-structure.

The office was cluttered, with an accumulation of files and manila folders piled precariously high on a Formica topped table. A Toshiba laptop computer sat on the corner of his desk, hooked to a printer. The carpet, a threadbare plush pile in muted pink, showed multiple signs of spilt substances, and a large, faded poster of a football team took centre place on the wall. The lone vertical window was narrow and fortified with what looked like chicken wire. A trickle of fresh air managed to penetrate the overly hot, cheerless room.

Reggie sniffed. 'I take it, sir, that you do not have air-conditioning.'

'No, sorry, we haven't. I'm Edgar by the way. Edgar Ormrod.' His handshake was limp and brief. He was a short man, mid-fiftyish, with a stubble of greyish-brown hair. 'I'm sorry for your loss, Mr Grosvenor Smythe.'

Ormrod sat down indicating that Reggie should follow suit. 'Mr Grosvenor Smythe, Reginald – if you don't mind my using your first name.'

'No, not at all – it's Reggie actually. Now then, I assume you have the post-mortem results on Miss Cressida Smythe.'

Edgar lifted a hand in apology. 'Unfortunately, no. The police are now involved.'

'The police! Why, for God's sake?'

'They haven't told me. But when I informed them that you would be here this afternoon, the officer insisted on seeing

41

you.' He checked his watch. 'D S Clapp should be here in ten minutes ... or so.'

At that juncture, the door opened. It wasn't the police.

'Where've you been?' Edgar grumpily greeted a peculiar looking young man with a stiff, clumsy gait and no style.

'On the loo for the past half hour, Dad. I think it was yesterday's Indian curry I had for breakfast.' Struggling to carry an object into the room, he eventually managed to lean it against the wall – a life-sized cut out of a bikini-clad girl wearing a *Miss Bournemouth* sash across her shoulder.

'I told you not to bring it into the office,' Edgar scolded. Then using a Captain Mainwaring cliché, added, 'You stupid boy.'

'Sorry Dad. It's hot outside and I'm starting with a cold. They say the hot weather's due to Al Pacino.'

There followed a moment's silence. 'Al Pacino?' Edgar forlornly shook his head. 'Red, my boy, I think you may mean El Ninio.'

Grinning like a gurning gargoyle, he muttered, 'Oh yea, that's it.'

'Anyway, you'd better go to the chemists and get something for your cold.'

He sniffed. 'Should I get euthanasia tablets like last time?'

Edgar held his gaze for a moment. 'No Red, it's Echinacea ... although ... ,' he shook his head. 'Now go into your room and stay there 'till I tell you to come out.'

'But Dad. I've got to learn the legal stuff, let me stay.'

'Not now, Red. Go to your room.'

Mumbling and sniffing, he did as he was told, taking Miss Bournemouth with him.

'I apologise for that.' Edgar exhaled noisily. 'He's er … so much smarter when he keeps his mouth closed.'

Reggie nodded. 'I take it he is your son, the other half of Ormrod and Ormrod? I noticed only your name on the outer door.'

'Ah, yes. Bit premature the *O and O* bit, he's not qualified yet … keeps failing his exams.'

'Really! But after meeting him, I can't say I'm surprised. Remember the saying – if at first you don't succeed, then maybe failure is your thing.'

Edgar sighed. 'And that sums Redknapp up to a tee.'

'Redknapp! Not Ormrod?'

'Redknapp's his first name. Redknapp Ormrod. He was born on 8th January 1984.'

'Really! Is that piece of trivia supposed to mean something?'

'Oh yes, it was a momentous day. You see Bournemouth played Manchester United in the cup.' He pointed to the poster on the wall.

'Did they indeed.'

'Yes, Bournemouth, bottom in Division Three, beat the mighty United, two nil. It was the best day of my life - two magical events on the same day – the birth of my son and beating United. Harry Redknapp was the Bournemouth manager. So, what better way to remember those amazing twin events than to call my son Redknapp.'

Reggie wished he'd never asked. 'Now Edgar, can we get down to business? I'm planning on returning to Kingston before the evening sets in. What date has been set for the funeral?'

Edgar shook his head. 'It can't be done until the police give their say so.'

Interrupted by a knock on the door, Mrs Pluck, looking like an airship with legs, ushered in a bespectacled man in his late fifties. He was dressed in a mid-blue suit, and chewing vigorously on a wad of gum, whilst smoking a cigarette at the same time. Pushing the gum round his mouth, he first made one cheek bulge and then the other.

'Ah, Dorian, er Sergeant Clapp.' Edgar rose, guiding the man to the chair next to Reggie. 'This is Mr Reginald Grosvenor Smythe, OBE, the gentleman I told you about.'

The sergeant's face was bulging and pink ... like a giant haemorrhoid, Reggie thought.

Slouching into his seat, he blew a stream of smoke out of the corner of his mouth. The smell of tobacco hung on him like a shroud.

'No smoking in here, Dorian, I've told you before. It's not allowed.'

Grudgingly stubbing his cigarette out, he gave a cough resembling catarrh, then used a soiled tissue to remove the gum from his mouth and placed it in the jacket pocket.

Reggie was not amused. 'Sergeant Clapp,' he boomed. 'As a gentleman, I try not to have an emotion that is unbecoming, but the ill-mannered performance I've just had the misfortune to witness does nothing to inspire any credibility in your ability to carry our any law enforcement duties.'

Taken by surprise, D S Clapp's stunned response was to open and close his mouth a couple of times, like a goldfish at feeding time. 'Er, what was that? Eh, but you shouldn't speak to a police officer like that.' His thick rubbery lips constantly worked his jaw.

Reggie pursed his lips to contain his irritation. 'Putting all that to one side, Sergeant, what grand illumination is it you think you'll be able to glean from me?'

Incensed, Clapp imperceptibly clenched and unclenched his fists. Taking a deep breath, he regained something close to his composure. Opening a file, he took out some papers. 'Well now, sir, in carrying out my orders re the death of one Miss Cressida Smythe,' his pedantic diction similar to that of a police constable in a television series Reggie had watched as a boy.

'From Mr Ormrod's records – thank you very much, Edgar,' he nodded in his direction, 'I have here your name and date of birth. But, as I understand, sir, you lived out of the country for several years. I need evidence of your British citizenship … sir.'

Irritated by this abomination of a law officer, Reggie articulated slowly, 'If you need proof, Sergeant, I really do feel that my Saville Row tailored Harris Tweed jacket and MCC tie should be more than sufficient evidence that I am a British Subject – note the word Subject - not a citizen as you mistakenly put it, because citizens belong to republics and we, thank the Lord, do not.'

Clapp shuffled uncomfortable in his chair.

'And to add to the above, I received the Order of the British Empire from Her Majesty, Queen Elizabeth II, an honour bestowed on British subjects.'

D S Clapp knew that he wouldn't win in any battle of wits with this pumped-up pompous blockhead, and slowly ticked a box on the form, muttering loud enough for them to hear that the Order of the British Empires was a load of rubbish.

Hackles raised to a new level, Reggie gave Clapp a fearsome glare. 'Let me explain something to you, D S Clapp. We British led the world in the most important development in human history since the bronze age. We have lifted the human race out of abject poverty, making modern civilization possible, and bringing hope of betterment to every part of the globe. That's what the British Empire achieved.'

D S Clapp knew he had no answer to that.

Concerned that the situation was getting out of control, Edgar shifted uncomfortably in his chair. 'Now moving on, Sergeant, has the body been released yet?'

'No, Edgar. Tests are still being carried out.' Inwardly preening himself in the knowledge that he was privy to information unknown to the others, he smirked. 'What I am about to tell you is confidential - so please keep this to yourselves, gentlemen. Miss Smythe was murdered.'

CHAPTER NINE

'Murdered,' thundered Reggie, a shiver ran down his spine 'My Aunt, Cressida Smythe murdered! By the Sainted God's of Albion, who would do a thing like that?'

'And that, Mr Smythe, is what I am trying to discover.' The officer placed another tick on his form. 'Where were you on the 3rd of July, the day Miss Smythe passed on?'

'Passed on?' bellowed Reggie. 'I've been reliably informed that my aunt actually died on the 3rd of July, and as far as I know, she did not pass on anything. And let me assure you, D S Clapp, I resided in Kingston upon Thames all that day.'

'Hmmm. Were you with a person or persons on that date, sir?'

'No.'

'So, you were alone all day.' Rolling an unlit cigarette dextrously around his mouth. Clapp referred to the form once more. 'Were there any witnesses to you being alone?'

Reggie's well-cultivated and bristling eyebrows rose in disbelief. 'How could anyone be witness to that? I was alone. Nobody came to check that I was alone because if they had, I would not have been alone.' It was like holding a conversation with a lobotomised simpleton.

The smile Clapp attempted was purely a mechanical adjustment of his lower face and devoid of any humour. Slowly taking off his glasses, he carefully placed them next to the form on the desk. 'Just checking, sir.'

'Can we move on, Sergeant?' Edgar butted in.

'Of course, Edgar,' Clapp smirked. 'It's my trusted method of questioning, you see. I compare it with colonic irrigation - I like to get rid of the easy bits first before concentrating on the serious business.'

Edgar pulled a face. 'Your analogy does you no credit, Dorian. And you haven't told us how she was murdered.'

'No, I haven't, have I? She was poisoned. It seems that during the post-mortem, traces of thallium were found in her bloodstream ... or so they say. Thallium, being the poisoners poison, is untraceable in most cases - the main clue for the pathologist being hair coming out in clumps.' He turned his attention to Edgar. 'Have you been able to locate Miss Smythe's housekeeper yet, Miss Dorothy Smerdal?'

'No, Sergeant. I was hoping that you, the police, would have traced her by now.'

'We haven't, but we've put a nationwide search out for her.'

'And?' questioned Reggie.

Clapp gave a deep sigh. 'No luck so far, sir.'

Reggie's dislike of the man was increasing by the minute; the blatant overuse of 'sir' was clearly and deliberately patronising – a covert sneer.

Edgar began to stand, and then thought better of it. 'Dorothy Smerdal is one of the beneficiaries of Miss Smythe's will.'

'Yes, I know. And that conveniently leads my questioning onto you, Mr Edgar Ormrod.' Clapp referred to his file once again. 'Unlike Mr Smythe here, I note you and your son Redknapp are beneficiaries of Miss Smythe's will. You stand to receive quite a handy sum.'

Edgar appeared to shrink under Clapp's steady gaze. 'Oh, that,' a faint line of sweat gathered along the twin furrows on his forehead. 'Yes, I was surprised myself. Very generous of her but I don't expect to er ... you know. The amount won't be much.' Edgar's neck was getting warm. 'Miss Smythe wasn't a rich lady.'

'And do you know that to be a fact, Edgar?' The tone of Clapp's plodding voice had taken on a suspicious note. 'Ten percent of her estate each for you and your son, Redknapp, would be significant. Her financial affairs were handled by an accountant, I believe.'

'Yes, it's mentioned in the will.' Edgar's eyes were as unrevealing as black holes.

Turning to Reggie, Clapp added, 'Although not a financial beneficiary, you are mentioned in Miss Smythe's will.'

'Am I indeed? In unflattering terms, I would imagine.'

'I'll come to that later if you don't mind, sir. In fact, Mr Grosvenor Smythe, I am officially requesting that you remain in Ringwood for the next few days to help with our investigation. Please do not leave town.'

'Not leave town!' Reggie laughed, 'Balderdash, don't be ridiculous. Am I under arrest?'

'No, nothing like that, sir.'

'For your information, Clapp, I will leave town at a time of my own choosing. I will not be dictated to by a perfunctory.

Being a free-born Englishman, I possess and enjoy individual liberty under a free and democratic government and reject any aphorism to the contrary.' He continued putting on a Churchillian intonation. 'Freedom from arbitrary detention is the oldest human right dating back to Magna Carta.' Then mischievously added, 'Did she die in vain?'

'Erm ... er,' was as far as Clapp got. Self-doubting his own intelligence, he decided to leave that alone and change his approach. 'We have here, sir, a murder, and experience tells us that close family members are often involved, either directly or indirectly. You are the late demised nearest relative. But you are not, as such, a suspect, but, there again,' he paused to marshal his thoughts, 'you are an un-suspect.'

'An un-suspect!' Reggie ridiculed. 'What a relief,' and theatrically mopped his brow.

Ignoring the sarcasm, D S Clapp took an envelope out of his folder. 'This was attached to Miss Smythe's will; it's addressed to Reggie Smythe. No mention of the "Grosvenor".' He slid it across the table, 'or the OBE.'

'The old girl disliked the Grosvenor side of the family.'

'Oh, I see, sir.'

Picking it up, the seal on the back of the envelope had been broken. 'But it's been opened!'

'Yes sir, we did that.'

'But you can't do that, Sergeant,' Edgar chipped in. 'It's against all procedures.'

D S Clapp's lips pulled into a thin line, the closest he got to a smile. 'It's a murder enquiry, Edgar. Of course, we had the right. We want Mr Smythe to tell us who this lady is.'

'What lady?' Reggie frowned. There was an awkward silence as he read the slip of paper. 'Who in the blue-blazes is Gertrude Dogberry.'

'We were hoping you would tell us, sir.'

'Never heard of her.'

Edgar looked at the note himself. 'This lady is due to receive sixty percent of Miss Smythe's estate. All our enquiries have so far failed to identify or locate her.'

'And Aunt Cressy wants me to find her. Can't you do that Sergeant? You boys in blue have got the where-with-all.'

'We are trying, sir, but it's usually the solicitor or next of kin who has the information, isn't that right, Edgar?'

'Well, I guess in a way, we have tried. Reggie. You should contact Percy Blimp, he's the man.'

'Percy who?'

'Blimp. He's our local expert in, you know, family trees, ancestry, that sort of thing. He knows how to find people.'

'Well, I'm not interested,' Reggie emphatically declared.' You find her.'

A scowling D S Clapp declared, 'It's wrong to ignore the wishes of the dead.'

'Not really,' Reggie intoned calmly. 'Cressida Smythe is dead, beyond trouble, toil and disarray, nothing can upset her now. That's the great thing about being dead; you don't even mind what the weather is.' Looking at his watch, he noted that it was after three o'clock. 'As it is getting late, I and my friend Mr Lee are prepared, reluctantly, to stay overnight. Edgar, kindly asks Mrs Pluck to book two rooms at the Struan Hotel.'

'The Struan's gone. Knocked down about fifteen years ago for housing.'

'Oh, that's terrible. Where do you recommend, then?'

'The best hotel near here is *Forest Glenn*, a 4-star hotel just out of town. I'll get her to book it for you.'

Just then, Redknapp opened the door and gave an enormous sneeze.

'Ah, Redknapp.' D S Clapp smiled. 'Come on in, I have a few questions for you.'

Gleefully, Redknapp joined the others. 'Call me Red please, Inspector.'

D S Clapp gave him an encouraging smile. 'Red, the late Miss Smythe has left you cash in her will. Do you know why?'

'No, but it'll make my girlfriend happy.'

Edgar glowered. 'You silly boy, you don't have a girlfriend.'

'Oh yes I do, Dad.'

'When did this happen?'

'We met on July 4th. She was holding an American flag. She said it was their birthday.'

Still smirking, Clapp continued. 'July 4th, was it? The day after Miss Smythe died'.

'Yea, it was. 'I think it were before Rigoletta set in – I read about it in your law book Dad.'

Edgar gives a deep sigh and nods at Clapp. 'He means rigor mortis.'

'I guessed as much. Now Red, where did you meet this girlfriend of yours?'

'I met her, she's Tiffany, on the corner at Friday's Cross. She'd just been to the dentist – she had loose morals.'

This brought the conversation to a halt. 'I think Red,' Edgar eventually said, 'that if she went to the dentist, it was because she had loose molars.'

'Oh yea. Anyway, she were standing there when I walked past. She was working the street. I stopped to have a word with her.'

'Working the street, Red? What exactly was the work she was doing … in the street?'

'Just that – street working,' he said in a matter-of-fact tone.

Clapp eyed him with amusement. 'Was this in er … should I say in a professional capacity?'

The question puzzled Redknapp. 'Yes, I suppose so.'

Clapp rapidly scribbled on his pad. 'And how did Tiffany know Miss Smythe?'

'Cos she were always complaining, that's why. She hated her.'

'Did she now? Was it because of her profession?' It was said in the same amused tone, but the words suggested something else.

'Oh, yes. It was - definitely. Tiffany drives one of those small steamrollers that road crews use. She'd just got back on it and was sitting with a cigarette in her mouth and bent down and asked me if I had a light. I didn't, but I said something about her steamroller, and we started to chat.'

A beaming Reggie reached across and shook Redknapp by the hand. 'And jolly well done, old chap. There is nothing like a steamroller to bring two young people together. A match made by JCBs should be rejoiced.'

CHAPTER TEN

The *Forest Glenn Hotel* proved to provide pleasant enough accommodation, especially for Reggie who decided to upgrade to a suite. Located on the top floor, it had agreeable views over manicured gardens and the New Forest beyond. His heart give a thud of applause – yes, it is, without question, beautiful countryside. It brought back memories of school holidays cycling the many pathways in the sun-kissed days of summer, a sanctuary away from the unloving Aunt Cressy. He felt that if England had a heart, it had to be here.

He ordered a bottle of single malt and would have happily remained in his room. The room service dinner menu looked inviting enough, but he couldn't leave Mr Lee all evening, particularly as the poor chap had waited in the Rolls for several hours that afternoon. They met in the dining room at seven.

'Did you finish *bwisness*, sir?' Mr Lee asked, polishing the lenses of his glasses.

'I think, Mr Lee, now that we are better acquainted, you should call me by my first name, Reggie.'

'Ah ...I call you *Weggie?*'

Reggie had a faint inkling that he'd heard the term before – what could it be? 'Is that acceptable to you?'

'Oh yes sir.' He faltered again. 'I have confession - in my head, my name for you is *Keon Ko*.'

'You call me what?'

'Keon Ko. I *sowwy* it make me *wacist*. In *Kowea*, we call westerners Keon Ko which mean 'big nose'. I sowwy.'

'No need to be sorry, Mr Lee.' Placing his index finger on the end of his nose, he smiled. 'I guess compared to the Asian races, we do have large noses. I think it an appropriate term, and it's not racist.'

Mr Lee burst into a grin. 'Thank you sir … oh, I mean *Weggie*.'

'That's quite alright, Mr Lee. And what, pray, should I call you?'

'Mr *Ee*,' he bleated.

'Mr Lee. Not one of your other names, Su or Won?'

'No please. Call me Mr Ee. It custom in my *countwy*.'

'Well, Mr Lee, I've almost finished my business here, but before we return to Kingston in the morning, I have to visit the police station to make a statement.'

'*Powice*?' A note of alarm in his voice. 'They *awest* you?'

'Awest! Ah, you mean arrest. No, no, nothing like that. You see, Mr Lee, the business I had referred to was about my aunt. She used to live here in Ringwood. She's dead now – murdered.'

Mr Lee almost choked on his drink. '*Muwder* – that when *men'ses* kill on *puwpose'es* – is it?'

'Yes, that is correct. But I am not a suspect. In fact, I am an un-suspect according to the police officer, D S Clapp.'

'*Cwapp*?'

Reggie laughed. 'Yes, I like the way you pronounce it – *Cwapp*. I think *crap* is an appropriate description of the man.'

Clearly not understanding, Mr Lee added. 'We have saying in my *countwy*. When bad *men'ses* kill, a dove *cwashes* in water and *dwoun*. You have same saying?'

'I don't believe we do. No.'

'It mean ... '

'Thank you, Mr Lee.' Reggie gently cut him short, 'I understand what it means.' The last thing he wanted was another incomprehensible Korean saying. 'The date for my aunt's funeral has not yet been set so I will have to come back to Ringwood. Will you be able to drive me down again?'

'Of course, *Weggie*. I be honour.'

'Very kind, Mr Lee. Oh, by the way, both Ormrod and Ormrod have to attend the police station as well to make statements.'

'They *awested*?'

'No, they haven't been arrested, but Crap said they are *people of interest* and mustn't leave town. Crap is also looking for my late aunt's housekeeper, who went missing on the date of the murder. He also is trying to locate a person who may well be a distant relation of mine. She is, by the way, the largest beneficiary of the will.'

Giving a quick laugh, Mr Lee said, 'Ah, this is good, it *compwicated* puzzle. *Wike* a Agatha *Cwistie mystewy*.'

'Yes indeed,' Reggie smiled. 'Like Agatha Crispie.' Pushing his half-empty plate to one side – his dinner had been disappointing. He signed for both meals. 'We should meet here for breakfast at nine o'clock in the morning.'

'Yes *Weggie*. But first I now go *Wingwood*. I go *nite'es* club.'

Somewhat surprised, Reggie didn't realise that the vertically-challenged Korean gentleman was a frequenter of exotic nightlife, and certainly not in Ringwood. Thinking back, he remembered summer nights when the market square would be thick with teenagers drinking beer from cans, smoking and feasting on fish, chips and burgers. No nightclubs, only *The Regal* provided any entertainment. 'I hope you find what you're looking for, Mr Lee, but a word of caution - beware of young ladies driving steamrollers.'

'Ooo,' came his high-pitched response. 'I like *steamwower* and massage.'

Oh dear, Reggie thought. Mr Lee will be in for a disappointing night.

CHAPTER ELEVEN

Comforted with a tumbler of single malt, Reggie did his best to settle in a large, but lumpy armchair to read the newspaper; the pure, clean flavour of the whisky beginning to cancel out the aftertaste of his woeful dinner. Through his window, he could see the last golden light of day fading to a dusky pink.

A knock on the door brought him back to the present. Thinking it would be the maid to turn down his bed and, hopefully, leave a chocolate on his pillow, he opened the door. A man of middling age stood there. Staring hard at Reggie, tension gathered along the line of his jaw. Unflinchingly, he maintained eye contact as though searching for something. It seemed to Reggie that this unannounced visitor's posture bordered on the confrontational.

'Can I help you?' He was tall, similar in height to Reggie, with blue eyes and broad shoulders. A lock of dark-brown hair strayed over his brow.

'Are you Reginald Smythe?'

'May I know who's asking?'

'I'm Chester Makepeace.'

'Well, Chester Makepeace, kindly tell me why you are here.'

The man's shoulders moved up and down as if to relieve inner tension. 'Please answer me. Are you Reginald Smythe?'

'Well, Mr Makepeace, if it will satisfy your curiosity and let me return to my newspaper,' Reggie spoke as charitably as he could, 'My name, as registered at reception, is Reginald Grosvenor Smythe OBE. Now, I would love to stand here and talk ... but I am not going to. Go away.'

The man flinched like someone cut by a rapier tip. 'Oh my God, it is you,' he exclaimed. 'I thought so. You are my father.'

Reggie's eyebrows arched like a croquet hoop. Keeping his voice under control, he said, 'Mr Makepeace, I don't know what kind of nonsensical deception you are scheming. You are, however, trespassing on my space, and let me emphasise, I am not your father. Consequently, I would be obliged if you would kindly remove yourself. I have a newspaper to read.'

Nervously, Makepeace wiped the mounting perspiration from his brow, but remained standing on the threshold. 'You are my father,' he blurted out again, his heavy black eyebrows anxiously rising and falling in unison.

Annoyed, Reggie increased the volume of his voice. 'I'm about to close the door, and if you don't leave immediately, I'll phone security to have you forcibly removed.' He started to close the door forcing Makepeace back as he did so.

'My mother is Sylvia Makepeace.' He pushed lightly back against the closing door.

'Well, bully for you.' Reggie pushed harder. 'Now, go away.'

As it was about to close, Makepeace managed to shout through the disappearing crack, 'She was Sylvia Fox.'

The door closed.

It was now Reggie's turn to stand rooted to the spot. His heart beating rapidly, reaching the top end on his personal

Richter scale. Sylvia Fox – my Foxy. Slowly, he reopened the door. Makepeace was still there. Reggie dropped his air of control. 'Tell me once again, what is your mother's name?'

'Her maiden name was Sylvia Fox.'

Staring at the younger man for several seconds, Reggie's brain raced at top speed. Could it be true? He tried to remember how he looked forty years ago to see if there was any resemblance. There was. Great Chivas! Opening the door wide, he said, 'You'd better step inside.'

Exhaling heavily, Makepeace entered, standing awkwardly inside the entrance.

'Tell me erm ... Chester, what makes you think that I could possibly be your father. How old are you for starters?'

'Forty-one.'

'And your father is a certain Mr Makepeace?'

'Yes. He adopted me when he married my mother.'

'And when did you reach the absurd deduction that I am your father?'

'It was only this afternoon. I overheard my mother's next-door neighbour telling her that Reginald Smythe was in town. My mother almost had a fit and blurted out that something - it was hard to hear, and I almost missed it, but it sounded as if she linked your name with me. As soon as she said it, she tried to cover it up, blustering on about work or ... I don't know what. Anyway, that's why I'm here.'

'That's not very convincing,' Reggie said.

'I agree. I wasn't convinced myself, but I thought I'd try and find you, never ever knowing who my real father was. But when I saw you just now – well, I knew.'

'Your mother's neighbour seems to be very well informed.'

'Yes, Grace Pluck. She works for Edgar Ormrod.'

'Oh my God, her.' The image of that two hundred pounds of flab wobbling in and out of Edgar's office brought Reggie to a standstill. And being called Grace – how ironic. 'I think, Chester, that you have misunderstood what you thought you heard. I can't be your father.'

Chester mulled this over for a moment. 'Why don't I phone Mum now and ask her?'

'No, that would be ... well, iniquitous.'

Taken by surprise, Reggie was slow off the mark as Chester hurried over to the desk, picked up the phone and quickly dialled a number, warding off Reggie with an outstretched hand. 'It's ringing – you speak to her.' He held it out to Reggie.

A female voice answered. 'Hello, who's that?'

Reggie was stunned into silence.

'Oh, bloody hell, another deep breathing pervert.' Sylvia's voice was as he remembered, all those years ago, even in her scolding tone.

'Hello, Foxy, it's me, Reggie.'

There was silence. It took a few seconds before a hesitant reply came. 'Oh.'

'I hope I've not disturbed you. Chester is here with me.'

'Chester! Where are you?'

'He's in my hotel room ...the Forest Glenn.'

Another few seconds elapsed. 'Put him on.'

Reggie handed the phone back. 'Sorry Mum but ... I had to know.'

'You had no right to do this; it's none of your business.' Her angry voice was loud enough for Reggie to hear.

'But it is my business, Mum. I have a right to know who my father is.'

'I'm truly angry with you, Chester,' she countered. 'Put Mr Smythe back on.'

Chester passed it over. 'I'm sorry, Reggie,' her voice had calmed a little. 'Obviously, we need to talk. Can you come round and see me in the morning? Chester will give you the address.'

'Yes, of course I will.'

'I leave for work at eleven, so make it earlier than that.'

CHAPTER TWELVE

Breakfasting together in the hotel dining room, Reggie asked Mr Lee if he would mind staying in Ringwood for a few more days? 'I'll cover all the extra costs, of course.'

'Oh *Weggie*, I happy to stay,' Mr Lee gave one of his toe-curling grins. '*Wast* evening, I met *Kowean wady,* Mrs Kim. She work at massage p*awlour*. She *weceptionist*. Mrs Kim make me *Kowean* meal of *kimchi* and *galbi* with noodle and bottle soju. She also *awange* free massage for me with Thai girl. I *vewy, vewy* happy man.'

Reggie's usual vivid imagination was unable to picture the licentious events as described. He smiled, 'Well that's settled then, Mr Lee. I'll contact you later in the day.'

Chester had given Reggie Sylvia's address in Shady Grove Close, just off Southampton Road in the Poulner area of Ringwood. It was only a short distance from the hotel and Reggie found his own way there quite easily. Number 28 was a modest 1960s semi, set in a row of identical houses with pocket handkerchief-sized front gardens. The sun and wind had taken their toll on the door and window frames.

Checking for the second time that he had the right address, Reggie took a couple of deep breaths. All his life, he had not been one to suffer from nerves or faint heart ... except at that very moment. Could Chester Makepeace really be his son? On top of that, he was about to meet Sylvia Fox again, his Foxy. Did he actually impregnate her forty years ago before making off to the colonies? If he did, how was she going to react when she clapped eyes on him? Bloody furious probably. These questions, with all their ramifications, had driven all thoughts of Coralie out of his head for the first time in months.

The front door of the house opened. He recognised her immediately – it was Foxy. His heart missed a couple of beats.

She looked quite composed. 'Is it you, Reggie? Just look at you and your flash car.'

After a great deal of thought that morning, he had decided to wear a navy blazer, grey slacks, white shirt and tie, topped with his Panama hat. As usual, his trademark monocle was firmly fixed in place, and he carried his silver-topped cane. Still feeling uneasy, he gave a deep bow to cover his inner turmoil. 'Do I have the pleasure of addressing Mrs Makepeace?'

'God, you don't change, do you, Reggie? Still suave with the posh accent.'

The nerves he had felt earlier began to melt away – but only slightly.

She pointed to the neighbour's house. 'Come in before the curtains start twitching.'

She was the still the same Foxy. Older of course, with a tracery of faint criss-cross wrinkles around her face, and a little thicker around the waist. Her hairstyle had hardly changed, thick auburn, shoulder-length fixed back with a clasp, which fell onto the collar of a white blouse. The hem of her navy skirt fell exactly to the knees, and the curve of her full calves tapered to narrow ankles. An image flashed into his head of her standing naked before him all those years ago – it almost seemed like yesterday – no it didn't.

Still unsure of himself, he stood awkwardly inside the door.

'Don't stand there like a dummy, come through to the kitchen.' Her perfume smelled of jasmine. The click of her heels echoed off the terracotta floor tiles, as the swing of her hips was emphasised by the fullness of her skirt. There was something innately provocative in the movement.

'You look so ... I don't know ... so English.'

He saw in her the young Foxy, flashing eyes and a wide smile.

'Cup of tea?' she asked.

'That would be nice.' He would have preferred something stronger. Sitting at the kitchen table, he watched her plug in the kettle and take two mugs down from a wall cabinet.

'Just tea bags I'm afraid.' She dropped a bag into each mug.

But this welcome, meeting after all those years was too composed, too ordinary, almost as though he'd just popped in after being away for a few days. Why isn't she angry, why doesn't she yell and curse? Yet here he is, beside himself with anxiety, wanting to ask the one question that could change his life forever. 'Before we have tea,' he wavered, 'there's something ...'

'What is it?'

His heart beat a tattoo in his chest. 'I need to know if Chester is my son.'

Pausing, she turned towards him, blue eyes questioning. 'Yes.'

'Oh my God.'

The kettle started to boil.

'But how?' Oh, for the knack of never saying silly things.

'The usual way. Milk and sugar?' She turned and smiled, her full lips turned up at the corners, and glint of laughter in her eyes.

Although he'd been half-expecting this news, it still came like a shattering shock. Full of emotion, his head slumped onto his arms resting on the table. He was a father. Remaining bowed for several seconds, tears sprang into his eyes.

'It's alright, Reggie?' she said. 'I thought Chester had told you.'

Looking up, he gazed at her through blurry eyes.

'You don't have to do anything.' She poured water into both mugs.

'Why didn't you tell me you were pregnant?'

'I did – or at least I tried to, but I'm guessing you didn't receive my letters.' She was going to say something else but thought better of it. 'After our last night together, remember, that's when it happened. You left the following morning to go and conquer the world. We'd had your *Farewell to England fuck*.'

'No, it was never just that.'

'That's what you called it.'

'Did I really? I feel ashamed now.'

'If you recall, you'd brought the usual protection with you for ... how should I delicately put it, one go?'

The steam from his mug misted his monocle. 'Yes, I remember, but what happened?'

She held up three fingers. 'Artificial respiration you called it.'

'Oh.'

She gazed at him. 'You were wild that night. Nocturnal osmosis – I think you called it – I guessed it was more becoming than common or garden shagging. We even thought of installing a fire extinguisher in case we combusted.'

He shook his head and smiled. 'Yes, I remember.' In fact our last night together – the recollection of it, has remained top of his personal memory bank. 'Like Romeo and Juliet.'

'Unlike Henry Miller, I don't believe Shakespeare even wrote as descriptive as our antics.'

Reggie laughed. 'Yes, you're right.' Not only had Sylvia kept her looks, above all she'd kept her sense of humour. She could always make him laugh like nobody else could, and take the rise out of him.

'Oh, er, what were the letters you mentioned?'

'As I said, I did try to contact you.' Her fleeting smile touched Reggie's heart. 'It was a month before I realised I was pregnant. You'd left the address of the company you were joining, their London office that is, and I was told that you didn't work for them anymore. I then went to see your Aunt Cressy, but she didn't know or care and gleefully told me to piss off – well, words to that effect.' Her voice lowered to almost a whisper, 'I waited and waited for a letter, but nothing came.'

Reggie was at a loss. 'I promise I didn't receive any letters from you – *what a bugger,*' he swore, making and unmaking fists at his side before shoving them into his pockets.

'I wrote to you from hospital - three times I wrote to you. I gave money to the orderly for stamps and he promised to post them. But when I didn't receive a reply, I assumed that ... what? Well, I assumed you were glad to be rid of me and spreading your wings in pastures new.'

'Oh, good God, Reggie, no!' She took a tentative sip from her mug, the tea scolding her mouth. For a few moments there was silence, save for the sound of a motorbike racing along Shady Grove. They were both lost in their own thoughts.

'I assume you have children,' Sylvia ventured. 'You were married, I imagine.'

'Yes er, but no, no children. I married Coralie a year or so after I arrived in Africa, thirty years ago. She died last year.'

'Oh, I'm sorry. So is Chester your only child?'

He nodded. 'It's such a strange feeling after believing I'd never have children. How about you? Did you have any with Mr Makepeace? Is he around?'

Finishing her drink, she took the mug over to the sink. 'No, we didn't, he died almost fourteen years ago. You see, he was quite a bit older than me, eighteen years, but he was a lovely man and was willing to accept Chester and adopt him.' Slowly, she sat in the opposite chair. 'It wasn't a marriage of grand passion, if you know what I mean, but we were happy and loved each other.'

'Is there anyone else in your life now – you know, a man?'

Sitting in an easy chair, she pulled her knees up under her chin and hugged her shins. 'I've had a few liaisons over the years, but nothing serious. I hadn't expected to be in my 60's quite so soon – like taxis in the rain, birthdays go whizzing by.' Giving a little laugh, she continued. 'At my time of life, the main feature I look for in a man is whether he has full bladder control!'

Reggie laughed. 'I know what you mean. With men around my age, the topics are pensions, politics, and comparing how many times they have to get up in the night.'

Returning his laugh, she suddenly stopped by the radio, turning the sound up. 'Oh, my Lord! How's that for timing.'

The song, *Don't go breaking my heart* from their youth, caught them both by surprise.

'That is incredible,' Reggie mused. 'The stars above must be in alignment foretelling an extraordinary event has taken place. Music, certain songs, provide a memory marker, don't they? Transporting us back through time to when we were together.'

'Me too – but they were good times, all life smiled upon us,' she sighed. 'Whilst they lasted.'

Reggie nodded. 'Oh, and Chester, does he live with you?'

'No. He lives in Bournemouth and lectures at the university there. He lives with a young lady called Pandora. They've been together a year now, but I don't believe it's a love match – more a convenience. There'll be no children - you're not a grandfather as well as a father.' Her smile was the alluring smile he remembered, the upturned corners of her lips, the creases around her eyes.

'Tell me about Chester. Oh, why did you call him Chester of all names?'

'My mother sent me there when I started to show. The shame, you know.'

'You went to Chester to give birth?'

'I did. Just outside the city in Upton. My Mum's sister, Auntie Margie, lived there.'

'I see. When did you return to Ringwood?'

'With Freddie – Freddie Makepeace, three years later. We married there so that Chester would have a father. This was partly to spare my Mum's old-fashioned sensibilities.'

'Poor you.'

'No, I was very lucky. Freddie was with Lloyds Bank and was able to transfer here; knew I wanted to come back.

By then, nobody knew for certain if Chester was conceived out of wedlock, except those who bothered to count.' Trying to gather her jumbled thoughts together, she said. 'I have a question, Reggie. What would you have done if you'd received my letters?'

'I'd have come back, of course, to make an honest woman of you.' He grimaced slightly. 'That's a terrible cliché, but you know what I mean.'

Her thoughts raced to and fro speculating how their lives would have changed, but it was too complicated for now. 'Anyway, what were you doing in hospital?'

He pointed to his left eye with the monocle. 'I was taken off the plane in Bombay as the injury had worsened – probably because of the altitude. It was unbearable.'

It was Sylvia's turn to look shocked. 'That's not the one I ...'

Reggie nodded.

'Oh my God, I'm sorry. I didn't realise it was that bad.'

'I didn't either, at the time, that is. It turned out part of the eye socket had fractured; a piece of bone was pressing on a critical nerve. I had two operations to put it right. Instead of being in Singapore with my new employer, I was stuck in a Bombay hospital for over seven weeks.'

'And that's because you didn't duck when I threw that bottle of perfume at you.'

'It served me right for being a cheapskate. Woolworths was not a good enough present for you, so I blamed myself – not you.'

'Is that why you're wearing a monocle?'

'It is. Without it, the focus is not so good. I could wear spectacles of course, but the monocle fitted in with the image I was trying to create.'

'And did it help?'

'Yes, I think it did. It goes well with my posh accent and smart clothes – naked people have very little or no influence on society ... don't you think?'

'Maybe,' she smiled. 'But of all the mighty cockups in history, this must be amongst the biggest. You never received my letters, and I didn't receive yours. It was the international postal service in both directions which kept us apart.' Reggie took her hand and gave it a gentle squeeze - the enormity of this communication failure was not lost on either of them.

'Have you ever seen a TV programme called *As Time Goes By?*'

He shook his head, unsure of the relevance. 'Tell me more about my son – I should say our son, our only child. I want to know everything about him.'

She checked her watch. 'Look Reggie, I have to go to work soon. Why don't you come round for dinner tonight and we'll continue from there?'

'Yes, I'd be delighted. Where do you work?'

'I'm a part-timer at Sainsbury's.'

'Oh, I thought you'd be a university lecturer yourself. You did get your English degree, didn't you - Nottingham Trent wasn't it?'

She shook her head. 'I was well into my final year when well ... you know.'

Reggie looked puzzled. 'What do I know?' Suddenly, the explanation hit him. 'Oh my God, it was me, wasn't it?'

'Things were different in those days. Breast feeding in lectures was definitely not on.'

'Oh, I'm so very, very sorry. Our passion deprived the world of a poetess extraordinaire. I hope you forgave me.'

She was silent for a moment. 'Not at first I didn't - I bloody well hated you. With not hearing from you, well, what could I think? I assumed you'd just lost interest and found someone else. I called you every rude word I could think of – I even shouted out a word which scholars have so far failed to discover in any dictionary.'

Reggie laughed. 'I don't blame you. But after sending three letters with nothing from you I thought … well, I didn't know what to think. Except I missed you – missed you very much. I didn't date anyone for years thinking I'd eventually hear from you. It was ten years after I left England that I married Coralie.'

She pushed some strands of hair off her face and rested her forehead in her palms. 'But time heals. Marrying Freddie Makepeace and baby Chester's sort of compensated for not hearing from you, as well as not getting my degree. I was so proud of Chester. He grew up to be an exceptional, well-behaved boy, excelled in school and the sports field. He ended up Head Boy.'

'And I missed all of that,' His voice unsteady and full of emotion.

'Anyway, I'm late for work,' she said. 'I enjoy working at Sainsbury's, the people are genuinely nice. Some of my best friends work there, especially Pam. You could drop me off outside if you like.' Smiling she added, 'I'd like to be dropped off by a handsome gentleman in a big Rolls Royce. It'll do my street cred no end of good.'

They drove to Sainsbury's nearest entrance. Taking her time in the hope that some of her work colleagues could be watching, she turned to Reggie and gave him a long, lingering kiss. 'See you tonight, darling,' her voice was husky, barely above a whisper. 'Around six o'clock. We can start all over again - it'll be like old times.'

Chapter Thirteen

The eleven o'clock chimes from the Parish Church faded into the distance as Reggie arrived back at the *Forest Glenn Hotel*, his mind adrift in a sea of uncertainty. He was a father and he had been without knowing it for forty-one years. His eyes misted over with the cruel sadness of it all. Missing all the supposed landmarks of life like bonding with one's child, school and sports, and, of all things, him being Head Boy. 'And with my genes,' he said to himself, 'no wonder.' He'd also missed his later years like voting for the first time, getting a driver's licence and - losing his virginity. And now they were total strangers. How could he make up for it? He poured himself a large whisky to help put his thoughts into focus.

And then Foxy. What was the message she had just signalled? What had she meant saying *"We can start over again"* and something like *"just like old times"* followed by a passionate kiss? It didn't make sense. Old times for them had mainly been spent, hard at it in the bedroom. So, what, *Mon Dieu*, was she planning for tonight? Surely not that ... or maybe she was.

Apart from Mr Lee, the hotel lounge was deserted except for a young couple deep in conversation in the far corner. A sullen waitress with a botched peroxide job on her short hair brought two coffees to their table, whilst scratching a nose ring.

Reggie pulled a face after his first sip. 'As soon as we finish coffee, I'd like you to drive me to Lymington Police Station. I've written the address on this paper.'

'Of course, *Weggie*.'

They headed off through picturesque New Forest scenery, ancient woodlands and heather-covered heath, interspersed with grazing areas dotted with gorse bushes. 'This is the land of yeomen, poets and artists,' Reggie declared theatrically. 'My England.'

Mr Lee nodded, but remained silent. Suddenly, a pony roamed onto the road, forcing Mr Lee to come to a halt. 'It *howse*, can I *kiw* it?'

'Good God, Mr Lee, no. The forest is full of ponies like this, and they are protected. It is a crime to kill them.'

He gave his customary, oriental sigh. 'That too bad, good to eat.'

Observing the speed limits, it only took twenty-five minutes to reach the outskirts of Lymington. Studying his satnav, Mr Lee found the quickest route to the main entrance of the Police Station. 'It no parking,' he squeaked.

'Don't worry, stop right here.' Reggie commanded. 'I will go inside. You stay where you are in the car.'

'I do that, *Weggie*.'

A uniformed policeman hurried over. 'You can't er ... oh.' Hesitating on seeing the Rolls, and an impressively attired Reggie, including the Panama and silver-topped cane, he paused.

'Take care of my limousine, constable.' Reggie instructed, using his Falstaffian brand of speech. 'Official business, my man.'

'Oh, er ... yes sir,' he touched his helmet in a hesitant salute. Peering into the driver's window, he saw Mr Lee, looking inscrutable.

There was no police station in Ringwood, so D S Clapp had asked Reggie to use Lymington - the files on Miss Smythe were there. Clapp wasn't in, but the duty officer was expecting him. On a form provided, Reggie briefly wrote his statement, signed it and marched out, receiving another salute from the constable. Intuitively understanding his part in the pretence, Mr Lee gave a deep bow as he opened the rear car door for Reggie.

'I want the nearest chemist or pharmacy in Lymington, Mr Lee.' Reggie had written both words out for him. Like Morton's Fork, Reggie was still pondering the duplicitous message Foxy had given him about that evening. Since Coralie's death, the thought of having sex with another woman had not entered his head, and not having done it since then, wondered whether he was still up to it. When Sylvia had kissed him in the car, there had been no stirrings. Was he dead down there?

And what would Coralie have thought? Reggie knew she would want him to find a new, loving relationship. On the flimsy basis that Sylvia possibly wanted him to perform that evening, he would probably need some help, and the only thing he could think of was Viagra. Just to be prepared. Not having lived in the UK for a long time, he was not sure if the drug was freely available.

After turning down several narrow streets, Mr Lee found a parking space outside a small chemist shop. 'Thank you, Mr Lee. I'll just be a minute.'

Apart from two elderly ladies chatting together as they examined a shelf full of vitamin pills, the shop was empty. This made Reggie a little more comfortable. An unsavoury looking male attendant was behind the counter. He had acne and a chronic sinus problem. 'Yes, mate,' he sniffed.

Reggie bristled. 'Young man, I am not, and never will be your mate, so kindly refrain from using that impertinent term.'

Taken aback, the man sniffed again, breathing through his mouth. ''Ere 'ang about, mush. So, what yer after?'

The creature looked as if he had four or five generations of inbreeding behind him. 'I would prefer to be served by an attendant proficient in the English language.'

'Just me 'ere at the moment ma...' he mumbled, wiping his nose on his sleeve. 'Me dad's not 'ere. Back in ten.'

'In that case,' Reggie reluctantly asked. 'Do you have Viagra?'

A nasty smirk spread across his disagreeable face. 'Viagra, is it?' He loudly gave notice to the two elderly ladies and gave an exaggerated wink.

'Your ocular gyrations, young man, do you no credit. Do you have Viagra?'

The two ladies put their pill bottles back on the shelf and moved stealthily towards the counter. This was going to be fodder for several days' coffee mornings.

Slowly, it dawned on the young man that the puffed-up customer could be an inspector from head office. Quickly wiping the smirk from his face, he held out his hand, clicking his thumb and finger together.

'And what, pray, does your wretched finger rotation mean?' Reggie's voice was now like bottled thunder.

'Perscription,' he stuttered.

'If you mean a *prescription*, I don't have one.'

The brow-beaten young man's shoulders slumped. 'Not qualified er ... sir.'

Storming out, Reggie raised his hat to the two ladies. 'Good day to you, dear ladies. If it's Viagra you require in this dreadful establishment, I'm afraid you'll both need prescriptions.'

Back in the car, Reggie gradually calmed down. 'Mr Lee, I'd like you to do me a favour.'

'Favour for *Weggie*. I *wike* it. We have saying in my *countwy*. If man find *dwagon* eggs, it is *fwiend* who helps *cawwy* them – like favour. You have same saying?'

'Yes, we do, Mr Lee. Exactly the same - word for word.'

Chapter Fourteen

Back at the hotel, Reggie phoned the local medical centre. After a tedious recorded message giving numerous options, he pressed number three for appointments. Two tortuous choruses of Des O'Connor singing *"My Way"* did nothing to improve Reggie's disposition. The call was eventually answered. 'Reception, Kathleen speaking.'

'Good day to you, Kathleen,' Reggie turned on his effortless charm. 'My name is Reginald Grosvenor Smythe OBE, and I need to arrange an appointment for a colleague of mine to see a doctor as soon as possible – it is rather urgent.'

'I'm sorry, but all appointments have been taken for today.'

'You see, Kathleen, my colleague is an important scientist from the Republic of Korea, doing nerve agent research in this country.' He paused before adding conspiratorially, 'Official secrets, and all that. The appointment has to be this afternoon; five minutes would be sufficient.'

'*Oooh*, I *vewy impowtant* scientist,' Mr Lee gave a squeaky giggle. 'I *wike* it.'

'Oh, just a moment, sir,' Reggie heard whispers doing the rounds for a few seconds. 'Well sir, I've just spoken with the practice manager, and we can squeeze him in, at five past three this afternoon with Doctor Rollins. What name is it?'

'Thank you most kindly, Kathleen,' Reggie purred. 'His name is Professor Lee. Now, he struggles a little with the English language. He may need help.'

'I visit doctor?' Mr Lee asked, open mouthed. 'I not sick.'

'Of course you aren't Mr Lee.' Reggie gave him a beaming smile. Taking a sheet of hotel notepaper, he wrote *"I, Professor Lee from Korea. My brother die. I have very important meeting with his widow lady this evening. Korean tradition make it necessary for me to be ready to bed with widow lady if she so demands to free his spirit. It important for me to save face. I need Viagra to do this. Kindly issue a prescription."*

'Please sign this note, Mr Lee.'

Dutifully, he did as he was told. Only then did he start to read it. 'My *bwother* dead! I have no *bwother*.' He read further. 'Oh no, you say I need *Viagwa* to bed *Kowean wady*? I not need it.'

Re-assuredly patting him on the shoulder, Reggie phoned room service and ordered coffee and cakes. 'Let me explain, Mr Lee. The Viagra is for me.'

'For you?'

'Yes.' Reggie wondered how he should put it. 'You see, Mr Lee, because I am known here, I can't be seen asking for Viagra at the doctors in Ringwood. So you go, see Doctor Rollins, and give him this paper. The doctor will give you another piece of paper called a prescription so we can get the Viagra together at the pharmacy.'

'Doctor *Wowins*?' Mr Lee grinned. '*Weggie*, I think you *embawass*, so I go.'

'Thank you, Mr Lee. This is the favour I asked you for.'

'Okay. I do it.'

Reggie drove the short distance to the surgery in good time for Mr Lee's appointment. He parked close to Reception and left the car window open. Smiling to himself, he heard Mr Lee's high-pitched shriek introducing himself. '*Ee su won*'. The sound of a cup crashing to the floor and a look of shock-horror on the receptionist's face could be seen as she peered over the counter at the tiny Korean.

After allowing for a possible delay in seeing the doctor, Reggie was beginning to be concerned. It was nearly four o'clock before a bedraggled Mr Lee stumbled out of the surgery, staggering as though he'd been on a drinking binge. His tie was unfastened, and the buttons on his uniform were in the wrong holes making the garment skew-whiff.

'I *vewy* unhappy,' he bleated forlornly.

'What in the blue-blazes happened to you?'

'Oh *Weggie*. I *vewy, vewy* unhappy.' Trembling, he got into the car.

'Tell me what happened. Are you in pain?'

Taking several deep breaths, he slowly calmed down. 'Doctor *Wowins*, she not a nice *wady*.'

'Doctor Rollins was a *wady* ... er lady?'

'Yes, *Weggie. You not tew me*.'

'I didn't know, Mr Lee. I assumed it would be a man. Anyway, what did she do?'

'I give her paper, she *wead* it and ask me things I not understand.'

'What was it she asked?'

'I not know. She make me take off jacket for *bwood pwesure*. It *vewy* high, she say. She tell me take shirt off and put stethoscope over me. Then *twouser* come off.'

'I'm so sorry, Mr Lee,' Reggie sympathised.

'She then said about *ewection*.'

'What an impertinent thing to ask an important gentleman of your standing.' Reggie was about to boil over. 'What did you say?'

'I told her conservative *pawty* win *ewection*.'

Reggie beamed. 'Brilliant, Mr Lee. Absolutely brilliant. Well done.'

'But when I say that she got *angwy* with me - why?'

Reggie shrugged his shoulders, holding the palms of his hands out in a questioning gesture. 'Why indeed?' He moved his head from side to side. 'Women!'

'*Oooh*.' Lee joined him, shaking his head in a similar fashion. 'Women,' he squeaked. 'Same in *Kowea*.'

'Ah, but did she give you the prescription?'

'She not do that. She say something I not understand, and paper not needed for boots. *Weggie*. I not need boots.'

'Boots? I wonder if she meant Boots the Chemist?'

'I not know. She say no paper for boots.'

'Mr Lee, I'm deeply sorry you've had all these problems. Doctor Rollins should not have done this. However, I know there's a Boots the Chemist in Ferndown, so we will go there now. You sit back and relax.'

The assumption about Boots the Chemist selling Viagra without a prescription was correct. Consoling Mr Lee once again, Reggie drove them back to their hotel. Going straight to the bar, Reggie ordered doubles of whisky to sooth their nerves. Gradually, Mr Lee regained his composure and Reggie booked him a dinner in the hotel's restaurant. Reggie would be at Sylvia's for dinner, armed with his potency enhancer – just in case.

CHAPTER FIFTEEN

Deep in thought, Reggie drove slowly through Poulner for his dinner date with Foxy. He had a lot on his mind. What were his feelings towards her? Now he'd found out that she is the mother of his only child. Before he left England all those years ago, he had loved her in a young at heart sort of way; not in a 'let's settle down and marry' way. He was young, in search of excitement, travel, adventure and he'd had it all in spades. But if their letters to each other hadn't gone missing, he would have returned. How different his life would have been?

And then there's this other matter. Had he made a huge mistake taking one of the little blue pills before leaving the hotel? Had he taken leave of his senses? He now wished he'd left things as they were and if Sylvia wanted to pursue *faire de l'amour,* and he knew it was only an 'if', he should let nature take its course. If it wasn't to be, it wouldn't be the end of the world. He consoled himself thinking that the one little pill probably wouldn't work.

Reggie had two bottles of wine, a twelve-year *Aberfeldy* single malt and a bouquet of red roses. Alighting from his car, he took a deep breath. It was one of those generous summer evenings when daylight persists until late, and the air still warm on his skin. A woman walking a dog, an old-looking terrier, gave Reggie a cheery 'hello' and, 'oh, do be careful' when she saw him balancing flowers and bottles.

The front door of the neighbour's house was open. Leaning in what she assumed was a provocative pose, was the voluminous Grace Pluck. Reggie did a double take. She had the sort of figure that makes one realise God does have a sense of humour. Her top half stuck out abnormally, and her hippo-sized rear end was hard against the house wall. She'd done something extraordinary with her hair and even from a distance; he could see she was heavily made-up with bright red lipstick smudged around her mouth. In one of her compendious fists, she held a bottle of wine. She had turned into a parody of herself.

'Hello, Mr Reginald Grosvenor Smythe, OBE,' she slurred.

'Good evening to you, dear lady.' Juggling his purchases, he headed speedily for Sylvia's door. 'Mrs Pluck, you look er ... how should I put it? Astonishing.'

'Why don't you come round for a drinky?' Her longing all too apparent.

'A kind offer, Mrs Pluck, but I'll be otherwise engaged this evening.'

Saved by Sylvia opening the door. He said goodbye before obtaining sanctuary.

'What was all that about?' she chuckled as he scuttled inside.

'Your capacious neighbour, Mrs Pluck, has just accosted me.'

'Poor Grace, on the booze again. She's desperate for a passionate relationship with a new man. 'Play your cards right, Reggie, and you could be in luck.'

'Good God, woman! I'd rather have sex with a Sherman tank.'

Sylvia laughed. 'Your coarse humour, Mr Grosvenor Smythe, hasn't changed in forty years.' She was wearing a light coloured, flowery dress and, in Reggie's eyes, looked marvellous.

'Dinner should be ready in an hour.' Leading him into the kitchen, Reggie noticed a half empty wine bottle on the table. 'Oh dear,' Sylvia blustered. 'I meant to er ... I got a bit nervous, so I've had a couple or ... you know.'

'Of course.' He handed her the flowers.

'You remembered,' she grinned, 'they're beautiful.'

'No more beautiful than you, my dear.'

'Oh yuk, Reggie, that's so corny. I'm sixty-two, past my *best-before date*, and don't look beautiful.' Pointing to the empty bottle, 'I smell more like a distillery. '

'And that, my dear, sounds like my perfect date.'

She ignored the chauvinistic jibe.

'What I meant to say was, you look very nice.'

'Very nice is okay, thank you, kind sir.' There was warmth in her smile. 'You're not too shabby yourself.'

He bowed. 'It's taken me sixty-three years to look this good.'

She laughed.

Reggie noted that since he saw her that morning, she now had pale coral lips with delicate grey shading around the eyes and mascara applied to her lashes. Her thick glossy hair was released from its clasp and brushed through. It was true, she did look beautiful. Without realising, he murmured. 'I've missed you very ...' awkwardly, the sentence was left unfinished.

'I missed you too, Reggie. We were going to change the world together.'

'Yes, we were.'

They looked deeply into each other's eyes.

'You left ...' she whispered softly, wiping a tear from her eye.

'I know. I er ...'

'I loved you, Reggie.' She gulped down the rest of the wine and shakily placed the glass on the table. 'I loved you from the first day we met. I've loved you all the years you weren't here.'

He crossed the kitchen in three steps, they kissed ... and the world stood still. Reggie knew he was full of love and desire and, oh gosh, was it the pill or were the stirrings his own?

Calmly, she took Reggie's hand to lead him to the stairs, her voice hardly above a whisper, 'Dinner can wait.' He now knew for certain the pill was working. He tried to adjust his stance.

'Something wrong with your back?'

'No ... well, it's a bit of sciatica,' was the only excuse he could think of. He needed a drink as the pill had left a nasty taste in his mouth - as though some creature had crawled in and died.

A couple of knocks on the door startled them as they were halfway up the stairs. A key inserted in the lock and the door opened.

'It's only us, Mum.' It was Chester and his lady friend, Pandora.

They hurried back into the kitchen.

'Don't worry,' Sylvia quietly whispered. 'They'll go in the living room first.' Quickly, she placed mats and cutlery on the kitchen table. 'We'll eat in here.' She gave him a concerned look. 'Hey, you're almost doubling up - your sciatica. Why don't you sit down?'

'I'll be okay in minute,' his voice almost falsetto. Taking a seat, Reggie made a noise that was between a sigh and a groan. The blasted pill had gone into over-drive.

'Ah, there you are,' Chester greeted them as he entered the kitchen. 'Reggie, is that your car outside?'

Swallowing to relax his throat, Reggie's voice steadied a little. 'And greetings to you, Ches my boy. Forgive me for sitting but my sciatica is playing up again. And if it is the Rolls you're talking about, yes, it is mine.'

'Very nice too. Reggie, I'd like you to meet my friend, Pandora.'

The woman who walked in could have graced any magazine cover; the kind of *femme fatale* that would make a bishop kick in a stained-glass window. From his seated position, Reggie bowed, his smile a little pained. 'How do you do, Pandora.'

The beautiful creature, with almost faultless features, wore a cerulean blue top over skinny pale, grey jeans. Curly, ash-blond hair fell in soft layers around her shoulders, while blue eyes, like the sea, were calm and emotionless. She wore a number of gold bracelets on her forearm. Casually brushing a loose strand of hair away, she revealed long, spear-shaped nails, lacquered in the same hue as her top.

'May I call you Reggie?' She had a tight-lipped way of speaking as if she was practising to be a ventriloquist. Reaching across the table, her bracelets chimed as she proffered a hand which Reggie held limply, concerned her talons might inflict an injury.

'Of course, you may, dear lady. Reggie beamed.

'We're just about to have dinner,' Sylvia said, 'but there's only enough for the two of us, I'm afraid.'

'That's okay, Mum. We just called in to say "hello" and meet my er ... Reggie again to see if you ...'

'If we were still talking to each other,' Sylvia added smiling.

'Yes, something like that.'

'Well, we are, thank you, son,' and abruptly changed the subject. 'Would you mind for a moment; I'll just go and check the oven.'

Chester helped Pandora into a chair on the opposite side of the table from Reggie. 'When are you going home, Reggie? Kingston, Surrey, isn't it?'

'Yes, it is. As you already know, I came to Ringwood to see the lawyer chappie, Edgar Ormrod, who is handling the affairs of my late Aunt Cressida Smythe, but much to my astonishment, the police are involved, as her death was considered to be suspicious.'

'Suspicious!' Chester frowned. 'In what way?'

'In a murder sort of way.'

'Oh, cool,' Pandora fluttered. 'Are you a suspect?' Her expression was hard to read.

'No, I'm not. According to D S Clapp, I am an un-suspect. But the fella did request that I stay a couple of days in case I could help in any way.' Looking over at Sylvia, he added. 'And new circumstances arose, so I was more than happy to oblige.'

'You're the first un-suspect I've ever met.' Pandora's expression still unfathomable.

Chester pointedly looked at his watch. 'We must go, Mum, we're meeting people at seven.' He gave her a gentle peck on the cheek and reached over to shake Reggie's hand.

'Before you go, I'm hoping you may be able to help … you too, Sylvia. Do either of you know a lady called Gertrude Dogberry? She is mentioned in Aunt Cressy's will.'

'Never heard of her,' Chester said.

'Ormrod and the police are trying to find her – seems they're roping in a chappie called Percy Blimp.'

'Oh him,' Sylvia laughed. 'Percy knows everybody's business round this neck of the woods. Yes, if anyone can find her, he will.'

'In addition, there's a lady called Dorothy Smerdal. She was my aunt's housekeeper but vanished on the day of her death.'

'I know Dorothy, or Dottie as she's known.' Sylvia tucked a strand of hair behind her ear. 'She attended church every week with your aunt. But why would she go missing? Surely she's not the murderer.'

'I've no idea, but she's a named beneficiary in the will … unlike me.'

'Sorry can't help,' Chester said, 'but I'll check around. Bye for now, you two.' Winking at his Mum, he added. 'Enjoy your dinner.'

'She's a pretty girl,' Reggie said after the front door closed. 'She seemed perfect – though a bit artificial, like plastic.'

Sylvia laughed. 'She purports to be a model, but as far as I know, she's only ever modelled handbags for a mail order catalogue and I assume her faultless, wrinkle-free face is due to plastic surgery. She's living a champagne lifestyle on a tap water salary and abuses Chester's hospitality shamelessly. Oh, and one other thing, she always leaves the toilet seat up.'

What this last piece of information meant, Reggie had no idea. 'Poor Ches. It is odd but they don't seem to go together, as a couple that is. Of course, he's forty-two and she is what – mid-twenties?'

'Ha, much older. Most women are not as young as they're painted. I don't know what their relationship is but I'm sure it can't be a sexual one.'

'Oh, why do you say that? He's a fair looking chap and she's, well ...'

'That's as maybe, but until she moved in, Ches was either alone or living with other men. I wonder if he's either gay or sexually neutral.'

'Oh dear, are you sure?'

'No, I'm not sure and also, he's not *outed* himself, or anything like that.'

'Outed?' he questioned. 'Oh, I see.' He thought for a moment. 'In my opinion, if homosexuality were the norm, instead of Eve, God would have created Adam and Bruce.'

This was one of Reggie's homilies that Sylvia did not find amusing. 'Anyway, enough about them. Now Reggie, what on earth is wrong with you? And don't try and fob me off saying it's sciatica.'

'Oh, bugger.' Reggie's heart sank. 'I'm afraid I have a confession to make.'

CHAPTER SIXTEEN

'Before I start, I need a fillip or two of Dutch courage from that over there.' Adjusting his monocle, Reggie pointed to the bottle of *Aberlour* Single Malt, the drink of the gods. The anticipation of quaffing the elixir was a balm to Reggie's troubled soul. Metaphorical oil, upon metaphorical troubled waters. Pouring himself a measure, he held the bottle towards Sylvia. 'How about you, my dear?'

'Not for me, I'll stick to wine.' Sitting quietly, she waited. 'So, Reggie, come on now; what on earth is wrong with you? Your pitiful shuffling just now was like a rehearsal for the Ministry of Funny Walks.'

He greeted her comment with a blank expression. 'What?'

'Oh, never mind. Anyway, I'm still waiting to hear about the funny walk and your confession.'

Taking his first sip, he sighed deeply. 'I've made a bit of a clown of myself, I'm afraid.'

'Go on.'

'Okay, I'm coming to it.' He was going to tell her in his own time. Finishing what was left in his glass, he poured another. 'You see, Foxy, all my life I've felt in control of any situation, in whatever direction my life has taken. Always on top of things. But then, when Coralie died - well, I lost it - control, that is. I loved her very much and it hurt like hell. I came back to England for treatment ... depression, actually.' He gave a self-effacing shrug. 'Although, through my own efforts, I'm over it now.'

'Well, I'm sorry about all that, but you're not telling me what's wrong with you now. And stop fiddling with your monocle.'

Slightly irritated, he said, 'Please hear me out. After I heard of Aunt Cressy's death, I expected to be in and out of Ringwood in a day. And then my, er *lever de Rideau.*'

'In English please.'

'Sorry. I was completely knocked for six – clobbered, when I found out I had a son. You can imagine how flabbergasted I was, can't you?'

'Yes, but go on.'

'And then clobber number two is you, my lost love. The girl I had loved all those years ago and lost touch with. I had no idea where you were, alive or dead, married with kids, or what. If I'd traced you, you probably wouldn't want to know me. Something like *"Hello, er ...sorry, but what's your name, oh, and this is my husband. Did we know each other once?"*'

Sylvia's expression softened. 'Is that what you thought?'

'Well, wouldn't you?'

'Probably.'

'This was why I hesitated to come back to Ringwood. I felt like the mythical pushmi-pullyu creature in Dr Dolittle stories, my emotions oscillating between opening Pandora's Box ... oh, there's a coincidence, Pandora ... or staying safe in Kingston. But when my neighbour, Mr Lee, offered to drive me here, I took the plunge to meet the solicitor and then return the same day.'

Sylvia gave his hand a squeeze. 'Go on.'

'Well, you know the rest.'

'No, I don't. When you said you had to make a confession, I thought it was something serious along the lines that you'd killed someone.'

'No, no, nothing like that. It was when I took you to Sainsbury's.'

'Sainsbury's! Why would taking me to Sainsbury's have anything to do with it?'

'You invited me to dine with you, remember? And then you gave me that full-on loving kiss, whispering that you wanted to rekindle our passion tonight ... or something like that.'

'I didn't say that ... did I? I agree I kissed you in your gleaming Rolls-Royce so that my work colleagues would see – and they did. I was the talk of the canteen after that,' she smiled. 'Pam made me give her the full story. But that still doesn't explain your funny walk or confession.'

'Yes, it does.' Reggie gave a forced smile. 'I thought you wanted ... now, how would a gentleman put it? I thought you wanted to have er ...'

'A good fuck!' She finished off his dithering ramble. 'Is that what you thought?'

'Not put as crudely as that, but yes. I thought that is what you were hinting at. You see, when Coralie died, my libido closed down for good, or so I thought. All the time I was married, I never once thought of sexual relations with any other woman. Not once, and ... not since. But then your kiss and the clear proposition, was, it seemed to me, a return to er ... *geschiechtsverkehr.*'

'Damn it, Reggie, in English if you don't mind.'

'I think you know what I mean.'

Relenting, she said. 'Yes, okay, I do.'

'*Post facto*, I acted foolishly. My control well and truly shot ... gone. So, I thought I would need help to, how should I put it? To perform.'

'You needed some help?' She put a hand over her mouth. 'Oh no.'

'Oh yes,' Reggie replied. 'I asked Mr Lee to help.'

'What?' She cried, horrified. 'You wanted Mr Lee to service me.'

'No,' Reggie yelled back. 'Don't be ridiculous, of course not. I asked Mr Lee to help me buy Viagra.'

Opened-mouthed, she gasped. 'You took Viagra?'

Reggie nodded.

'Viagra.' She started to giggle. 'And that's why you were ...' her giggle turned into laughter.

'It's not funny,' Reggie's embarrassment soared several notches.

'Oh, it is.' By now, tears of laughter were streaming down her face. It was one of those compulsive half laughs/half giggles that once started are hard to stop. 'So, is that your confession? You didn't murder anyone, but you bought Viagra for me. You naughty, naughty man.'

'That's it. The bloody pill worked, hence the funny walk.' Reggie grinned apologetically. 'It's clear you're not offended then.'

Still laughing, she used a tissue to wipe her eyes. 'No, not at all.'

'Life's a bugger, isn't it? When you've the strength for it, you're too young, and when you've got the age, you're too old.'

'Oh, poor you.' Bringing her laughter under control, she still had a cheeky look on her face. 'Out of interest, Reggie; the Viagra - is it still working?'

'Not a bloody chance, madam,' he barked. 'It's as dead as a dodo.'

Wiping the last few tears from her eyes, she suddenly stopped, jumping to her feet as smoke billowed out of the oven. 'Oh shit, the dinner's ruined.'

CHAPTER SEVENTEEN

Through light, early morning traffic on Southampton Road, Reggie headed back to the *Forest Glenn Hotel*. The less than formidable D S Clapp had contacted him to arrange a meeting in the hotel lounge at nine-thirty.

After a leisurely bath, Reggie dressed in fresh clothes, the sleeves of his shirt were neatly folded up to the elbows and his fawn jacket carefully arranged over the back of a chair. He phoned Mr Lee's room. 'Good morning, Mr Lee.'

'*Hewwo, Weggie*, I not see you *wast* night.'

'That is correct, old chap. I dined with a friend and imbibed a tad too much, so decided to stay overnight. Was everything pukka with you?'

Getting used to Reggie's use of English, Mr Lee knew that *old* didn't really mean *old,* and *pukka* meant good. He couldn't understand some individual words, but the friendly tone was clear. 'I had good time with Mrs Kim and massage. You *wike* I take you for massage?'

'Very kind of you, Mr Lee, but maybe another time. I have a meeting with Crap the policemen this morning, and after that, I'd like to return to Kingston.'

'Ooh, we go Kingston, back there today? I hope we come *Wingwood* another day.'

'Yes, we will, Mr Lee. Let us dine in the hotel restaurant at noon and discuss our plans.'

'Noon is *tweve o'cwock*. I *wike*. I ask for noodle.'

'Jolly good idea, Mr Lee, and fingers crossed for noodles.' Checking his watch, Reggie found he had fifteen minutes to spare before seeing Clapp. Time to think. After Sylvia's dinner had been incinerated last night, she'd ordered a Chinese takeaway delivery. For him, the lingering aftertaste was somewhat diluted by finishing the bottle of *Aberlour*.

They had talked for what seemed hours about their missing years and reacquainting themselves with the present. For Reggie, reaching a life changing decision was like watching the slow-motion picture of an arrow heading for a target. As the arrow flew, he thought of his first love, Foxy – on and on the arrow went, then life in Africa, thirty wonderful years with Coralie until her sudden death. The arrow flew on – depression, return to England, loneliness, Aunt Cressy's murder then POW, the arrow hit the target. Decision made. He knew, beyond a shadow of doubt, that he wanted a lasting relationship with Sylvia, his Foxy, matching her declaration of *amantēs* āmentēs, and how deeply they loved each other.

Following the Viagra fiasco, and by mutual consent, Reggie had slept in the spare room. He had asked Foxy if she would like to go to Kingston with him for a few days, but after a good deal of to-ing and fro-ing, she'd decided that for the time being, she would remain in Ringwood. They both had a mountain of issues to soberly think through. He would return shortly when the full impact of their decision had sunk in.

Fifteen minutes of contemplation up, Reggie entered the hotel lounge carrying his jacket over his arm. The sense of being well dressed gave Reggie a feeling of inner tranquillity which religion was powerless to bestow. The shabbily suited D S Clapp was already there; his thick, animated lips effortlessly moved an unlit cigarette around his mouth.

'D S Clapp,' Reggie said. 'Just to let you know I'm leaving Ringwood this afternoon.'

Taken by surprise, Clapp murmured. 'But I have questions, and there have been a few developments,'

'Positive developments, I trust.' Reggie ordered two coffees. 'But I'm still going.'

Taking a file out of his briefcase, Clapp said, 'The accountant handling Miss Smythe's affairs has given an estimate. Her estate, including house and contents, is worth between one point nine and two million pounds.'

'Great Scott! Two million quid, I can't believe it. She lived from hand to mouth when I stayed with her.'

'Yes sir. The bulk of the value was in shares purchased by your grandfather. On his death they were split between Miss Smythe and your father. She left hers untouched. Your father sold his and put the value into a trust fund for yourself, sir, for your education.'

'Really – I didn't know. So that's where the funding came from for Rymers Academy. He did ask Cressy once, shortly before starting at Oxford, but she'd angrily replied it was none of his business, so he'd left it at that.

They were interrupted by a young blonde waitress delivering their coffees. 'Thank you, my dear,' Reggie smiled. She was a big solid girl, buttocky, carrying a heavy tray with ease. As she sashayed away and, much to Reggie's surprise, Clapp followed her departure with an appreciative stare.

'Eyes off, Clapp, you're on duty,' Reggie admonished affably. 'Young women seem to be all blondes these days, whether by birth or bottle. Although,' he mused, 'the body of a young woman is God's greatest achievement. Of course, he could have built it to last a bit longer, but one can't have everything.'

Giving a timid cough, Clapp's dexterous lips discarded the cigarette and broke into what a generous soul could interpret as a smile. 'Yes, sorry sir, back to business. Following a discussion with the Chief Constable, D I Farting ...'

'Did you say Farting?' Reggie exclaimed. 'As in breaking wind?'

'It's Farthing actually, but it is unfortunately mis-pronounced at times.' There's that smile again. Reggie is gradually warming towards P C Plod. 'He wants to pursue the beneficiaries of the will, as they have a motive. He's busy on another case but expects to take over in a week. Unless, of course, it's been resolved by then.'

'Ah, you're under some pressure from Farting then?'

He gave a deep sigh and nodded. 'The beneficiaries, as you are aware, are the mysterious Gertrude Dogberry, whom your aunt wants you to find. She gets sixty percent. Mr Percy Blimp is still trying to find her.'

'Perhaps we could get Bletchley Park to work on it.' Reggie suggested mischievously.

'Bletchley who sir?'

Reggie couldn't be bothered to answer. 'The others I believe are Edgar Ormrod and his son Redknapp, and the missing housekeeper, Mrs Smerdal. All of whom will receive ten percent.'

'That is correct, sir. The final beneficiary, with another ten percent, being the church.'

'We're talking big lolly here, Sergeant. Now, has the quack finished the autopsy?'

'Ah, yes sir. I meant to tell you earlier. The pathologist has released the body of Miss Smythe. She was definitely poisoned by Thallium, and Mr Ormrod has arranged the funeral for eleven o'clock on 25th July.'

'Ah, at last,' Reggie said. 'I'll see Ormrod later for the details. So, to recap, as far as your murder investigation is concerned, it's the beneficiaries who are the only suspects.'

'No, not quite, sir.' Looking slightly awkward, he took another file out of his briefcase and handed it to Reggie. 'We were tipped off that you are acquainted with a certain Mrs Sylvia Makepeace, of 28, Shady Grove Close, Poulner. She will be interviewed later this morning.'

'Tipped off?' Reggie bellowed. 'Interviewed? What in the blue-blazes are you talking about? Sylvia Makepeace has nothing at all to do with this unsavoury business.'

'Well sir, if you read this charge sheet, Mrs. Makepeace's maiden name was, as you know, Sylvia Fox.'

Peering through his monocle, Reggie read. *"Local woman charged with threatening behaviour. Miss Sylvia Fox confronted local resident, Miss Cressida Smythe outside Ringwood Parish Church yesterday, threatening to kill her. The incident was witnessed by several members of the congregation who reported Miss Fox was about to attack Miss Smythe but was held back. Miss Fox will appear at the Bournemouth Magistrates court on Monday."*

'What in the blue-blazes ...'

'It's all true, sir,' Clapp only just managed to keep a straight face. 'The implication is quite clear. Anyway sir,' Clapp rose to leave, 'You may be required to return to Ringwood as our investigation continues.'

Back in his room, Reggie wasted no time in phoning Sylvia.

'Have you become gullible in your old age?' she mocked. 'Didn't you think of asking when this happened?'

'Oh blast! No, I didn't. But he made it seem as if you threatened to kill Cressida.'

'Reggie, you moron, it happened forty years ago. Anyway, can't stop now, I'm rushing to catch the bus to work. Call me this afternoon.'

'Foxy, my dear, I'm sorry, but please humour me a little.' There was a plea in his voice. 'Take a taxi to work – I'll pay but tell me everything that happened.'

She sighed. 'Oh, poor Reggie, I can tell you're upset, but your policeman friend is having you on. It happened at the time when I was trying to find your address, to tell you about me being pregnant. It was a Sunday morning: I was just about to go into church when your dear aunt saw me. She pointed directly at my face and bellowed at the top of her voice: *"There's the whore".*

'Oh, my Godfathers!'

'And that's not all. Word for word, and I have a good memory for that sort of thing, she shouted *"Thou shall not let a prostitute into the house of the Lord, Sayeth the Lord".*

'She said that? Two *Lords* together in front of all those people. Her grammar certainly let her down.'

'Are you taking this seriously, Reggie?' she snapped,

'Yes, of course, sorry m'dear. She was definitely *odium theologicum,'*

'God help me,' Sylvia sighed. 'English would help, but anyway, I went for her.'

'Good for you.'

'But I did not threaten to kill her. Oh no, just something along the lines that I was going to kick her teeth in and bash her silly head about a bit.'

'And that, m'dear, was a very reasonable response.'

'As soon as the plods got around to interviewing bystanders, they got the true story and dropped all charges. I was assured that your aunt received an official warning that any repeat of the accusation would end up with her being arrested.'

'Oh, Foxy, I'm extremely sorry. On behalf of my blessedly deceased aunt and the whole of the Smythe and Grosvenor families, I offer my sincere apology and will make it up to you when I'm next with you. That is after I've castrated that snivelling toad Crap who, I believe, is heading for Ormrod's office as we speak. I'll go and gently remove his testicles one by one, have them mounted into gold earrings, and present them to you as a token of my love.'

'Ah Reggie, how sweet of you. And they say romance is dead.'

Bursting into the office of Ormrod & Ormrod, Reggie was met by the enormous Grace Pluck. Before she could stutter a word, he went on the attack. 'You stand accused, madam of being in cahoots with the fuzz against the protocol of your duties of a *juridique secrétaire*.' Her face went pale under her face powder. 'You tipped off Crap that I was with Mrs Makepeace last night.' He banged his cane down hard on her desk.

She went limp ... or as limp as someone the size of Albania could go.

Squeezing past her table, he burst into Ormrod's office. 'Ah, there you are Clapp, you absolute bounder,' Reggie hissed. 'You're either mischievous or dim-witted telling me that story about Mrs Makepeace, but why did you not tell me that the so-called assault was forty years ago, and that all charges had been dropped? I await your apology, you ... you dishonourable varmint.'

In front of a shocked Edgar, a rattled D S Clapp faced the fuming Reggie, his trademark lips flapping together like pieces of wet haddock. 'Now then, sir,' he whined pathetically, 'you can't abuse an officer of the law like that.'

'Can I not?' He questioned aggressively. 'The law of these islands permits free speech, which the police should uphold, and free speech encompasses the right to offend and abuse another. Freedom only to speak inoffensively is not worth having.'

Clapp's voice had fallen to a whisper before recovering slightly. 'We, in the force, sir, have methods to, as you say, light the blue touch paper, so to speak, and see what develops, if you see what I mean?'

'Well then, D S Clapp. If you dare give Mrs Makepeace any strife over this matter, I will get my top London law firm, Snipe and Snortle of Regent Street, to have you up for *harcèlement sexuél*. The sooner Farting takes over this case, the better.'

'It's Farthing, sir, D I Farthing,' a worried Clapp corrected. 'I can assure you that it will not be necessary to interview Mrs Makepeace after all.'

'That is just as well, Sergeant. And while I'm *in situ*, have you informed Ormrod here that he, along with his son, is a suspect in the murder of my aunt?'

'What?' Edgar yelled, looking intently at Clapp.

Ignoring Edgar's cry of alarm, a shaken Clapp prepared to leave. 'I've finished my business for now. I suggest we three meet again after Miss Smythe's funeral.' And with the faintest flicker of serpentine menace, he left.

'What on earth was all that about me and Red being suspects?'

'Oh, not to worry, old crap-Clapp is scratching around like a headless chicken, so I thought it my turn to light his bloody blue touch paper and give him a kick up his shiny-suited arse.'

'I know what you mean,' Edgar nodded. 'He's still trying to locate this Gertrude Dogberry woman in the hope that, as she inherits sixty percent of the estate, she must be the killer. And there's still the missing housekeeper.'

'But the beneficiaries of such a large estate are bound to be suspects. And you are one of them.'

'That's ridiculous. I was her friend, and she didn't have many of those.'

'In the eyes of the law, it is not ridiculous. You are a suspect.'

'Of course, I'm not, that's utter nonsense.'

'Edgar, you are in denial.'

'No, I'm not.'

'There you are, denying.'

'I'm denying that I'm not in denial. That's not denial.'

'Have it your way, but if it isn't denial, then what the hell is it?' Reggie didn't wait for an answer. 'Look Edgar, I'm going back to Kingston now, but I'll see you at the funeral.'

Edgar rose. 'Of course. Would you like something to eat before you go?'

Shaking his head in mock disbelief, Reggie said, 'Edgar, old chap, a gentleman never eats. He breakfasts, he lunches, he dines, but never eats.'

CHAPTER EIGHTEEN

M r Lee, a beaming smile on his face, was ten minutes late arriving for lunch. *'Sowwy Weggie,* I come from kitchen.' A waitress had earlier placed two cushions on his chair so he could sit at a normal height.

'From the kitchen? What on earth were you doing there?'

'Kowean noodle, I teach them.'

The waitress, her vivid red hair cascading down her forehead like lava from an exploding volcano, placed a bowl of steaming hot noodles in front of Mr Lee.

Reggie wondered if he had heard correctly. 'You taught the chef to make noodles?'

'Yes, *Weggie.* Yesterday, I make *compwain* as no noodle on menu. Manager take me to kitchen. I teach them just now.' Taking a tentative mouthful from his bowl, he gave an appreciative burp. 'It good. You want noodle, *Weggie?*'

'An exceedingly kind offer, but I'll stick to what's in front of me.' Reggie looked approvingly at slices of delicious medium-rare roast beef on his plate with roast potatoes, Yorkshire puddings and a variety of fresh vegetables.

'That okay, *Weggie,* maybe another time.' He leant forward, inhaling the *fragrance of Asia.* Then using one hand to hold the bowl to his lips, he dextrously used a chopstick to scoop the contents into his mouth, only pausing to use a serviette to clean his steamed-up glasses and wipe perspiration from his face. The whole performance was accompanied by several pleasurable oohs and aahs and a couple of satisfied belches.

Reggie was not amused. With a pained expression that suggested he might be passing a kidney stone, he desperately wanted to shout, *"For God's sake, eat like an Englishman"* but tactfully managed to hold his tongue. Mr Lee had clearly not taken to British table manners.

The pervading aroma of hot spices, garlic and God knows what else reached Reggie's twitching nostrils ruining the enjoyment of his meal. Strongly flavoured foreign food, eaten with appalling manners in an English hotel, was difficult to tolerate, almost as bad as eating asparagus with a knife and fork, or serving instant mash.

As the waitress cleared away their dishes, Reggie, his eyes watering slightly, reminded Mr Lee that they would leave for Kingston in one hour.

'Of course, *Weggie*, I be *weddy*.' He emitted another belch before vigorously wiping his face with his stained serviette. 'What date we *weturn* to *Wingwood*?'

'On 24th July, in five days' time. My Aunt's funeral is on the following day.'

'Ooh, do *peoples-es* burn her?'

'Burn her? Oh, I see, no. She will be buried in the ground in Ringwood church graveyard. Burning the dead in Britain is called cremation.'

'*Cweam-mation*?' Mr Lee queried. '*Wike cweam* tea?'

Reggie laughed. 'No, nothing like cream tea. Cremation means to burn the dead.'

'Ooh, thank you *Weggie*, I *wemember* that. But I *gwad* to return *Wingwood*. I tell Mrs Kim, she be *pweased*.'

Reggie wasn't sure how much of his private life, principally Sylvia and Chester, he should reveal. But there again, why not? He had nothing to hide, and he would eventually meet them. 'You see, Mr Lee, I have a lady friend here in Ringwood.'

'Ooh, a *wady*.' Mr Lee smiled. 'Is she *wady* you need *Viagwa*.'

'No Mr Lee,' he thought it better to lie on this occasion. 'She is a lady I have known for over forty years. We are good friends. I also have a son.'

'A son with *wady*? Ooh, I not know you had son. We have saying in my country.'

Oh, God help me, Reggie sighed, awaiting another *suppression veri* of the English language.

'We say the hungry *dwagon dwink* kimche over the *wover*. It mean a good man sleep with woman and make many sons. You have same saying in England?'

'No Mr Lee, I don't believe we do.' Quickly putting an end to that line of discussion, he added, 'We should get our bags and I'll pay the bill. Toddle along now.'

Settling himself in the rear of the Rolls, Reggie looked up at the sky. It was painfully dark. Heavy, purple clouds had built up in the east and the first drops of rain splattered on the ground. As they drove out of Ringwood on the A31, up Poulner Hill towards Picket Post, heavy rain set in, puddles formed on the edge of the road, and thunder clouds clapped their giant hands.

Mr Lee said. 'You want I speak and drive today?'

'Thank you, but not in this storm,' Reggie replied. 'I find it difficult to hold any sort of conversation during a car journey, especially competing with the angry hammer of Thor, the god of thunder and lightning, so my friend, a Trappist silence would be appreciated.' The meaning must have been clear as Mr Lee didn't speak for the rest of the journey.

After two and three-quarter hours, delayed by the constant heavy rain, they arrived back in Kingston. Aida greeted Reggie with a beaming smile. 'I make dinner, sir. You want British roast beef?'

Reggie, and his grouchy stomach, declined saying he would prefer to dine simply and suggested scrambled eggs with smoked salmon. He needed time to relax after the recent life-changing events in Ringwood. Seated comfortably in his favourite armchair, he helped himself to a large malt before drifting off into the arms of Morpheus.

CHAPTER NINETEEN

Half asleep, Reggie squinted through gritty eyes at the luminous hands of the clock. Eight twenty-five. With so much on his mind, he hadn't slept well, but he hoped a hearty b reakfast with a gallon of coffee should gently ease him back to face the day.

Getting gently to his feet, he went onto the balcony, appreciating the view of the Thames, meandering its majestic way towards London and beyond. A low mist hung over the river with thin veils sweeping in and masking the sounds of a passing barge. An old song sprang into his head and he sang quietly, *"He never seems to worry, doesn't care for fortune's fame, he never seems to hurry, but he gets there just the same"*. Was there a message in there for him?

'Are you alright, sir?' Looking concerned, Aida stood by the kitchen door.

'Yes, Aida, just singing to the river.'

'Oh! That's nice.'

Reggie remained on the balcony for a while mulling over his situation. Foxy, the girl he'd been crazy over all those years ago was back in his life, which was truly fantastic. It wasn't her face or figure that first attracted his youthful desire, or even her prominent breasts, no, it was her positive attitude, her gentleness and sense of humour, the way she dressed and her bubbly personality. And not only was he in love all over again but, out of a clear blue sky, he discovered he also had a son – a forty-one-year-old son.

Feeling in need of an understanding ear, he phoned Miles, inviting him to lunch at his favourite local dining establishment, *Ruffles* on Richmond Road. He needed someone he could open-up to without everything being distorted into some form of Freudian psychoanalysis.

It was turning into a beautiful summer's day, and Reggie took a deep breath of what Rupert Brooke described as English air. Walking briskly, a slight breeze stirred the leaves above his head. A brown puppy with a huge head and floppy ears playfully ran in front of a lady heading for the river. They exchanged greetings.

Miles was already at the table when Reggie arrived. He appeared to be studying his reflection in a concave shaped spoon.

'Greetings Miles. What on earth are you doing?'

'Ah,' Miles acknowledged solemnly. 'Contemplating life and my huge hooter if you must know.'

'Oh dear, are things that bad?' A gleam of humour flashed in Reggie's eyes, 'Although you're right about your hooter. Remember the joke, Miles, about the horse that goes into a bar and is asked by the barman "why the long face?"'

He gave a hopeless shrug, 'Vaguely.' He ran a tired hand around his jaw. 'You see, Reggie, here I am, rapidly approaching my over-allotted three score years and twenty, five foot eight and shrinking, with a bus pass, a replacement hip and sky-high blood pressure. My doctor, however, assured me that there's nothing really wrong with me that reincarnation won't cure.'

Laughing, Reggie looked around to catch the eye of a waiter. 'Miles, old chap, you should avoid doctors at all costs. I consider there are only two types of medical cases – those that involve taking the trousers off, and those that don't. But there are worse things in life than death - have you ever spent an evening with an insurance salesman?'

'That's true,' Miles's sigh was immense. 'At least he told me the secret of longevity – keep breathing.'

'Very sound advice – but a little on the *insanus omnis*, maybe.'

'Ah yes, maybe indeed. Insanity, by the way, is heredity – you can catch it off your children.'

Reggie laughed. 'I'll remember that one. But Miles, I came here for an in-depth chinwag concerning my own fraught situation. For a verbal pick-me-up. And speaking of which, we both need a strong tonic to help lighten our discourse.' Reggie's regular waiter, Pedro, recognising him as a generous tipper, immediately took their order while they checked the menu to see if anything exciting had been added since their last visit.

'So, old man,' Reggie solicited kindly, 'What brought on all this despondency?'

'It's the whole of humanity - a mess - a complete shambles.' he exhaled noisily. 'Everywhere you look these days there's decadence – I saw a bishop with a moustache the other day.'

Reggie shook his head. 'Look old fluff, stop watching television, reading newspapers and get a hobby. We men need hobbies now we no longer hunt in packs.'

Miles pressed his fingers and thumb to the bridge of his nose. 'I'm sure you're right and I need a radical change in my life. I had vaguely thought of joining a monastery, become a monk, keep bees, make wine, and lead a life of quiet order and contemplation on the meaning of life.'

'Well, if you work it out, be sure to let me know. I once questioned the school priest at Rymers on this very subject and about the Trinity. He replied it's three in one, perfectly straight forward, and if in doubt, I should see the maths teacher.'

'Ha, ruddy typical.' Looking closely at Reggie, he said, 'My God, I've just noticed, you're looking disgustingly cheerful. I was too swallowed up with my own misery, you know, *ipse dixit,* to notice. Your trip to Ringwood must have been a success?'

'Yes, it was, and I want to get some of your astute feed-back.' Appreciatively sipping his whisky, Reggie began telling him about his new friend and chauffeur, Mr Lee, the meeting with the solicitors and police, and the shocking fact that Aunt Cressy had been murdered – poisoned by Thallium.

Miles eyes lit up. 'Oh, bloody marvellous, how brilliant is that?' Realising he may have overstepped the mark, he apologised.

'That's quite alright,' Reggie's look was far from one of reproach. 'My first thought was that at eighty-three, it was a jolly acceptable time to pop one's clogs. But her *corpus delicti* was carried out by some dastardly assassin. The motive may have been money as, much to my complete surprise; she was worth a ruddy fortune.'

'Interesting.' Miles nodded sagely.

Reggie continued his account describing D S Clapp and his theory that the four beneficiaries were the only suspects. 'Strangely, only two of them have been found. The main beneficiary, Gertrude Dogberry, was not known to anybody.'

'What a marvellous name,' Miles enthused. 'Gertrude Dogberry, purloined from a Shakespeare play is my guess. I'm sure I could find her.'

'What do you mean, find her?'

'I can trace almost anybody. Searching family records is something I do - like being a detective. You see, Reggie, I do have a hobby after all. I'm with several websites, and whether it's censuses, electoral roles, parish registers, birth and death certificates or whatever, I have never been stumped for long in finding anybody. Tell me her age and where she lives.'

'I've no idea.'

'Ah, that makes it a little more difficult. But if you like, I'll drop everything else and start on her. No charge of course.'

'Well, that would be wonderful. Thank you, Miles.' Reggie didn't tell him that some chap in Ringwood was already working on the same search. 'Let's have another drink to celebrate before lunch is served.'

Noting that they had finished their beef *en croute*, the attentive waiter presented them with the *Ruffles* speciality dessert menus. 'Before that, Pedro,' Reggie pointed to their empty glasses. 'Refills are required.'

'Not for me, old chap.' Miles placed a hand over his glass. 'I've consumed a tad too much already. I must be on my way soon.'

'I'll have one, Pedro, but make it a double. Now Miles, I hope you're not in a hurry because I still haven't got round to telling you the most important thing that happened in Ringwood.'

'You mean more important than a murder and a missing person?'

'Yes, I do.'

'Well, that'll take some beating.' He glanced at his watch, 'I've got another half hour.' Having just finished another of Reggie's *gratis* lunches, he felt an obligation to at least listen.

Taking a sip from his refilled glass, Reggie went into detail about meeting the first love of his life, Sylvia Fox, and their plan to live together. He said it may seem strange, but their feeling of love for each other was as though they had never parted, even after forty years. He told an opened-mouthed Miles everything that had happened, except for the unfortunate Viagra incident.

Miles almost choked on his coffee. 'After forty years! Are you serious? No, surely not, that's Mills and Boon stuff and nonsense. For goodness' sake, Reggie, you've only just got over the death of your late wife. Take my advice, love is a delusion - a delusion that one woman differs from another.'

Reggie hoped his severe expression would warn Miles that he was being serious.

Oblivious of this, Miles said. 'Now here's a coincidence.'

'What is?'

'It's about being careful at our age - you know, with a lady. I have at home a sex manual for the mature on how to tell an orgasm from a heart attack. I'll bring it in next time I see you.'

'I'd rather you didn't,' an exasperated Reggie replied. 'My other news is that I have a son.' Emptying his glass and calling for another, Reggie explained that Sylvia had conceived on his last night before going overseas.

'Are you sure about that?' Miles looked thunderstruck. 'You have a son? A son you had no idea about. My God, whatever next. Have you met him?'

'Yes, I have. He's a forty-one-year-old academic at Bournemouth University called Chester – he prefers Ches actually.'

'Amazing.' An astounded Miles drained the last of his coffee. 'Finding out that you have a son must have knocked you for six. Interesting though, isn't it?'

'What is?'

'Fate, old chap. Our lives are made up of random events that determine what's going to happen to us. Look at you for example – you were reluctant to go to Ringwood and only went because your unloved aunt had died, and then all this - fate. Anyway, Reggie, why are you telling me?'

Reggie hesitated. 'I have no-one else. I hope you don't mind.'

'No, I don't mind, but what do you want me to do? Say you're bloody crazy, that you're on the rebound and to back off, and to have DNA tests – it could all be a trick – a con. Does he have children?'

'No, he doesn't. In fact, Sylvia isn't sure about his sexuality.'

'Oh, I see, a modern man in touch with his feminine side, is he?'

'Whatever that means,' Reggie acknowledged. 'You're obviously more *au fait* with contemporary parlance than I am. He has a lady partner who leaves the toilet seat up.'

'Good heavens. Why would she do that?'

'I have no idea. As I have been told on many occasions, I am from a bygone era struggling to come to terms with society as it is now. I grew up in a world when there were only two sexes, but from what I can decipher from today's media, that is no longer the case.'

Miles gave another of his deep sighs, shrugging his shoulders.

'I read about it in today's *Times*. It is to do with different gender, or at least I think it is. It seems anyone can decide to change their sex, and at the drop of a hat, it's all done free of charge on the NHS.'

'Okay yes, I have heard of that,' Miles frowned. 'In a way, it's a good job people are different – otherwise they wouldn't sell many mixed biscuits.'

'Where on earth did you get that from?' Reggie couldn't help but laugh.

'But what I don't understand,' Miles continued, 'is after the op, what happens if you're still not happy? Maybe you keep what's been cut off in a jam-jar and then if you change your mind, ask them to stitch it all back again.'

This time, Reggie was not in the mood to appreciate Miles's piece of frivolous nonsense. He had hoped that Miles would have sensibly discussed the ramifications of the Ringwood events, but this had not happened.

In a contemplative mood, Reggie left the restaurant. Could Miles be right about him being on the rebound?

Aida greeted him when he arrived home, asking what he wanted for his dinner. 'Surprise me, Aida, something to cheer me up.'

She had become accustomed to similar requests in the past and knew that anything with chips was usually acceptable. 'I do that, sir.'

The day's mail was neatly stacked on his side table. Settling with a sigh into his armchair, he leafed through the pile. Mainly junk mail – desperate Technicolor exhortations to avail oneself of take-away meals or invitations to retirement villages were unceremoniously tossed into a bin. A letter in old fashioned copperplate writing had originally been addressed to R. Smythe Esquire at his last London address. This had been crossed out and his present address written underneath. He roughly tore open the envelope and, like a duck in thunder, was shocked to the core and yelled out loud. 'It can't be ... it's impossible.'

Chapter Twenty

Pouring himself a *shock-remedy* measure, Reggie vigorously wiped his monocle and stared again at the name at the end of the letter. 'Come on now,' he cried out, 'from Cressida Smythe, it can't be.' Taking a stiff drink, he sat back and took a deep breath.

'Ah, wait a minute.' He looked at the envelope to check the postmark. It was very faint, but he could just make out the 2nd of July. 'Phew, that explains it - it was posted three days before she was murdered..' The redirection of the letter had taken eighteen days.

Refilling his glass, he settled back in his armchair. The letter was undated and covered one side of a sheet of Basildon Bond. *"Reggie, I need your help. When I got home from Church yesterday morning, I got a terrible shock as all my private papers were scattered across the floor. Someone, other than Dotty, had been in my house".* Glancing over to a calendar, Reggie confirmed that the 1st of July was, in fact, a Sunday. It continued: *"An hour ago, Mr Fabian, my accountant of Torkle and Pout, phoned and told me attempts had been made to steal my identity – someone had tried to transfer a large sum of money from my portfolio to an account in the Cayman Islands, but Mr Fabian had stopped it. He said I should immediately report it to the police. What am*

I to do Reggie? I don't want nosey police poking their noses into my private affairs".

Reggie ran a hand around his jaw. Poor Cressy must have been desperate to write asking for help – to me, of all people. And her plea went to the wrong address. Moving his gaze to blink up at the ceiling for a few silent moments, he massaged the back of his neck knowing full well that he should have notified her of his new address weeks ago. If he had, maybe he'd have been in Ringwood before she was murdered. What price his stubbornness?

'Dinner - it ready,' Aida announced as she placed a plate and dishes on the dining table.

Feeling guilt amongst other emotions, he put the letter on his side table. 'Thank you, Aida, what is it?'

'I make for you chips and egg. You ask for dinner to cheer up, so I do it. You see, there British film on television, it was something like Surely Balentine, and they all like chips and egg. I grill some gammon to go with it. Is that happy for you?'

What could he say? The enjoyment of food was important to Reggie, and this was the first time she had let him down. He manufactured a smile. 'Once a year, Aida, I have chips and egg, and this is that once a year occasion.'

Putting up with unappetising food brought back more memories of Aunt Cressy. Her culinary activities past all understanding. It had always been the same. Sunday, a joint; Monday, cold joint; Tuesday, minced joint; Wednesday, cottage pie; Thursday, beans; Friday, fish fingers; Saturday, macaroni cheese. Cholesterol hadn't been invented in those days and he was ordered to *"eat your fat, boy"*.

He winced at the memory. In her way, she had done her best, although she took pleasure in correcting any sign of bad manners. Not saying "please" and "thank you" was a sin, which ranked above belching. On one occasion, he'd timidly suggested a change in the weekly routine diet, but this was rebuffed in no uncertain terms. *"Going to that posh boarding school has given you ideas above your station, boy".* He never asked again.

Thinking back, the food was actually worse at boarding school; snoek, the poor relation of cod, served with cabbage. The boys stuffed it straight into their pockets to be discarded in the lavatories, where it would float, even after two flushes. The Gestapo dinner commissar, Ghastly Gutty Garter, one day introduced us to sweetbreads – what a misnomer. We all laughed when the ever-smiling dinner assistant, Miss Pinkerton, explained what sweetbreads were, and said her dad used to call them the Beverly Sisters. And then for pudding it was usually frogspawn tapioca, jamless roly-poly or spotless dick.

But now Aunt Cressy was dead – could he have stopped it? Needing to stop thinking about what he had failed to do, he thought it was the right time to phone Foxy. His heart missed a beat when she answered.

'Good evening, my dear.' He felt he should have said something more romantic, more meaningful than just *my dear*, but words of affection like *darling* or *beloved* or worse still, *sweetheart,* did not come naturally to him. He was a man after all.

'Hello Reggie, I'm, er, already on my second glass of vino.'

'And here's me, sober as a judge, sobbing my eyes out and counting the days until I'm in your arms again.'

'You're a liar, Grosvenor Smythe. I can tell you're already two sheets to the wind, but I wish you were here now.' This was exactly what Reggie wanted to hear – she hadn't changed her mind. 'I should have accepted your invitation to see the spectacular highlights of Kingston upon Thames, but a shy country girl like me would have been at the mercy of a lecherous old city-man.'

'Less of the *old* if you don't mind,' Reggie chuckled, 'but I'll accept that the lecherous bit is spot on as far as you're concerned. I miss you very much.'

'Oh still my beating heart,' she mocked.

After their somewhat juvenile love-chat, Sylvia told him she'd done her part-time job at Sainsbury's with her friend Pam. 'I quite enjoy working there, and we meet some interesting people – you know, customers. And Pam is fun to work with.'

'On my next trip to Ringwood, I'll pop into Sainsbury's to check their range of whiskies.'

'And I, sir, will give you my personal attention.'

'I should jolly-well hope so. Now then, moving on - my recent acquaintance, a chap called Miles, considers himself an expert in all things relating to ancestry and tracing people. He's put finding Gertrude Dogberry as his priority.'

'So that's your man versus Percy Blimp – may the best man win.'

'Indeed.' He decided not to tell her about Aunt Cressy's letter until he had had more time to think about it.

'Oh, I almost forgot,' Sylvia said. 'There are a couple of developments. Ches has moved back in with me for a few days; he's split up with his lady friend.'

'Oh dear,' Reggie sympathised. 'A lover's tiff?'

'Ha, I don't think so. He said he'd tell me all about it later.'

'What was the second thing?'

'Oh yes. Grace Pluck, you remember her?'

'How could I possibly forget the Jurassic creature of Shady Grove?'

'Well, she told me Edgar Ormrod's son, Redknapp, has gone missing, and the police are looking for him. I don't know if it's anything to do with your aunt's murder but, it's a bit strange, isn't it?'

'Yes, it is strange. Surely not Redknapp. He's unhindered by any possible talent, and to think he may be involved in a cunning murder plot is ludicrous. I'll phone Edgar tomorrow to get the lowdown – I'll let you know what he says.'

CHAPTER TWENTY-ONE

The following morning, Reggie phoned Edgar Ormrod in the off chance that he would be in his office.

'Good morning, Ormrod and Ormrod. How may I help?'

'And a very good morning to you, Edgar. You are highly industrious working on Saturdays. Business must be good.'

'Ha, if only it were true,' he sighed. 'No, I'm afraid business is slack - it's what we in the profession call, *light contact*, there being no term other than death to describe the situation where absolutely nobody has written, phoned, faxed, emailed, or even sent a bloody smoke signal.'

'Oh dear.' Reggie commiserated. 'Anyway Edgar, what's this I hear about Redknapp going missing. Is it true?'

'No, well not that I know of. Anyway, who told you?' He paused before adding, 'Oh, don't bother, it was Grace Pluck, wasn't it?'

Reggie thought it wise to ignore that question. 'I'm getting mixed messages here, Edgar. Why was old Clapp seeking him high and low? It must be to do with Cressida's murder.'

'Reggie, you've met Red,' Edgar said. 'The thought of him masterminding an almost undetectable murder is crazy.'

'I take your point, Edgar, but he may know something.'

'I very much doubt it. Occasionally, he goes away for a few days without checking with me first. He is an adult, after all. So, I don't think he's missing as such. Old Clapp is struggling with his investigation, clutching at straws and getting nowhere. Dorothy Smerdal is still AWOL and old Blimp hasn't found Gertrude Dogberry yet.'

'What about Redknapp's so-called girlfriend? Tiffany with the steamroller. Is she involved? Are they having an affair?'

Edgar gave a forced laugh. 'Are you kidding? He wears fleece-lined vests and long-johns all year round and covers himself in enough cheap deodorant to defoliate the New Forest.'

Reggie wondered what Edgar's motive was to deliberately paint a picture of his son being useless. 'Methinks, Edgar, you exaggerate somewhat. Aunt Cressy made him a beneficiary in her will for some reason. Are you hiding something from me?'

'Definitely not.'

'In that case, who prepared her will? It wasn't you, was it?'

'Good God no, I'm a beneficiary so that would have been unethical. The lawyer involved was a Mr Jacob Pinch, and he was the other executor.'

'And where might Mr Jacob Pinch be located?'

'He died nine days ago and cremated yesterday; I was at the service.'

'Great Gods of villainy, Edgar, this gets more like a conspiracy every day.' The words of Mr Lee flitted through his mind; *"it wike Agatha Cwispy"*. He'd thought of telling Edgar about his aunt's letter, but his trust in him was rapidly diminishing. Reggie brought the conversation to an end by asking Edgar to keep him in the picture with any developments, including the whereabouts of his son.

With a mixture of confused thoughts circulating around his brain, Reggie decided he needed a breath of fresh air and a walk into Kingston to buy socks seemed just the ticket. A contrite Aida had earlier confessed that for the second time since she'd been in his service, another of his socks had gone missing. She said she would pay, but Reggie wouldn't hear of it. He told her, 'Aida my dear, they disappear in a Bermuda Triangle of socks,' but her blank expression showed it was yet another of his *lost in translation* statements.

The weather was sunny and warm. Strolling along Barge Walk, a pleasant riverside path along the Thames, he entered Canbury Gardens where ducks were bickering like children in a playground. A barge painted red, chugged along at walking pace - a small brown terrier stood in the bow wagging its tail. His attention was then drawn to a pair of buzzards circling lazily against the liquid blue of the afternoon sky. He stopped to gaze as they rode the thermals and a poem from the recesses of his mind came to him:

> *"You've slipped the surly bonds of earth,*
> *Up, up, you've topped the wind-swept heights*
> *The high un-trespassed sanctity of space"*

What a glorious line – the high, un-trespassed sanctity of space. Not realising he had spoken the verse aloud; a genial man with a big belly smiled and gave a round of applause. Reggie bowed and moved on.

He now wondered if continuing into Kingston on a Saturday afternoon was such a good idea. He hated crowds and judging by the large number of people in the gardens, he decided to interrupt his expedition by stopping for a tincture or two in the relative calm of the conveniently located *Rowers Inn*.

He was greeted by a barman of the *Hi-de-Hi* school of hospitality and was on the point of leaving when he noticed a bottle of Ledaig Tobermory 20-year-old single malt on the shelf. He pointed. 'Would you mind letting me see that bottle.'

'A special whisky, sir.' A middle-aged man in a smart, three-piece suit had taken over from the barman. 'My name's Alexander William, the manager. Are you familiar with this particular malt?'

'Indeed, I am, Mr William,' Reggie smiled, introducing himself. 'May I ask where you got it?'

'Of course, sir. I go to the distillery's annual auction each year. I bought this a month ago, but you are the first customer to show an interest. Would you care to sample it?'

'I certainly would.'

William took a tulip shaped glass and poured in a small measure. 'A drop of Tobermory water should increase the pleasure, sir.'

Savouring his first drink, it was an exceptional whisky, with an almost seamless blend of flavours. Holding the glass under his nose, he murmured, 'I sense a waft of smoke, very delicate, of moss and burning embers. Mr William, you have made my day. Would you care to join me?'

'That is extremely generous of you sir, I'd love to.'

Sampling some more, Reggie was in his seventh heaven. 'I'd say it's a, how can I put it? A creamy malt with an oaky spice.'

'Very well judged, sir,' William nodded shrewdly, 'and it's backed with ... could it be toasted almonds.'

It was almost two hours later that a somewhat intoxicated Reggie bade farewell to his new friend, Alexander William, and walked unsteadily back to his apartment. The purchase of socks would have to wait.

CHAPTER TWENTY-TWO

Miles was waiting for him by the flat's front entrance, holding a manila file in his hand.

'I have some news for you, young Reginald.'

'*Wondershul*,' Reggie slurred. 'Come and have a drink - dinner in fact.'

'Well thank you.'

One of the lifts had an 'out of order' notice, and someone had added their own note – *"This Otis regrets it is unable to lift you today"*.

'How wonderful,' Miles laughed as he pressed the button for the second lift. 'Very clever ... and funny.' Miles had purposely timed his visit in the hope he might receive an invitation. 'Reggie, you look, how should I delicately put it? A little ... unsteady.'

'Are you saying I'm drunk?' Reggie questioned sharply as they entered the flat.

'Maybe a little.'

'For your edification, old chap, the only true definition of being drunk is when you can't lie on the floor without holding on.' This well-used response to that most disrespectful of charges always made Reggie chuckle.

Miles dutifully snorted with laughter. Reggie poured him a whisky.

'There was a more tolerant attitude to the consumption of liqueur in Asia and Africa,' Reggie pronounced, 'But in the UK, it is different, even frowned upon erroneously linked to debauchery and pleasures of the flesh.'

'You're right; I blame it on the Liberals. Tell me Reggie, did you ever consider leaving the UK for good and settling in alcohol tolerant foreign climbs?'

'No, never. It was always my firm intention to spend my golden years here in the Sceptred Isle of good old England. This is my home.'

Miles sipped from his glass. 'You know, old chap, I'm getting a sort of HMS Pinafore moment – how about you?'

'Ha, yes, why not. I'm well-oiled enough.'

Still grinning, they stood, saluted, and burst into song:

> *"But in spite of all temptations,*
> *To belong to other nations,*
> *He remains an Englishman,*
> *He remains an Englishman."*

'Bloody marvellous,' Miles laughed. 'Absolutely, bloody marvellous. Of course, you would never leave Blighty forever. You're an Old Rymerian, for God's sake.'

Aida peeped round the door, shook her head in bewilderment, then immediately withdrew.

'Now, where were we before the G and S sonneteer took over? Ah yes, you have some news for me, Miles - what is it?'

After another whisky taster, Miles opened the folder, 'Well, I've trawled through every single avenue looking for a Gertrude Dogberry, and my first foray would indicate that the lady does not exist.'

'But she must exist. Aunt Cressy would never make a mistake like that.'

'There is one area I haven't checked - the register of deed polls. The illusive Gertrude Dogberry could be living under an assumed name. So, saying, I do have something to show you which may be of interest.' He had brought with him a bottle of claret which he'd handed to his host. Politely, Reggie declined the offer. 'Miles, old friend, claret is the liquor for boys, but they who aspire to greatness drink whisky.'

Being the guest, Miles didn't take offense as he much preferred a fine claret to anything that came out of Scotland, including Nicola Sturgeon.

Aida served them *olia-podrida,* an Asian style beef casserole which, fortuitously, she'd been preparing that afternoon for the freezer.

'She's rather special, isn't she?' Miles observed after she'd cleared away the dishes and left a cheese platter with crackers and grapes. 'What are you going to do with your delightful Filipina once you and your Ringwood ladylove set up home together? Won't she be in the way?'

'No, not at all, Sylvia will not be my housekeeper, but a lady of leisure.'

'So, you still plan to stick to Lady Sylvia of Ringwood.'

'Of course I do.'

'I hope you don't mind me saying this, but I did mention something along the same lines when we dined in *Ruffles.* Don't you think you're rushing things a little? After your trauma following your loss of Coralie, maybe you should look around a bit, go out with some different women, you know, just to be sure. You're about to make a huge commitment.'

'What in the blue-blazes are you getting at?'

'Well, Reggie, look at me, with my rather disappointing marriage. Over the years, I've had the pleasure of knowing several delightful ladies. In fact, older women are best because they always think they may be doing it for the last time.'

Reggie shook his head and sighed. '*Iūs prīmae noctis.*'

'*O temporal o mores!*' Miles smiled. 'We men are designed to take up with as many women as we can - it is something to do with genetic survival. Women are designed to do exactly the opposite – to raise children.'

'Ha,' this time, Reggie laughed out loud. 'You take the biscuit, Miles. The *hashtag MeToo* generation will have your guts for garters.'

'Hashtag?'

Reggie shook his head. 'No, I don't know it either.'

'There was this barmaid I met at the *Old Kettle Inn* in Surbiton. She was quite a looker and I tipped her over generously.'

'And do I want to know where this anecdote is leading up to?'

Miles smirked. 'Maybe not, but all I'll say is that copulation was her uncomplicated way of saying thank you – a tenner well spent.'

Reggie shook his head. 'But Miles, you randy old goat, aren't you a bit old for this sort of thing?'

'Unfortunately yes. My 'randy days', as you put it, are well and truly over. This happened a while ago but ... I do like revisiting the memories.'

'A couple of weeks ago, Miles, you accused me of being from a bygone age, out of touch with modern Britain, and now here you are with more of a caveman attitude towards women. Anyway, I'm not a bloody twenty-year-old; I am sixty-three, ready to settle down with one wonderful lady ...*fortes fortuna adiuat*. And my genetics, old chap, are none of your damn business.'

'No offence, young Reginald,' Miles chuckled.

'You are amusing company, Miles, but probably not the oracle I'm seeking to help me plan a happy, fulfilled life.' He repositioned his monocle to have a clear look at what Miles had brought.

'I've made a few notes on my research to date,' Miles pointed to the first page. 'My first assumption was her age; I've put her between forty and sixty. Then location; I envisaged her in southern England and these assumptions have revealed something which may - just may lead to finding her. After wading through scores of false leads, Eureka, up came this, a certain G S Pinch-Dogberry of Seaton, Devon. Her late mother was named as Amelia Pinch, but alas, there was no record of the father.'

'Did you say Pinch-Dogberry? Well, that is interesting. One Mr Jacob Pinch, who died just a few days ago, was the solicitor who wrote Cressida's will. He was also an executor. Well done, old chap - very interesting. It gets curiouser and curiouser. Once Cressy's funeral is over, methinks a trip to Seaton will be called for. Did the register give an address?'

'No, but if you can get Jacob Pinch's address off Edgar Ormrod, you could start there.'

'Excellent, what a clever old stick you are. The Hercule Poirot of the bureau of missing persons. Are you sure you don't want another drink?'

'No, not tonight. I'll leave you with your thoughts. 'I'll call a taxi before I turn into a pumpkin.'

Miles left, leaving Reggie in a thoughtful mood. 'Well, well,' he murmured. 'It looks as we're onto something now.'

Chapter Twenty-Three

Suffering from yesterday's overindulgence, Reggie propped himself up in bed. 'That bounder, Miles, led me astray,' he growled like a bear with a two-day hangover. 'Will I ever learn? A few cups of strong coffee and full English breakfast should help, followed by a dry day. *Ah now that's a wee bit hasty, Reggie, old boy, maybe a dry-ish day.*'

Despite feeling under the weather, he'd enjoyed the evening with Miles who was always amusing. It was good to have a chum. He'd left his well-cultivated friends in Africa and hadn't, thus far, identified new *faire des amis* in England. He knew he had to make more of an effort to develop friendships, but where would that be, Kingston or Ringwood or wherever? The decision of where he and Foxy would live in their *bower of bliss* hadn't been seriously broached. His own preference would be Kingston. The proximity to the sophistication of London with its theatres and galleries was a big draw. Ringwood's proximity to Ferndown and Verwood did not, somehow, set his pulse racing.

After Aida had cleared away the breakfast dishes, he sensed the fug in his head had cleared a little, and his churning stomach had calmed. The outlook for the day ahead suddenly brightened.

'Aida,' he called, 'Would you kindly go and tell Mr Lee that he and I should leave for Ringwood at ten o'clock on Tuesday morning.'

'Mr Lee? You mean downstairs Mr Lee.'

'That is correct, Aida. Please give *downstairs Mr Lee* the message. We are going to Ringwood again.'

'I do that, sir. You go for many days?'

'A few days, Aida. My Aunt's funeral is on Wednesday and after that, I have some other matters to attend to. I'll call you when I've set the date for my return.'

'I understand, sir.'

'Oh, and one more thing. I expect to bring a friend back with me, so prepare the spare bedroom, the one at the front with the nice view.'

'I do that sir.' Hesitating, unsure if it would be improper to enquire further, she asked, 'Your friend, sir, is it woman?'

Reggie smiled. 'Yes, Aida, my friend is a lady.'

Aida forced back a smile holding her hand over her mouth. 'Oh.'

They had an uneventful drive to Ringwood and, with Mr Lee's talented chauffeuring; the journey from Kingston to the front entrance of the *Forest Glenn Hotel* took only a fraction under two hours.

'Well done, Mr Lee, it's nice to be back in Ringwood.'

'It good, *Weggie*, it *wovewy* here.'

'Yes, it is *wovewy*,' Reggie laughed. His previous doubts had faded about ever returning to his childhood despondency, housed as he had been, with his stern, unloving Aunt Cressy. Any difficulty in becoming re-acquainted with Ringwood was surely to be expected. One consolation was that the streets and people were more or less the same as he'd left them forty years ago and, of course, it was mainly meeting Foxy and falling in love all over again.

'After lunch, Mr Lee, I will take the car and call on my friend, Mrs Makepeace. I don't expect to be back until late this evening.'

'Ah *Weggie*, you see the same *wady fwiend*? The *Viagwa wady*?'

'There is no need for Viagra, Mr Lee.' Reggie's tone was firm, hoping the subject would not be mentioned again. It was an episode in his life he'd rather forget. 'But you are correct, Mr Lee, it is the same lady as before.'

'Ah, that good. I go Mrs Kim, she *wike* me.'

'I'm sure she does. Therefore, I suggest we meet for breakfast here in the hotel at nine o'clock tomorrow morning.'

'*Nine o'cwock.* That okay.'

'And then after breakfast, I'd like you to take Mrs Makepeace and myself to the funeral at the church. Is that convenient for you?'

'Of course. We have saying in my *countwy*.'

'You know, Mr Lee,' Reggie smiled, 'I had a feeling you would.'

'We say, *pewson onwy* die once, but it for a *vewy wong* time.'

'Indeed, it is for a long time, Mr Lee. That is a particularly good saying.'

'Thank you, *Weggie*. I take Mrs Kim *funewal*?'

'Er ...oh!' Reggie hadn't thought about who would be there, or indeed, how many. Edgar Ormrod had arranged to hold the wake in the nearby *Star Inn* - probably more like a cocktail party for the geriatric-set than a sad farewell. The appearance

135

of Mr Lee accompanying Mrs Kim may well be a welcome distraction to what could be like an over-seventies care home for the terminally bewildered. 'Yes, Mrs Kim will be most welcome as your guest. I look forward to meeting her.'

'Thank you, *Weggie*. Mrs Kim will be my *guest-es*. Will *powiceman Cwapp* be at funeral?'

'I think so. I expect Policeman Crap-Clapp will be checking everyone at the church. He's still not arrested anyone for my aunt's murder. I have a meeting with him and Mr Edgar Ormrod on Thursday morning.'

'Okay *Weggie*.'

Reggie had already decided to give Clapp a copy of Aunt Cressy's revealing letter. That should befuddle the buffoon.

Chapter Twenty-Four

Drawing up outside 28 Shady Grove, Reggie was relieved that Sylvia's neighbour was not outside standing guard. The last thing he wanted was to be accosted by the humongous Grace Pluck. Carrying a bag under one arm, he hurried down the drive and rang the bell. Sylvia opened the door.

'Hello Reggie.'

'Hello.' He caught her perfume as they embraced.

She tilted her head and they kissed; a kiss full of tenderness. Pulling away, she smiled. 'You know something, your mouth fits mine in a way that no other mouth ever did – our mouths were meant for each other.'

'And my mouth agrees.' He gazed into her eyes. *"You walk in beauty, like the night, thus mellowed to that tender light."*

She laughed. 'You do talk total crap at times but thank you anyway. You used to sing love songs to me – remember, with the sole aim to try and seduce me.'

'Yes, I did, didn't I?' he reminisced. 'In those days I was a bright young chap full of zip. I could run, jump, spring ...'

'I don't ever remember you actually springing or zipping.'

'Well, no, probably springing is an exaggeration, but I could bowl a good ball.'

'Yes, I went to see you play cricket in what you described as an international test match, Ringwood versus Ferndown. You scored a lot of runs. To anyone within earshot, I said "that's my boyfriend". I was proud of you. After the match, they gave you the ball as a souvenir, and you gave it to me,' her eyes fluttered, 'I still have it.'

'Do you really? Nestling within your drawer of lacy underwear and G-strings, I trust.'

'G-strings! Oh my God. Why did we ever wear thongs? An entire decade lost to crack.'

They laughed together.

'Anyway,' she led him into the kitchen, 'If you're interested, and I'm sure you are, I am of an age when I no longer wear support underwear, it can make you look like a vacuum-packed sausage. Let's face it, fleshy bits have to spill out somewhere.'

He stood back to look at her. 'And, if I may be so bold, it's *spilled out* rather nicely in all the right places.'

'Thank you, kind sir. Your juvenile babble has made me thirsty, let's have a cup of tea.' Seeing the bag, he'd brought, she smiled. 'I see you've brought your own supplies.'

He produced two bottles of *Ancestor* whisky from his bag. 'You boil the kettle and I'll pour myself a little snifter.'

Drinks in hand, they settled in the compact living room and talked. Reggie hoped the arrangements for the following morning's funeral were alright with her. With Mr Lee driving, they would collect her at ten-fifteen and go straight into the church. Even though Reggie was Cressida's closest relation, all the arrangements had been made by Edgar Ormrod, for which he was most grateful. Edgar had also arranged refreshments for the wake and sent invitations to the few people he thought should be there, but, as he'd told Reggie, excluding those of the lower levels of the social heap.

'Is that what he said?' a shocked Sylvia demanded.

'His exact words.'

'What a bloody snob. I thought he was better than that.'

Reggie wished he had never told her. 'He probably only said it to humour me.'

'I hope you're not like that, Reggie. You never used to be.'

'No, of course not, my angel. As you can tell, I am the model of the perfect English gentleman, impeccable manners and social graces, all included at no extra cost.'

'Of course, you are,' she nodded. 'But what should I wear?'

'Wear? What do you mean?'

'For the funeral.'

'Not an area of my expertise, I'm afraid, but I'll be in a grey suit and black tie. I don't think Aunt Cressy would want flamboyant apparel. She'd prefer traditional.'

'Traditional – what, like Trooping of the Colour?'

'Oh yes, she'd have loved that; canons blazing away and buglers playing the last post. Incidentally, Mr Lee is bringing a guest, a Mrs Kim from the local massage parlour, and he told me that it is a Korean custom to wear bright clothes at funerals.'

'Well, that should be interesting.'

'I'm meeting Edgar and D S Clapp the following morning to see if the police are any further forward in their investigation. And then I'd like to go to look around Cressy's house; one last journey down memory lane. I would be grateful if you'd come with me; hold my hand and give me a shoulder to cry on. Would you do that?'

'Yes, of course. And after that?'

'I'd like you to come back with me to Kingston. You can take your time to look around and see what you think of it. I also want you to finish work, I want you all to myself. I'm sufficiently well-off to care for us as long as we both shall live.'

'That would mean I'd be a kept woman.'

Reggie puckered his brow. 'Not the phrase I would choose, old girl.'

She thought about it. 'A kept woman, what a wonderful expression. It's so ... well, exotic isn't it, like the description of a fallen woman. But I can tolerate, without discomfort, being waited on hand and foot. Too much of a good thing can be wonderful.'

'You're in your own fantasy land, aren't you?'

'Maybe. By the way, Reggie, don't get too comfy just now as Chester will be here anytime. I did tell you he'd moved back in, didn't I?'

'Yes, you did. Even more reason for you to come back to Kingston with me.'

As if on cue, the front door opened, and Chester called out that he was home.

'In here, Ches,' Sylvia called.

'Oh, hello Reggie. Down for the funeral?'

'That's right, Ches. Would you like to come? She was your Great Aunt but, of course, you never knew that.'

'No, I'm not going. I don't want to even think that I was related to the old misery-guts. On the few occasions I met her, she was always complaining about something or other. Oh,' he laughed, 'I forgot to tell you, Grace Pluck is outside, drunk to the gills, caressing your Rolls with one hand and emptying a bottle of wine down her throat with the other.'

'Oh God,' Sylvia quickly got to her feet. 'Edgar Ormrod made her redundant this morning. Come on both of you, we'll have to get her in the house.'

'Not me,' Reggie resisted. 'You'd need a forklift truck to move her.'

'Yes you,' Sylvia sharply rebuked. 'It's your fault. She's besotted with you, Mr *Sex-on-Legs*. And you'll have to come as well, Ches. I'll need all the help I can get.'

CHAPTER TWENTY-FIVE

Looking through her front window, Sylvia saw Reggie's Rolls arrive. Closing the door behind her, she walked up the drive. After a good deal of dithering that morning, she'd decided to wear a navy-blue suit with a white blouse and medium heeled shoes.

Reggie gave a warm smile. 'You look very nice, m'dear.'

'Well, thank you,' she replied while, at the same time, eyeing-up the tiny Asian man opening the car door for her.

'Sylvia, I'd like you to meet ...'

Before he could complete the introduction, Mr Lee bowed deeply from the waist, announcing in a falsetto screech, '*Ee su won*.'

The ear-piercing shriek almost made Sylvia jump.

Seeing her surprised reaction, Reggie quickly took over. 'Mr Lee, I'd like you to meet Mrs Sylvia Makepeace. This is my friend and neighbour, Mr Lee.'

Being so small, she wasn't sure whether to shake his hand or pat him on the head. Regaining her composure, she managed a smile. 'Hello Mr Lee, I'm pleased to meet you.' Speaking quietly as Reggie helped her into the car, she said, 'He's rather short to drive your car?'

'Yes. His legs are, perhaps, shorter than they should be, but he's fitted his own special pedals. We're quite safe.'

Mr Lee piped up. 'This your *wady fwiend, Weggie?*'

'Indeed, Mr Lee, Sylvia is my very good friend.'

'Thank you, *Weggie.* We go church now.'

Sitting together in the back, Sylvia nudged Reggie. 'Did he call you Wedgie?'

'No, no,' he shook his head, 'Reggie.'

Starting to giggle, she whispered, 'No he didn't, he called you Wedgie.' Her giggling was beginning to get out of hand.

Reggie whispered back. 'Kindly stop your tittering.'

'Okay, Wedgie.' This set her off again. 'I've got a *wedgie image* of you in my head,' she chuckled, 'and it won't go away.'

'You'll upset Mr Lee,' he admonished through gritted teeth. 'And remember, we're heading for a funeral.'

Taking a deep breath, she managed to stop herself giggling, and apologised.

It was a fine, sunny morning and the air in Ringwood was pleasantly warm. In the market square, leaves on the trees fluttered gently in the moderate south-westerly breeze. There weren't many people heading for the church, just a few diehard locals who went to every funeral and a handful of Cressida's neighbours, curious as to who would turn up – specially to see if her dissolute nephew appeared. Reggie wondered if the murderer was amongst them; he'd read that often happened, taking a macabre pleasure in witnessing grieving relations. The mournful, slow tolling of the church bell summoned to those gathered that the service was about to commence.

Before they reached the doorway, two elderly ladies thrust themselves forward directly in front of Reggie. The taller of the two leaned forwards, her face only inches away from Reggie's. She drew back her head like a snake about to strike. 'It's you, isn't it?'

The ill-mannered approach irritated Reggie enormously. 'Madam, as you haven't indicated a proper noun, implicit or unspecified immediately after the pronoun, then the answer is "No".'

'I know it's you,' her voice grated. 'Look ... it's me.'

'Indeed, it is you, Madam,' his voice taking on a stentorian tone. 'And I offer you my congratulations for you knowing that you are you.' For this pompous, mocking remark, Reggie received a sharp kick on his ankle from Sylvia.

The lady, however, didn't pick up on his sarcasm. 'I was Miss Smythe's neighbour. You must remember me.'

Reluctantly, in the recesses of his memory, he did. 'Unfortunately madam, I can't remember your name, but please don't bother to tell me.'

'It's Mrs Snout – you must remember me.'

'Oh yes.' Aunt Cressy had never liked her and irreverently described her as *"Snout by name, snout by nature"*. How could he forget that? 'Erm Mrs Snout, it was interesting meeting you again, but we must go now.' Turning his back, he gently guided Sylvia towards the church.

Giving the departing couple a withering look, she murmured to her companion, 'That's Miss Smythe's nephew. He had a reputation for a wandering eye and a restless groin.'

Walking away, Reggie and Sylvia overheard her comment and smiled.

'By the way,' Sylvia whispered, 'I know the other woman with Mrs Snout, she's Mrs Golightly, Tiffany's mother.'

'What, you mean the one looking like Joan of Arc after she'd been burnt at the stake is the mother of Tiffany, Redknapp's friend, the one with the steamroller?'

Sylvia couldn't help chuckling. 'Don't be so cruel, Reggie, she can't help looking like that but yes, the very same.' She suddenly stopped and pointed to another lady heading for the entrance. 'Oh gosh, look, that's the person you've been looking for. Dotty – you know, Dorothy Smerdal, your aunt's housekeeper. You told me she was missing.'

'She is missing ... well was. Are you sure?'

'Of course I am.' She was small and plump with a sad, lined face, her hair mousy-coloured and in poor condition. 'I'll introduce you after the service.'

'Please do. I see D S Clapp hovering over there by the entrance. He'll obviously want to speak to her. She's on his list of murder suspects.'

'What! Dotty, a murder suspect? That's total nonsense.'

As they entered the body of the church, they were met by the vicar. Reggie was not impressed by the man of God as his dog collar was shabby and perspiration trickled down his forehead. 'I'm Reginald Grosvenor Smythe, Cressida Smythe's nephew, and this is my friend, Mrs Makepeace.'

'Oh, hello.' They shook hands. 'I'm the Reverend Duke FitzPeter.' He was a thickset man of medium height, beneath a head of black hair touched here and there with grey.

'Duke?' Reggie questioned, wondering what role the nobility was about to play.

'It's short for Marmaduke. I'm pleased to meet you but, of course, it is a very sad day.' His voice was like the rehearsed intonation of a costume drama thespian. 'It must be a mistake to take her from us too early.'

Reggie sighed. 'I tend to differ, Duke. God doesn't make mistakes - that's how he got the job.'

'Oh, well, of course,' Giving Reggie wounded scowl, FitzPeter gave a soft, inaudible laugh not wanting to draw attention.

Edgar Ormrod came to stand next to them. 'Hello, Edgar, FitzPeter purred.' It was like being bathed in warm custard.

'Ready to kick-off, your Reverence?' Edgar asked.

Checking his pocket watch, Duke nodded and then, turning his head, gave a thunderous sneeze which echoed around the entrance porch. To a startled Reggie it sounded like something between a vomiting donkey and an explosion in an arms factory. This was immediately followed, like an encore, with a loud hic.

What in the blue-blazes? None of the others turned a hair at Duke's proboscis outburst, Reggie assumed they were used to his sternutations and diplomatically held his tongue.

The service was mercifully short. Two choruses' of *Abide With Me*, followed by a eulogy given by Edgar, espousing the selfless dedication Cressida had given the community. Then the Reverend Marmaduke FitzPeter read the King James version of the Twenty-third Psalm, putting in dramatic pauses and theatrical gestures where none were needed, followed by the Lord's Prayer. After a long pause, he rocked back and forth before announcing in a loud voice, in case anyone had fallen asleep, 'I now quote from Corinthians chapter fifteen. "*To the sound of trumpets, the dead will be raised imperishable, and we will be changed*".

The organ played recessional music from the hymn, *The Day thou Gavest Lord is Ended*, indicating to the congregation that it was time to troop out for the committal and burial.

As they left the churchyard, Sylvia took a sombre looking Reggie's arm. 'Are you alright?'

'No, not really. Full of remorse if you must know - seeing the coffin being buried upset me. It was ... oh, I don't know. I should have been more attentive to her over the years, and now it is too late. But even though she's gone, the way she died was terrible – she was actually murdered – of all things. She didn't deserve that, no, not my Aunt Cressy. And now it's in the less than capable hands of the police in the person of D S Clapp. Will he ever find out why and by whom? I have my doubts.'

Slowly, they walked arm in arm to the *Star Inn* for the wake.

Chapter Twenty-Six

Neatly laid out in the *Star Inn* were plates of assorted sandwiches, cold meats, sausage rolls, porkpies, salt and pepper prawns and duck, and something greenish yellow in wraps, along with green and potato salads. Reggie was impressed.

'There's plenty,' Edgar smiled reassuringly as they arrived. 'Care to try a pie before kick-off? The manager here wouldn't provide them, so I ordered the pies myself from Belch the Butcher.'

'Not for me, old chap,' Reggie's expression said it all. 'They look as if they contain enough grease to fuel the QE2.'

Sylvia nodded in agreement. 'A wise decision, Reggie. I once tried one of Belch's pies – not an experience I care to repeat. So, tell me, Edgar, why did you order them?'

Slightly hurt, he chose not to answer. Pointing to the far corner of the room, he said there's free tea and coffee over in the alcove.

'And what about proper drinks?' The saliva in Reggie's mouth was already drying up.

'Anything from the bar has to be paid for.'

'What absolute nonsense,' Reggie protested. 'I know Cressida was a difficult person at times, but she still deserves a proper send-off. Her estate can afford it.'

'As her only living executor, I feel it my duty to limit the cost.'

'You're a miserable old Scrooge, Edgar. I'll pay for the drinks myself. Kindly inform the manager accordingly.'

'Be it on your head, old chap.'

A smartly dressed lady joined them by the buffet. 'May I convey my deepest sympathy at your aunt's death, Mr Grosvenor Smythe, I'm the manager here at the *Star Inn*.'

'Very kind of you, dear Lady Manager,' Reggie gently shook the proffered hand. 'And may I convey my gratitude to you for the excellent spread your staff have provided today. If the budget the miserly Mr Ormrod here gave you is insufficient then add the extra onto the alcohol bill I'm paying.'

She gave a gracious smile. 'Thank you, sir.'

Edgar scowled. 'Moving on, I suggest, Reggie, you stand with me at the entrance. I'll greet everyone as they arrive and introduce them to you.' He looked at his watch. 'They'll be beating down the door in a few minutes.'

'I see the formidable D S Clapp is already hovering around the place,' Reggie pointed him out at the back of the room. 'By withholding the fact that Cressida didn't die from natural causes, the police hope it will make the murderer think he's got away with it; the perfect crime - and then he'll get careless.'

Edgar nodded. 'You're probably right, but I'm not convinced Clapp knows what he's doing.'

'Now then my dear Foxy, please join me in the receiving line. I'd like you by my side.'

'Only on one condition.'

'Oh, and that would be?'

'Under no circumstances are you to be pompous, patronising, or like the way you spoke to Mrs Snout earlier; you can be very rude at times.'

'But she's a very annoying, sabre-toothed old bat. She has the face of an exhausted gnu, the voice of an unstrung tennis racquet, and a figure of no discernible shape.'

'That's enough, Reggie,' she scolded. 'I don't care, it won't hurt you to be nice.'

'In that case, m'dear, I promise to be on my absolute best behaviour.'

Edgar opened the door and the first people entered, all eager to sample the food - it was lunch time after all. The initial sombre mood lifted dramatically when they were told there was a free bar.

As he'd promised to Sylvia, Reggie greeted everyone, including Mrs Snout, with overzealous courtesy, including several people he vaguely remembered from forty years ago.

'Not exactly the elegant mourners one would expect at a society wake,' Edgar muttered. 'Rather a shabby lot. I'm afraid.'

'Disapproval showed in Reggie's eyes. 'Don't be such a snob. Edgar, The good Lord prefers common looking people – that's why he makes so many.'

Edgar rubbed the stubble on his head. 'Well, it's just that ...' His shoulders slumped, and Reggie left a somewhat chastised Edgar and strode to the bar, overjoyed when the barman produced a bottle of Glenfiddich single malt. At Reggie's insistence, he poured a treble measure into a large glass, and then a glass of Pinot Grigio for Sylvia.

''Ello,' came a mumbled voice. Standing in front of them was Redknapp, accompanied by an orange-skinned lady wearing a skimpy top with a bare midriff, and a dark-blue mini-skirt. She held onto Redknapp, gracelessly tottering on bright red, high-heeled shoes. Her heavily muscled bare thighs wouldn't look out of place in the front row of an all-male rugby scrum.

Reggie shook Redknapp's limp hand. 'Are you going to introduce your lady companion?'

'I'm Tiffany.' Not waiting for Redknapp, she thrust a large, calloused hand into Reggie's and squeezed hard. She had a rather bovine face, the sort that one used to see on strike pickets – *cross this line if you dare, mate.*

'How do you do, Tiffany. I understand you toil and travail, protected by Saint Benedict of Nursia.'

'Eh?'

'Saint Benedict, the patron saint of steamroller operatives. The labours of Hercules pale in comparison to your steamroller endeavours.'

'What yer on about?'

'Never mind Tiffany,' Sylvia gave Reggie an exasperated glare. 'He was being humorous.'

'Oh well, that's alright then, aint it? I 'ear you related to the old Smythe woman, the one 'oo popped her clogs and left lots of money for Red.' Her voice was rough and heavily accented. 'She were nuffink but bloody trouble, that one - aint that right, lover?'

Reggie's eyes flashed with anger. 'Young lady, my late Aunt, Cressida Smythe, has just been buried and this is her wake. Speak nothing but good of the dead – or not at all.'

'Cor, yer voice ain't-alf posh, mate. I dunna understand a bloody word yus sayin'.'

Reggie seethed. 'In that case, Tiffany, I will ...' he stopped on seeing Sylvia's foot poised ready to inflict further damage to his ankle. Changing tack and taking a deep breath, he pointed them towards the buffet. 'Refreshments are over there. Off you go.'

''E may be bloody clever,' Tiffany whispered loudly as she tottered away, 'but I bet 'e can't waggle his ears like you, Babe.'

They tittered together as Redknapp bent his head to one side and jiggled his left ear.

Taking a large sip from his glass, Reggie took Sylvia's hand and they looked round hoping there would be no further vulgarity and disrespect.

Two tables away, Grace Pluck had purloined a plate of sandwiches and a bottle of wine. Her chair looked as if it had been built around her by someone who knew that armchairs should be tight around the hips this season. Mrs Snout, looking like she'd been weaned on a pickle, was holding a large wine glass and rabbiting on to some poor old dear wearing a large hearing aid, which whistled in protest.

Suddenly, all eyes turned towards the door as Mr Lee made a spectacular entrance wearing a yellow florescent shirt and tie. He was towered over by what seemed at first sight to be an ostrich – an apparition in feathers that began to bob slowly up and down. Spotting Reggie and Sylvia, Mr Lee led the feathered manifestation to their table.

'*Hewo, Weggie and Sywvia*, I introduce my *fwiend*, Mrs Kim.' Pleased with the distraction, Reggie helped to seat them, stifling a smile in order to maintain the sombre expression of chief mourner 'I'm very pleased to meet you, Mrs Kim, and your erm ... outfit is truly magnificent.'

Her face, stern at first, broke into a smile as she brushed away a stray piece of plumage that had found its way into her left nostril. '*Vewy* kind, *Weggie*, I dwess in Kowean tradition. It *honour* to be with you. I *sowwy*, my *Engwish* not good - better in my mouth.'

'We understand you perfectly, Mrs Kim.'

'Thank you, *Weggie*.'

Noticing that some people were preparing to leave, Reggie stood and tapped on his now empty glass, catching everyone's attention. Public speaking was his forte. First, he thanked them for coming and assured the guests that the buffet and bar would remain open for another hour. He then expressed his gratitude to Edgar Ormrod for making all the arrangements, and the *Star Inn* for the excellent buffet … choosing not to mention the Belch's pies.

There was light applause from the few without food and drink in their hands, led by an inebriated and over-stuffed Mrs Grace Pluck.

Reggie went on to explain that after his parents had died when he was only eight years of age, he'd spent his school holidays with Aunt Cressy, and he appreciated the kindness and hospitality given to him by the children of Ringwood who befriended him at that time, some of whom are here today. He asked everyone to raise their glasses and drink to the memory of his aunt, Miss Cressida Smythe.

Chapter Twenty-Seven

A rolled umbrella measured Reggie's steps as he crossed the market square towards West Street. The church clock chimed ten confirming his punctuality for the meeting. It had rained overnight, and the sky had an angry glare. Thinking back to when, forty years ago, he'd wooed the young maiden, Sylvia Fox, at the end of West Street near the River Avon, he smiled to himself, *la memoire deux heureux*. The street itself hadn't changed much, still a mixed bag ranging from Victorian varicose to a couple of King Charles's architectural carbuncles.

The seedy corridor leading to Edgar Ormrod's office was poorly lit confirming he was not effectively soliciting business. At least the smell from Satan's lavatory had gone, as had *The Incredible Hulk* of Grace Pluck. Entering the office, Edgar was in the process of opening the only window - whether to allow in fresh air, or to expel the smell of cheap cologne emanating from D S Clapp, was unclear. The sergeant sat sprawled in a visitor's chair, uncouthly chewing a wad of gum, which he dextrously propelled from one side of his mouth to the other.

Muted greetings were exchanged. 'Sergeant, may I enquire as to whether there have been any positive developments regarding Cressida Smythe's murder investigations? And did you manage to identify any suspicious characters at the funeral and wake yesterday?'

'That is something I'm not at liberty to reveal, sir.' Clapp opened his file in a manner suggesting he knew what he was doing. 'Unfortunately, sir, I was unwell yesterday evening, as I'd eaten two pies at the wake, which had adversely affected my wellbeing.'

Guiltily, Edgar looked away.

'But I can reveal to you gentlemen that I was unable to follow up on a couple of potential leads. I will, however, endeavour to question the persons of interest later today.' Droning on in his gravelly voice, he continued, 'Before the onset of my illness, I did interview Miss Dorothy Smerdal, Miss Smythe's housekeeper. It would appear that on the evening prior to Miss Smythe's murder, angry words had been exchanged between the two ladies, resulting in the said, Miss Smerdal, being dismissed.' Pausing for effect, he turned over a page. 'Being upset, Miss Smerdal took the opportunity to visit her sister in Wick, Scotland, only returning to Ringwood two days' ago. She alleges that it was only then that she learned of Miss Smythe's demise.'

'That sounds a bit fishy,' Edgar pronounced.

'I agree with Edgar,' Reggie said. 'I assume you have checked her alibi.'

'Of course, sir, we have made checks and can confirm Miss Smerdal did indeed, leave Ringwood at 0830 hours on 5th July, well before the murder took place.'

'And did she go straight to Wick?'

'As straight as humanly possible, sir, 'cos the road from Ringwood to Wick is not a straight line, if you see what

I mean.' Clapp stopped chewing for a second to give a satisfied smirk. 'We were able to establish, beyond any doubt, that she did not stop anywhere en route.'

'Does that mean she's no longer a suspect?' Edgar asked.

Clapp used a finger to tap the side of his nose. 'Not a *prime* suspect, no.'

'Well in that case, Sergeant, which of the other suspects is *prima inter parés?*'

'Prima what, sir?'

'Who are your main suspects? From our previous discussions, it leaves Edgar here, Redknapp, and the mysterious Gertrude Dogberry.'

'That is something I'm not at liberty to reveal, sir.' Clapp started chewing again. 'As far as Gertrude Dogberry is concerned, we are no further forward with our enquiries.' Then nodding in Edgar's direction said, 'We interviewed Redknapp Ormrod who, we discovered, has a police record, for 'aving a flawed character.'

Edgar protested. 'But Dorian, that was six months ago.'

'It was still a crime, Edgar.' Clapp removed the gum from his mouth, wrapping it in a tissue and placing it in his jacket pocket. 'Redknapp Ormrod was 'ad up for indecently exposing himself, adjacent to the delicatessen counter in Waitrose supermarket.'

'But that, in itself, was not a serious crime,' Edgar argued.

Clearing his throat, Clapp nodded. 'In itself, Edgar, it could have been overlooked. But then Redknapp, without using his finger – if you see what I mean, lewdly pointed a certain Miss Pinkerton in the direction of the fish counter. Unfortunately, Miss Pinkerton had a nervous disposition, but excellent eyesight, and fainted at the indecent spectacle that confronted her, and was rushed to A and E.'

'Look Clapp,' an irritated Reggie boomed, 'That's all very sad, but using the wrong digit to give directions does not make him a murderer. During my formative years, sodomy and whiplash domination were socially acceptable, but flashing old ladies is flagrantly lower class. Redknapp is too young to have been brought up in the *clip around the ear* generation.'

Neither Edgar nor Clapp showed reaction to Reggie's summary. Clapp checked his watch. 'Now then, Edgar, Redknapp was supposed to be here to see me this morning, but he hasn't appeared and he's not answering his mobile. Where is he?'

'I don't know ... I'm not his keeper.'

'That maybe true, but there is a pattern emerging here relating to Redknapp and elderly ladies. Miss Pinkerton, aged eighty-one, was assaulted by Redknapp, whereas Miss Cressida Smythe, aged eighty-three was assaulted at home ... well, murdered actually.'

Angrily, Edgar banged his hand down hard on the desk. 'If you're inferring, Sergeant, that Redknapp was ...'

'I'm not inferring anything at this stage,' Clapp interrupted, 'But kindly instruct your son to contact me asap. If I don't hear from him by later today, we'll issue a warrant.'

'That's an extremely tenuous connection, Sergeant,' Reggie said. 'I suggest, therefore, that we move on from Redknapp's little peccadillo – what other positive revelations have been unearthed during your forensic investigations into my aunt's death? You've had time enough.'

Clapp turned to another page in the file. 'You will understand, gentlemen, that details of murder investigations are highly confidential, and my senior officer, D I Farthing, is already breathing down my neck ... so to speak, so I have to be very careful. I do want to be helpful, especially as your co-operation may help the enquiry, but please keep anything I tell you confidential.'

'Understood, Sergeant.' Edgar replied. 'You have my word.'

Reggie said nothing.

Clapp's droning continued. 'We learnt from Miss Smythe's investment adviser that, prior to her death, someone tried to take money out of her account.'

'Ah, I know about that.' Reggie passed a copy of his aunt's letter to Clapp. 'Cressida wrote to me two days before her death but addressed it to my previous domicile. It was redirected onto my current address, but that took eighteen days, only arriving on Monday.'

Clapp took his time to read it, and placed a note in his file, mumbling out aloud as he wrote, 'Letter dated 3rd July from Cressida Smythe to Reginald Smythe. Do you know, sir, who it was who tried to take her money?'

'No idea, but you should check the suspects' bank accounts – that would be a good start. I'm sure, Sergeant, that you, using your famed *latest technology*, could do that.'

Not grasping Reggie's sarcasm, Clapp said. 'Well sir, now I have this evidence, my team will get onto it straight away.' Resting his chin on his hand in what he hoped was a thoughtful posture, he resumed, 'Is there anything else you are withholding from us, sir?'

Reggie took umbrage. 'Damn it man, I'm not withholding anything.'

'Just thought I'd ask, sir.' Clapp enjoyed any opportunity to wind-up Reginald Grosvenor Smythe and his sodding OBE.

CHAPTER TWENTY-EIGHT

Cressida Smythe had lived all her life in what was locally known as a two-bedroom Forrester's Cottage. The unlikely name of *la belle maison* painted on the front gate. It was set in Holson Avenue off Horton Road in Ashley Heath, two miles west of Ringwood. The bungalow, built at the turn of the twentieth century, had white rendered walls, brown woodwork - in urgent need of re-painting - and roofed with slate tiles.

Reggie parked his Rolls in the drive. He sat for a while with Sylvia, trying to control his feelings. Uncharacteristically, he was subdued. 'I was told by a doctor,' his voice hardly above a whisper, 'that the human memory has powers to commit to oblivion the things that would otherwise distress us. I can assure you, my dear, that is a load of bollocks.'

Sylvia took his hand and gave it a reassuring squeeze. A cat, a ginger tom, sauntered towards them and stopped a few yards away to stare at the intruders, before nonchalantly wandering off into next door's garden.

They got out of the car. 'You see that place with the tall chimney,' he pointed to a house two doors away, 'well Humphrey 'Fatty' Davison lived there. He was rather tubby and everything he wore was tight-fitting. I remember his party trick was to spit froth – bloody brilliant, it was, but his acne-blotched cheeks were like a scarlet aurora borealis. Ha, he got an acorn stuck in his nose once which had to be surgically removed.'

'For your information,' Sylvia said, 'a certain Mr Humphrey Davison is now the *acne-free* Mayor of Bournemouth.'

'Is he really, by George? I'm so pleased. Well done Fatty. His mother used to make wonderful scones and, oh, and another thing I remember, she wore a charm to ward off tigers.'

Sylvia laughed. 'That's incredible – an amazing coincidence because bizarrely, Mrs Davison died at Marwell Zoo. It was in the paper. But I don't think it was a tiger attack … or maybe it was. What a great story that would have made.'

In the tiny front garden stood a tall, thin poplar resembling an exclamation mark, and at the back were three Scots pines. One of the branches had a piece of rotted rope was tied to it. 'I did that,' Reggie said. 'It's all that's left of a swing I made. Luckily, gardening was not one of aunt's interests and she didn't mind when I played out there. Unfortunately, Mr Clinch–as in boxing, the neighbour at the rear, complained when my balls landed amongst his chickens, but Cressy, bless her cotton socks, didn't seem to bother. I did get a good ticking off, though, when I drop-kicked a rugby ball right on top of the hen house roof. No eggs for a week, but it was worth it.'

'Poor Mr Clinch-as in boxing and his chickens, you young scallywag, you.'

'But so saying, the area itself doesn't seem to have changed apart from those new bungalows further along Holson Avenue.'

Walking slowly, they approached the front door. 'Did Ormrod give you the keys?'

'No, he wasn't going to, but old Clapp said he wanted me to look around to see if there was anything suspicious.'

'Suspicious?' she laughed. 'What, like a trail of blood leading to the bedroom?'

'I know, but that's how Clapp's mind works.'

Inside, the house had a chill about it, and there was a faint smell of disinfectant. Dead flowers in two vases hung their heads as if in mourning and tatty cushions were scattered on the chairs and floor. It was the ultimate of *memory-lane* moments for Reggie. Even the off-white walls and sad, tawdry pink and orange fabrics were as he remembered.

The living room was small, or intimate as Aunt Cressy described it, with a two-seater settee, and two unmatched armchairs, along with a small pine-effect bookcase with a small television balanced on it. The wall behind the settee was painted red with several paintings – landscapes and two female African portraits facing one another. A low, stained coffee table in front of the settee held several copies of the Parish magazine.

'It's like entering a time warp.' Reggie sighed, taking a couple of deep breaths. 'I'm beginning to well up.'

Sylvia gently put her arms round him and held him tight. 'It's okay, Reggie. You lived here for all those years; it's bound to be emotional.'

Next to the living room, his aunt's bedroom had a police blue and white *crime scene* tape hanging on the door frame. 'I won't go in just now.' They went to the next door which was his old room. It was filled with clutter; cardboard boxes and some old books lay on the floor with curled yellowed pages. Motes of dust hung in shafts of sunlight. He opened the cupboard and was amazed to see some of his old toys stuffed in, a sad reminder of the past. He brushed away a tear. 'Why on earth didn't she throw them out?'

'Maybe she missed you,' Sylvia empathized.

'Yes, maybe. She didn't show it at the time, though.'

'What with staying here and boarding school, you didn't have a happy childhood.'

'Oh, I don't know. I just had to buckle down and make the best of it. I never felt loved though ... until I met you, that is. You were like a sunburst in a grey Ringwood sky.'

'Oh, you corny old bugger. Me, a sunburst? Anyway, thank you, darling. I'll think of myself as a sunburst from now on.' She pecked him on the cheek. 'But what puzzles me is I was expecting a much grander house with better furnishings. You told me her estate is around the two million mark, but you wouldn't know it from this.'

'It actually doesn't surprise me. She was just that type of person.'

The galley kitchen was old and needed updating, although the cooker and fridge had changed since Reggie's time.

'Through there is the bathroom.'

'You mean you have to go through the kitchen to get to the bathroom?'

'Yes. The house was originally built with an outdoor lavatory, but an extension was added in the thirties. I wasn't allowed to have a bath, though,' he gave a little laugh. 'Looking back now, I find it hard to believe but she scared me into thinking the bathtub had malicious powers. She showed me that when you put a stick in water it looks bent but isn't. Well, she made me believe that if I had a bath, I'd come out bent.'

'What a horrible thing to say to a little boy but having to go through the kitchen every time must have been very awkward.'

'It was, particularly if visitors came. But in all my time, the only visitor I remember was the ancient vicar, a Reverend Holehouse, who came for afternoon tea once a month to discuss parochial matters, and who always had the grace to control his bladder whilst here.'

'Well done the crossed-legged Reverend Holehouse.'

'Let's go and look in her room now.' There was a strong smell of disinfectant in there. The bed Cressida Smythe was murdered in had been made up and everywhere was tidier and cleaner than in the other rooms. Apart from the bed, there was a free-standing wardrobe, a desk, and two upholstered chairs. Opposite was a fireplace, the grate empty. It had an intricate, strangely bulky carved wood surround which looked out of character with the rest of the house.

'Ah yes, I remember now,' Reggie said excitedly. 'Somewhere in there is a hidden panel. I sneaked a peep through a crack in the door one night. She opened it – a safe I think - with a combination and put some papers in. Let's see if it's still there.' Examining it from close range, there was one area around a carved flower where a little of the varnish had worn away. After several frustrating attempts, Reggie pushed on one petal and a panel slid to one side with a click revealing a safe.

'Yes, I was right, look, it has a combination lock ... I wonder.'

'You mustn't open it – wait for the police.'

'What! wait for old Clapp. Not on your Nellie.'

'You could be in trouble if you do.'

Ignoring the well-meant caution, Reggie first entered four zeros - but no luck.

'Well if you must, try 1 2 3 4,' suggested Sylvia, 'or her birthday, when was that?'

'It was ... oh, hang on, I remember it was the same day as D Day, 6th June, but which year was it? It must have been eighty-three years ago ... making it 1935. I'll try 6635. Open sesame.' There was a click, and Reggie was able to turn the handle and open the safe door. 'Oh my God, it worked.'

Slightly nervous about what he might find, Reggie knelt in front of the open wall safe, and began to carefully remove the contents.

'Are you sure we should be doing this? I still think we should inform the police, first? This could be evidence.'

Only half listening, he took out a small album. 'Look at this,' his heart missed a beat. Photographs. 'Oh my gosh, look, my parents and me,' Tears prickled his eyes and his voice faltered. 'I've er ... I've never seen these before.'

Sylvia knelt next to him, holding him gently in her arms. 'It's alright, Reggie, you've had a shock. She had no right to hide these from you.'

'Why did she, why?' He wiped a tear away. 'I would have loved to have seen these pictures of my parents. Here they are, my mother and father, Fiona and Rex Grosvenor Smythe.' His voice grew a little calmer. 'Anyway, these have nothing to do with Cressy's murder or the police, and they're mine, no-one else's.'

'Of course, they're your private property.'

Turning the page, there were a few more photos. 'That's where we used to live. That's me, in my mother's arms as a baby; on my first day at school; in the garden and at the seaside.' Sliding the photo out, he saw it was Swanage. 'Yes, that's right, I remember.'

Taking a deep breath, he put the album to one side and took a file of papers from the bottom shelf. 'By all the saints in Christendom, I can't believe it. The old crow was a bloody gambler. Look, she had an account with Specawin in Ferndown. She's listed all her bets, stakes, wins and losses and there's a credit balance on her account of more than four hundred pounds.'

'Wow,' Sylvia exclaimed. 'You can give that to the police, it's part of her estate.'

'She also had an account with Tophire Taxis.' He ran a finger down a list and over the page. 'It looks as though she took taxis to Bournemouth Bus Station every month, and then back two days later. Where in the blue-blazes was she going?'

Sylvia shook her head. 'Why don't you phone Tophire and ask them.'

'No, I'll let the police do that.' The safe was empty except for one large, manila envelope, a company's name across the top in large letters CAMELOT. Inside was an A4 sized colour photo of a smartly dressed couple with well-practised smiles, holding a cheque out to a startled looking Cressida. A thick black line crossed through it with the words 'No Publicity'. A letter accompanied it from Camelot, congratulating Miss C Smythe, the holder of the winning lottery ticket. 'Oh my God, look Foxy, it's for three million, four-hundred and fifty-two thousand, six hundred pounds.'

Sylvia gasped. 'Is it a joke, could it be real?'

In the same envelope was a passbook in Cressida's name from Bagara Investments, Bond Street, London, showing a deposit in her name for the same amount.

Reggie gasped. 'It's dated 15th June - that's what?' He thought for a second. 'That's only six weeks ago.'

Sylvia's hand shook as she read it. 'It can't be real, can it? It's not possible.'

His response was laced with frustration. 'I guess anything is possible. Blue and green snow is possible. It's all a question of likelihoods. and as Cressida was a gambler, it's likely she bought lottery tickets every week, and six weeks ago, her numbers came up.'

Abruptly Reggie stood and closed the safe. 'I've had enough here. We're going. We'll take everything with us and decide what to do over an exceptionally large whisky.'

Driving back to Sylvia's house, Reggie was lost in thought, not saying a word, even when Sylvia pointed out that he'd taken the wrong turn off Southampton Road. Grunting, he turned the car around. Once inside the house, Sylvia knew her priority was to produce the bottle of whisky. She poured an extra-large measure for Reggie and a smaller one for herself.

He sipped it appreciatively. He took out his monocle, closed his eyes and massaged his eyelids with his thumb and forefinger. 'Now if all this is correct,' he held up the Camelot letter and bank passbook, 'then Cressida's estate is worth,' he slowly enunciated each word separately, 'Close – to - six - million - pounds.'

Sylvia pulled a face as she sipped the whisky, which spread through her veins, burning and spreading to her fingertips.

'Whisky, my dear, leaves you with a cask-strength, capillary reddening tingle of happiness that runs to the very tip of your nose.'

'If you say so,' she coughed. 'Look Reggie, about all the money, I'm as confused as you are. If she did win it, why in hell's name didn't she do something with it? She lived in poverty. She could have spent it on her house for starters.' She creased her brow as an idea came to her. 'Or, oh, wait a minute, of course, maybe someone found out about the windfall and murdered her for it.'

'You mean someone who would benefit from her will?'

'Yes – no – hey, I don't know. We know there are known knowns like the beneficiaries – these are things we know we know.'

Reggie continued the theme. 'But we also now know there are known unknowns, like her gambling, her trips to Bournemouth Bus Station and, of course, the unknown Gertrude Dogberry who gets sixty percent of the estate. That is to say, we know there are some things we do not know, but also, there must be unknown unknowns, the ones we know nothing about.'

'Interesting though, isn't it?' Sylvia said. 'I wonder who could have discovered her big win? Dorothy Smerdal, her housekeeper, possibly.'

'But what about her confidential solicitor, Edgar Ormrod? Both he and Redknapp get ten percent, that's close to six hundred thousand pounds each. And Edgar already told me he's broke and almost out of business.'

Sylvia nodded. 'I don't think Redknapp brings in any money. You know, Reggie, there are so many unknowns.'

'Stop right there,' Reggie laughed. 'We've already done that.'

'Sorry, but what are you going to do? You'll have to tell the police; this is definitely a motive for her murder.'

Reggie took another swig. 'Yes, you're right. I'll give Clapp a call and ask him to see me tomorrow. He can come to the hotel. I don't want Edgar to know any of this.'

'Agreed. Apart from this money business, what do you remember of them - your parents, that is?'

He thought for a moment. 'From what I recall of my father, he was very tall, a teacher and had thick, black hair and deep blue eyes. And my mother, oh, she was lovely. She had blonde curls that she dragged back into a ponytail. She had pale, freckled skin and large hazel eyes. She was a gentle person, always happy.' A stray tear appeared again which he quickly brushed away. 'She drove me to school in her pride and joy, that bright red Austin Healey 3000, look there, in that picture. The car they both died in. The driver of a lorry had fallen asleep on the A4 near Maidenhead and drifted across the carriageway. They died instantly.' He paused for a second, 'And my life changed forever.'

CHAPTER TWENTY-NINE

Diners in the hotel restaurant looked up when two sharp-suited men entered. After a cursory survey, they headed directly for Reggie's table. He and Mr Lee were having breakfast.

'Are you Mr Grosvenor Smythe?' The authority in the first man's voice showed he was used to people jumping when he spoke.

The ill-mannered approach annoyed Reggie. 'Unless the hotel's on fire or a nuclear explosion is imminent, and I don't believe either is the case, I'd be obliged if you would kindly go away.' Turning his back, Reggie calmly took another slice of toast from the rack, prepared to add butter and Coopers Old English Whisky Marmalade, a preserve he'd enjoyed all his life.

For a moment, the man looked dumbfounded. 'I am Detective Inspector Farthing.'

'Are you really, well, bully for you,' Reggie articulated in a sarcastic tone. 'But I am going to finish my breakfast at my own pace. If, however, you would care to wait in the hotel lounge, I will be available at 0930 hours, that is in fifteen minutes, the time already agreed with D S Clapp. Until then, I'd be obliged if you would leave.'

Completely taken aback, D I Farthing was about to respond when Mr Lee, banging his bowl on the table after slurping the last of his spiced noodles, gave his high-pitched squeak. 'Ah, you say you *pwocemans-es*. How I know you *pwocemans-es*, you no uniform.'

Angry at Mr Lee's intrusion, Farthing's temper rose, demanding to know who he was.

'I *Ee su won*,' he piped loudly. 'Where you *pwocemans-es* uniform?'

Reggie took pleasure in the look of irritation on Farthing's face.

'Mr Ee?' Farthing questioned.

Mr Lee's screech was shriller than ever. 'No, not Mr Ee, my name Mr Ee.'

Wondering what the hell he'd let himself in for, Farthing, looking heavenward for guidance, reluctantly took out his *badge of office* and showed it to Mr Lee.

'Ah, you Inspector *Fawting*.'

'It's pronounced Farthing.'

'That what I say, *Fawting*.'

Having remained silent so far, and now lamely trying to intervene, the constable introduced himself. 'My names D C Lott.'

'You name D C *Wott*.'

'No, not *What* sir, but Lott.'

'That what I say, *Wott*. What wrong with *pwocemans-es* make too many confusion?'

'There's nothing *wong* ...wrong,' Farthing stuttered. 'We're plain-clothed police officers.'

Mr Lee shook his head. 'We have saying in my *countwy*.'

Halfway through his toast and marmalade, Reggie held back a smile.

'And what country would that be, sir,' ventured D C Lott.

'In *Repubwick of Kowea*. We say, *"When you want dog shit to understand one pewson, there is none."* You have same saying in your *countwy*?'

Both police officers stood stock still, dumbstruck. Seeing that Mr Lee's mangled wordplay was going down like a plate of raw codfish, Reggie, the end of his breakfast already spoilt, told the officers he was ready to join them in the lounge. Relief on their faces was clear.

'Mr Lee, old friend,' Reggie patted him affectionately on the shoulder, 'I'll see you at dinner this evening and we'll leave for Kingston at midday tomorrow, if that is acceptable to you.'

'Of course, *Weggie*. That *vewy* good.'

'That's settled, then.' Mr Lee left to go to his room while Reggie casually strolled through to the lounge and settled himself into an armchair, the two officers sitting opposite. 'Can I get you gentlemen some tea or coffee?'

'No thank you.' Farthing replied for both of them. 'Mr Grosvenor Smythe, you left a note for D S Clapp saying you had some new information regarding the murder of your aunt. Can we have it, please. We have wasted enough time already.'

Reggie made a show of checking his watch. 'Mmm, almost nine-thirty, yes, of course. Oh, where is Clapp by the way?'

'He's working on another case, and I've taken over,' Farthing replied. 'Now, sir, what is the new information.'

Reggie took several papers from his jacket pocket. 'I found these in Cressida Smythe's house yesterday. They were in her safe.'

'Really, you went to Miss Smythe's house! It doesn't say this in the notes. Who went with you?'

'My friend, Mrs Makepeace.'

'No, I mean which officer went with you?'

'No officer.'

Farthing looked at Lott, who, in turn, looked blank. 'Who gave you permission to enter the house, a crime scene?'

'D S Clapp asked me to check to see if there was anything suspicious.'

'Suspicious!' Farthing furiously made notes on his folder. Poor old Clapp, Reggie thought, he's clearly in trouble now. 'A safe, you say,' Farthing stared at Reggie. 'Why didn't you let the police know. Was it locked?'

Reggie chose not to answer the first part of the question. 'It had a combination lock, but I opened it easily enough, and this is what I found.' He showed Farthing his aunt's account at Specawin detailing her gambling wins and losses, and her account with Tophire Taxis revealing her monthly *two day away* travel from Bournemouth. Almost speechless, Farthing looked them over before passing them to D C Lott.

'Did you know anything about ...? 'he waved his hands over the papers.

'Nothing at all. I think it's worth checking with her housekeeper, Miss Smerdal. Don't you?' Reggie was enjoying himself.

'We conduct enquiries in our own way, thank you very much,' Farthing snapped,

Finally, Reggie produced the CAMELOT letter, photo, and the Bargara Investments passbook. 'Maybe you'll conduct your enquiries into this.'

Farthing looked stunned. 'Three million, four hundred and ... my God, is this real?' Open-mouthed, he read and reread the letter and passbook. 'I assume you haven't checked with Bargara Investments.'

'No, I haven't.'

Picking up the papers, Farthing stood, looking well out of his comfort zone. 'You'll need to come to the station to make a statement and have you fingerprints taken. Mrs Makepeace as well.'

'We certainly won't,' Reggie replied calmly.

'We'll see about that. Mr Grosvenor Smythe, you've provided us with information which should have been obtained directly by the police service. I order you not to leave Ringwood without the express permission of the Hampshire Constabulary. Here's my card and I'm available twenty-four hours a day.'

'That's utter nonsense. Why would I agree to that?'

'Because sir,' Farthing said, 'of something of which you are unaware. For your information, Mr Redknapp Ormrod, the son of Edgar Ormrod, the sole executor of Miss Smythe's will, was killed last night. He was run over by a steamroller.'

CHAPTER THIRTY

It was nearing noon by the time Reggie reached Sylvia's house. As soon as she opened the door, he took her in his arms and almost hugged the breath out of her. Their lips met.

'Wow, that was rather special.' Holding him at arm's length, she studied his face. 'Has something happened? You look sort of ..., I don't know, troubled.'

'Have you heard the news that Redknapp is dead?'

'Yes, I heard about an hour ago.' Sitting next to him, she nursed a steaming cup of coffee. 'Grace next door told me he'd been killed by a steamroller, and not just any steamroller, but the one operated by his lady friend, Tiffany Golightly. She's been taken to Lyndhurst for questioning.'

'How in the blue-blazes did Grace Pluck find out?'

Sylvia laughed. 'She seems to know everything that happens round here.'

'And Redknapp, poor chap, was due to inherit ten percent of Cressy's estate, about sixty thousand pounds.'

'Yes, that's right. What will happen to it? Will it go to Edgar?'

'I don't know. My knowledge of wills and inheritance is rather limited. The legal boys will have to work that one out. Poor lad though, Edgar will be devastated.'

Going through to the kitchen, he gave a theatrical dry cough.

'Not a very subtle hint.' Smiling, she, poured him a whisky. 'Now Reggie, I'm sure you won't take offence, but I can't help but noticed that your significant consumption of whisky has become a habit with you.'

'Whisky … habit forming? Of course not. I ought to know, I've been drinking it for years.'

She laughed.

'I consider an abstainer a feeble person who yields to the temptation of denying himself a pleasure.'

'Hmm. If you say so.'

Sitting comfortably in a chair, Reggie took his first sip and savoured the rich, maritime nose and the blast of flavours. 'Ah, that's better.'

'Now then,' Sylvia folded her arms. 'Why the look of foreboding when you came in?'

Reggie sighed. 'The reason I'm a little uneasy is I'm trying to get my fuzzy old head around everything that's happened since Aunt Cressy died – make that murdered, and there's more happening by the day.'

'Did you have your meeting with the police this morning?'

'Yes, there is this obdurate police inspector who has taken over the case from old Clapp, his name's Farthing. I told him what we'd found in Aunt Cressy's safe yesterday.'

'Was he pleased?'

'Pleased! No, he was furious. The vulgarian said Clapp should have come with us. He then went on to say that we must go to the police station to make statements and have our fingerprints taken. The bloody cheek. I told him in no uncertain terms to sod-off.'

'Oh Reggie, that doesn't help, you know.'

'Yes, I know, but that's not all. He also said I should not leave town without his permission, knowing full well that I've arranged with Mr Lee to go back to Kingston at noon tomorrow.'

'So, what will you do?'

'Oh, I'm leaving alright. He has absolutely no justification for saying that, only excessive stupidity. Anyway, he knows where I live in Kingston which leads me onto the most important point.'

'And that is?'

'Will you come and stay for a few days ... weeks. I'd love you to see the place.'

'To see the place!' Sylvia faked a frown. 'Like an estate agent, is that it?'

He stood and took her in his arms. 'No, that's not it, you imp,' he kissed her. 'I want you to live with me, you know, give it whirl.'

'A whirl eh! Well, I've never heard it called that before. Do you mean to live in sin?'

'Come, come, young lady,' he admonished her with an expressive glint in his eye. 'I'm an English gentleman, but actually, the sin bit sounds rather good for me. Will you come?'

'If you're still a free man by tomorrow, and as long as you take your monocle out at night, I'll come. I'll let Sainsbury's know I won't be in tomorrow – I'm due some holidays.'

'Excellent. Mr Lee and I will pick you up at twelve noon.'

'I'll be ready. Now, I've prepared lunch for three of us, hotpot and dumplings. Ches is due in about half an hour.'

'I'm pleased Ches is coming. I'd like to get to know him better.' Holding out his empty glass, he added, 'And it gives us time for another refill.'

Halfway through his next drink, Reggie's mobile phone rang. It was Miles. After his customary juvenile banter, he came to the point of his call. 'I have a lead on your missing lady, Gertrude Dogberry.'

'You've found her?'

'No, I haven't actually found her - it's just a lead. A little on the flimsy side but, personally, I think it's worth following up.'

'Go on then.'

'One of my *off the record* contacts checked a police file covering Devon, and found that a lady called Cressida Smythe, and let's face it, it's a unique name, was charged with an affray two months ago, in Seaton.'

'By Jove, Aunt Cressy in a bust-up.'

'Yes, after receiving a warning from the authorities, she was released to a certain Miss Portia Barton. Her address is in Seaton which makes two leads in the same town. First the Pinch-Dogberry report I told you about, and now this.'

'You're a star, Miles. I'll definitely go to Seaton, hopefully next week. I'll be back in Kingston tomorrow afternoon, so why don't you come round for dinner, at say seven, there's someone I'd like you to meet.'

'Very kind, thank you squire. And may I assume the *someone* could be of the feminine gender.'

'You'll have to wait and see.' Just as he finished the call, the front door opened, and Chester strolled in. 'Hello, you two, I'm just going up to my room, I'll be down in five.'

As Sylvia started to get the plates and dishes out, Reggie gave her a summary of Miles's call and the lead to the mystery woman who would inherit around three and a half million pounds. 'Shouldn't you tell the police first? You're not in their good books, are you?'

'No, what would I tell them? That I have a flimsy lead and even with all their resources, they have nothing. No, so how would you like a few days' holiday on the Devon coast. It will be beautiful at this time of year.'

'What's that I hear?' Chester asked as he entered the kitchen. 'A holiday in Devon?'

'Talk your mother into it, Ches, she needs a break.'

'I need no persuading, thank you very much.' Sylvia said. 'I look forward to it. Now, lunch is ready.'

'Thanks, Mum. By the way, have you heard Redknapp Ormrod was killed last night?'

'Yes, but, my God, word gets around quickly. How did you hear?'

'Because I was there when it happened. I was going past the road works off Christchurch Road and saw Redknapp with Tiffany. The next thing I knew was the steamroller rolling forward; it must have been left on an incline. There were screams and a horrible er …crunch … and, well, that was it. I phoned 999 for an ambulance, but it was too late. There was another man in the background, but he immediately disappeared. I've just come from Lyndhurst Police station. A bloody narky inspector there, Farthing, made me give a statement, took my prints and said I should not leave town without his permission.'

Reggie laughed as he affectionately patted him on the shoulder. 'Join the club, son. You can come with us if you like – we could form an escape committee.'

That was splendid, my dear.' Feeling comfortably replete, Reggie leaned back in his chair, gazing fondly at Sylvia and Chester. 'In Kingston, you'll give Aida some stiff competition.'

'What?' Chester queried. 'You have another woman in Kingston called Aida, as in the opera?'

'Same pronunciation, Ches, but nothing of Verdi's Egyptian Grand Pasha, I'm afraid. Aida is a Filipina who takes particularly good care of me.' Thinking that he could have phrased that a little better, he immediately added, 'But definitely not in the biblical sense, if you see what I mean.'

Chester grinned. 'I'm sure Mum is pleased to hear that. Nice name though,'

'Speaking of names,' Sylvia chipped in. 'You said earlier that the police constable with Farthing, is D C Lott. I think it's probably Clive Lott. He used to live close by on Southampton Road. Unfortunately, he and his family had their legs pulled all the time. Poor Clive was known as Clott - you see initial C followed by Lott. His two sisters were Flott and Slott, and his parents Blott and Glott.'

They both laughed. 'Me thinks a worthy case for an appropriate name change,' Chester said. 'Anyway, Reggie, I'm glad you're here now as I'd like to know more about you and the Grosvenor Smythe side of the family – see what I've inherited.'

'I'll be happy to, Ches, but sadly, there's not a lot to say. You see my mother was an only child, my father had one sister,

Cressida, who was childless of course, and I, also, am an only child. My parents died together in a car crash, and I was placed in the care of Aunt Cressy. There I was, an eight-year-old orphan with no opt-out clause and no court of appeal. From spots to shaving, that was the hand I'd been dealt, and I just had to make the best of it. My plan, at the time, was to bypass puberty and go straight to adulthood, but it doesn't work like that.'

'No, it doesn't.'

'She sent me to the Rymers Academy, which, unlike Butlins and redcoats, was more like Colditz with snoek and communal toilets.'

'At least you went to a prestigious academy. Is that where you acquired your posh accent?'

'The very place and I'm stuck with it now, although it has served me well from time to time. At Rymers, they tried to make a man of me, doing manly things like tossing the caber and rugger. Academics came second to that of preparing young men for the colonies and to rule the empire. Shake hands nicely, elbows off the table, that sort of thing.'

Sylvia put her arms around Reggie's shoulders before turning to Chester. 'I was about sixteen when I first met Reggie. God, he was so aristocratic and charming, so public school.'

Reggie laughed. 'The first time I saw you, I stopped breathing.'

'Did you really? 'I didn't know that.'

'Yes. But I started again, obviously. But for that moment, there was nobody else in existence.'

'Wow,' Chester smiled at them both. 'So, was it love at first sight?'

They nodded together.

'I became one of those smarmy young shavers who called Sylvia's father 'Sir' and helped her mum with the washing up. Manners maketh a wimp. After university, I got an overseas posting and we swore eternal love for each other, but ... well, you know the rest, the world of international post offices conspired to keep us apart.'

'Yes, Mum told me all about it. Like a TV soap opera.'

'Just a minute, Ches, there is something I can show you.' Reggie went to get the photo album he'd rescued from Cressida's safe. 'I only saw these yesterday for the first time myself.' Turning the pages, he pointed out himself as a young boy, his parents, the house where they had lived and the car they died in. 'I have a few more photos at my flat in Kingston which I'll dig out next time I'm down here. But your Mum must have some others taken when we first met.'

'Yes, I have,' Sylvia confirmed. 'I didn't show them to you before, Ches, for the obvious reason you didn't know who your father was – now you do.'

'I'd like to see them myself,' Reggie said, 'as long as they're not too saucy.'

Chester laughed. 'Not intimate Polaroid's I hope.'

'Oh, good heavens, of course not,' Reggie glanced at Sylvia. 'Or do we?'

'Not now we don't. I sold them all to Playboy magazine,' she laughed. 'We both made the centrefold in August 1978.'

'Ah, so that must be why it went out of production,' Chester teased.

With mock severity in their voices, Reggie and Sylvia turned in unison to confront their son. 'You cheeky boy, go to your room at once,'

Chapter Thirty-One

The enigmatic Mr Lee got behind the wheel of Reggie's Rolls for their afternoon drive from Ringwood to Kingston. Reggie and Sylvia were comfortably ensconced in the back whilst Mrs Kim sat next to Mr Lee in the front. During the two-hour journey, the two Koreans talked nonstop, their unique language loaded with peculiar 'ahhs' 'ees' and other strangulated noises.

Glancing at Reggie, Sylvia whispered. 'What a weird sound, more like a creature being stuffed through a mincing machine than verbal communication.'

Reggie chuckled. '*Verbal communication* indeed, you're beginning to sound like me.'

'Oh my God, surely not - I need help,' she laughed, kissing him on the cheek. 'Do you realise, my dearest, it's only ten days since you suddenly sprang back into my life.'

'Sprang! It's reassuring to know I can still sprang, or even spring, at my time of life.'

'Well, you did. But forgetting your springing for a moment, we're leaving a lot of uncertainties behind us in Ringwood.'

'Yes, especially with Redknapp being killed last night and Chester on the scene when it happened.'

'I know. And what was Farthing on about saying you shouldn't leave town?'

'I think it's because D S Clapp's investigation was a load of clap-trap and Farthing wanted to demonstrate that he was in charge now. But before we return to Ringwood, I want to follow up on Miles's lead on Aunt Cressy being in a town called Seaton, and hopefully with the mysterious Gertrude Dogberry.'

After almost two hours of steady driving, they arrived at Reggie's flat. He helped Sylvia from the car and pointed to the top of the ten-storey block. 'That is my place, the top floor.'

'What, all of it?'

'Yes, it's the penthouse, although Aida and her daughter have a flat next to mine.'

'Oh, I see,' Sylvia's guardedly responded. This close cohabitation with his housekeeper was news to her. She was even more curious to see what she looked like.

Mr Lee ran round to open the boot. '*Weggie*, I help with *bags-es*. With you, I take Mrs Kim in *wift*. After, I take *Wolls Woyce* to *gawage*.'

'Thank you very much, my good friend.'

Getting out of the lift on the top floor, Reggie opened the apartment door.

'Welcome home, sir and madam,' Aida greeted them, giving a broad smile to Sylvia.

'This is Mrs Sylvia Makepeace who'll be staying a few days.'

Sylvia eyed up the other woman in Reggie's life. She was an attractive Asian lady and a lot younger than her. Should she be worried?

'Is Mrs Makepeace's room ready?'

'Yes sir, I go and take madam. It good room.'

'Please call me Sylvia.'

'Oh, thank you madam.'

'And Aida, Mr Miles Elderbeck will be joining us for dinner. Will it be ready by seven-thirty?'

'Oh yes sir. I do English roast beef, just what Winston Churchill like.'

'I could get used to this life, old boy.' Nursing a Scotch following Aida's excellent dinner, Miles sat in an armchair facing Reggie and Sylvia. 'Your lady housekeeper is a first-rate cook.'

'She certainly is,' Sylvia said. 'Reggie promised I could become a lady of leisure and the idea has become extremely attractive.'

'And my life suddenly feels a lot poorer,' Miles sighed. 'Reggie, you must give me the agency's address – I'd like an Aida of my own.'

'I hope you are jesting,' Reggie smiled.

'Oh, I'd never be unfaithful to my wife for the reason I love my house too much.'

'A very wise decision.'

'But in my state of decay, I deserve some extra care. My back hurts, my ears are stuffed with cotton wool, and then when I set off to go somewhere, one foot poised in mid-air, ... I've no idea where I am going. I grumble about murky lights in restaurants and can only decipher the menu by holding it at arm's length like a ticking time bomb. A sympathetic lady like Aida would understand.'

Sylvia sympathised. 'Well I think you're doing well, but old age isn't too bad when you consider the alternative.'

From his recumbent position, Miles gave her a salute and smiled. 'A point well made.'

'Sympathy over, Miles,' Reggie said. 'Now let us get down to business. What did you find out about Gertrude Dogberry?'

'Ah yes, of course. Gertrude Dogberry does not appear on any UK census, directory, electoral role or register. I spent ages on several websites but came up with nought.'

'But you have something,' Reggie said.

'Yes, I have. I called in a few favours, mainly from old chums specialising in probate and genealogy research, who had to bend the rules a tad,' Miles gave a broad wink, 'Nudge, nudge, if you see what I mean.'

'We do see what you mean, Miles, kindly get to the point.'

'Gertrude had an NHS number, no address but care of a certain Portia Barton. It took a bit of doing, but she lived in Seaton – it's in Devon. Please don't ask me how I got it.'

'I won't. Do you have an address for this Portia Barton?'

'I do, but here is the next problem.'

'Surely not another problem, what is it now?'

'Portia Barton was crushed to death in her car three weeks ago, by a stolen combine harvester.'

CHAPTER THIRTY-TWO

Mr Lee brought the Rolls to a gentle halt at the front of Beaufort Towers Hotel in Sidmouth, Devon. 'Too many *cars-es on woad,*' he complained. 'It *wike* Pusan in *wush* hour.' The journey had taken over three hours, with only a short break for lunch.

'Under the circumstances, Mr Lee, old chap, you've done extremely well.' Reggie placed his empty glass into the car's liquor cabinet located between the two rear seats.

Getting out of the car, Reggie thought that the Beaufort Towers Hotel looked like the sort of place that Hercule Poirot would visit to take a rest between cases, only to find the croquet lawn heaped with dead bodies. A weary-looking porter ambled out from the hotel, but quickly became an eager beaver on seeing the splendid limousine. No doubt hoping for a hefty tip, he filled both arms with their bags and headed inside.

Mrs Kim asked, 'We stay here, in this *pwace* – it *vewy* nice.'

'Indeed we are, Mrs Kim, but alas I'm afraid, only two rooms, one per couple.' Looking directly at Mr Lee, 'I trust that one room will be acceptable for you and Mrs Kim to share.'

The two Koreans jabbered at each other for only a few seconds before Mr Lee beamed. 'Thank you, *Weggie*, Mrs Kim with only one *woom* is okay.'

'Excellent.'

Sylvia nudged Reggie giving him a quizzical look. 'And do I have a say in this, sharing a room?'

'Of course you do, my dear. I volunteer to sleep upright in the wardrobe to protect your virtue.'

'Virtue indeed! she mocked. 'Do you know what a hollow laugh is?'

'I think so.'

'Well, if I knew how to do one, I'd do it now.'

He gave a humble bow, 'I have been warned.' Reggie then turned and marched majestically through the front entrance, as if expecting a band to strike up a fanfare at his arrival. To avoid other people obstructing his way, he'd learnt over the years to use his height and aristocratic bearing to walk purposely towards his goal without making eye contact with anyone. It always worked, but he knew he now had to put on one of his well-practised acts. 'Good afternoon, my good fellow.' His voice, created by nature to address multitudes, other than a nervous young man standing behind the reception desk. 'I am Reginald Grosvenor Smythe, OBE. You have two suites reserved in my name,' he bluffed. 'Kindly show us to our rooms.'

'Of course, sir.' Keying in the details, he scanned through the accommodation list. Thinking he must have made a mistake, he scanned for a second time. Nervously, he looked up. 'There is no booking for you, sir. We are full.'

'Nonsense, my man, get the manager. I spoke to him this morning.'

'Yes, sir.' With a trembling hand, he picked up the phone. Turning his back, he spoke rapidly into the headset. 'He's coming now, sir.'

'I should hope so,' Reggie thundered.

A door at the side of reception opened. A lean looking man appeared, thirtyish, with sandy hair and sharp features reminding Reggie of a fox terrier.

'Are you the manager?' Reggie boomed.

'Yes, sir. Mr Elbow.'

'What ... Elbow?' Reggie scowled. 'Oh well, if you're sure. I spoke to you this morning reserving two suites for three days.'

'Yes, sir, but I did say I could only try, but I'm afraid we're full.' Beginning to squirm under Reggie's fierce demeanour, he added, 'I called you on your mobile, but it was switched off.'

Reggie's next step was to bristle with anger, and brought his cane down hard on the counter. 'Nonsense, Mr Elbow. I spoke with Viscount Sir Finlay Carrington who assured me you would have two of your finest suites available for me and my guests.'

In the background, Sylvia squirmed with embarrassment.

The manager, his face shiny with perspiration, morphed from worry to panic. He had only been promoted to this position two months earlier, and had already had a couple of bad experiences.

'You can call Sir Finlay if you want,' Reggie snapped.

Panic turned into terror. 'Oh, I'll have to er ...' his reedy voice rose so high it almost disappeared. 'I could make some changes, er yes, sir, changes. Can you wait for half an hour or so, please sir?'

'If we must, Mr Elbow, if we must. Anyway,' Reggie softened his tone, 'I have complete faith in you, Mr Elbow, and I will let Sir Finlay know how you have helped. We will be in the bar. Send the keys over when the rooms are ready, there's a good chap.'

Imperiously, Reggie indicated to Sylvia and a stunned looking Mr Lee and Mrs Kim that they should follow him into a rather splendid bar with views over the bay,

'You bullied that poor man,' Sylvia frowned. 'You can be an overbearing bastard at times. How can the poor man find two suites, not just rooms? How did you do it?'

'It's all to do with style, m'dear.'

'What do you mean, style?'

'Style, in this case, is when one is definitely in the wrong – which I was - about to be thrown out of town, or in this case the hotel, and you make it look like you're doing them a great favour – leading the parade so to speak.'

Sylvia sighed and shook her head.

'Although I must admit I was rather naughty, wasn't I? But from my experience, the owners suite is usually kept vacant for such emergencies, and the manager must have his own suite.'

'So, you're turfing him and his family out of his home.'

'Only for three days. And I'm paying top-dollar for the accommodation which will double his takings for the month. It also might help him keep his job – even a bonus.'

'Well, whatever. I still feel sorry for him. By the way, who is this Viscount Sir Finlay something or other you spouted on about?'

'Oh him,' Reggie grinned. 'I've no bloody idea.' Turning to the others, he said, 'Right chaps, we all need a stiffener or two. Barman,' he called, 'Take our order if you will, mine's a double malt and no bloody ice. And send over some plates of sandwiches.'

While the others looked on, still a little confused, they ordered drinks which came surprisingly quickly, accompanied by four side-plates of rather insignificant sandwiches.

The hotel looked out from behind carefully tended palms across manicured gardens down to the sea. The glint off the water was particularly fierce that afternoon, like sunlight on tin.

Sipping a vodka cocktail, Mrs Kim gazed out of the window. 'It *gwatifying* scene.'

'Indeed, it is gratifying, dear lady. Of majesty and beauty and repose, a blended holiness of earth and sky.'

With mutual incomprehension, Mr Lee and Mrs Kim decided it was appropriate to nod sagely at Reggie's prose.

Emptying his glass, Reggie ordered another round. The clock over the bar showed it was nearly seven o'clock. 'Mr Lee and Mrs Kim, as it's getting rather late and all we've had to consume since lunch are those measly sandwiches, I would like you to join Sylvia and me for dinner in the hotel's dining room this evening.'

The invitation was immediately accepted with smiles and the nodding of heads.

'Very good. Now then, our programme for tomorrow. In the morning, I will drive Sylvia to Seaton, which is a small town just along the coast, and we will probably be out for most of the day. Will you be happy staying here in Sidmouth?'

'We happy, *Weggie*. It *wook* a good *pwace*.'

'Excellent.'

The waiter brought their drinks, followed by the bellboy with the two room keys, deferring to Reggie as if he had distant royal blood.

Standing, Reggie gave a wide smile. 'Dear friends, take your time and enjoy your drinks, and we'll meet at eight for dinner. I'll have a word with my friend the manager to see if the chef can rustle up some Korean food for you. I'm confident he will.'

'Oh, this is rather special.' Sylvia looked around their penthouse suite. 'It's just what we need before embarking on the hunt for Gertrude Dogberry. By the way, the dinner was excellent, and our Korean friends enjoyed it … whatever it was.'

'Yes, they did. But tomorrow, I'll order breakfast for us at eight-thirty, after which we'll head off for all the excitement of downtown Seaton.'

Walking through the lavishly furnished living room into the bedroom, Reggie smiled with satisfaction. 'Ah, two double beds and an en-suite.' He peered into the bathroom, the ultimate in modern luxury. Ultra-up-to-the-minute lighting shone from the opulent fittings. Everything looked expensive and new.

'Oh look,' Sylvia said, 'there's a balcony overlooking the bay.' Sylvia opened the sliding doors and leant against the rail. 'It's lovely out here.' The evening was warm, one of long shadows, lights twinkled, and a soft breeze caressed her bare arms. The smell of lavender was strong in the warm night air.

Reggie followed and put his arms around her waist. 'My *labas meile.'*

'If you say so.'

'Ah, and there's the moon, thou fairest angel of the evening.' Standing hand-in-hand, the stars winked one-by-one in the darkening sky.

'I want you to get used to the best things in life, m'dear. 'We're like Elizabeth Bennet and Mr D'Arcy.'

This made her laugh. 'Mr D'Arcy indeed. I hadn't quite seen you in that light before.'

'But why not? We're only just approaching middle age.'

'Yes,' Sylvia laughed, 'but from the wrong direction. Anyway, I'm rather weary and need a bath – then bed. It's been a long day.'

'I'll scrub your back if you like.'

'Yes, I'd like that. But take your monocle out in case it gets steamed up.'

'But of course.' Reggie had expected an instant rebuff to his mischievous suggestion – was romance in the air? 'I'll bring a couple of drinks through.'

Sylvia accidentally used too much of the bubble bath and poked her head through the foam, laughing as she spat out some froth. 'Not quite the image of Elizabeth Bennett. And Mr D'Arcy, where's my G and T?'

'Here you are, my darling. The owner of this suite has a fine taste in malt whiskies, I'm delighted to say. Now, let me see if I can find your back amongst all those suds.'

'REGGIE, THAT IS NOT MY BACK.'

'Oh, dreadfully sorry, is this it?'

'Of course it is, you old groper.' Reggie duly carried out his space-limited scrubbing duties.

'Thank you, my good fellow, I'm ready to get out now if you'd kindly pass a towel.' As she stood, Reggie held out a face cloth.

'You old lecher,' she laughed, 'I need a towel.'

'I do apologise once again, just a slight misunderstanding.'

Sylvia was happier than she had been for what, probably, forty years. She sat at the dressing table to brush her hair and apply night cream.

Reggie took a quick shower and slipped into one of the beds. 'I think it only right and proper, m'dear, that we use just the one bed tonight. We don't want to abuse the manager's hospitality.'

'Well, I'm not sure, but if you say so, sire, I trust you will respect my chastity.'

'That, my dear, goes without saying. Anyway, I would feel selfish sleeping alone in a double bed when there are people in India sleeping on the ground.'

Sylvia slipped off her bathrobe.

Reggie pulled a face. 'What's that you're wearing?'

'It's my new negligee. Contrary to popular belief, English women do not wear hand-knitted, tweed nightgowns.'

'Charming as it is, we do have a problem.'

'A problem?'

'I'm afraid so. The house rules clearly state that we are not allowed to wear anything in bed. Kindly remove your garment.'

'Is that so?'

'It is, and rules are rules. In any case, I always sleep in the buff … which isn't a bad thing except for maybe on those overnight flights.'

'That joke must be as old as you are. Anyway, before I strip, please put out the lights.'

In the darkened room, she spoke softly as she got into bed, 'One small step for woman, one giant leap for womankind.'

To which Reggie quickly added, 'And one giant leap for *coitus reservatus*.'

They snuggled into the soft mattrass and soon, Reggie put his arm around her shoulders.

Memories of those lost years flooded Sylvia's mind. 'If only,' she sighed.

'I know, it was fate that wrote the wrong script for us.'

'Fate and bloody Postman Pat.'

'Someone I know?'

'No, I strangled him years ago.'

They nestled together in the centre of the bed, facing each other. 'I love you, Mrs Makepeace.' They kissed. To Reggie, the softness of her body was both familiar and strange, like the memory of something once lived and lost.

'I love you too, whatever your name is,' She sank into his body instantly,

They kissed again.

Reggie felt a dampness on the pillow. 'Are you crying?'

'Just a little.'

He gently kissed her tears away. 'However, about tonight,' Reggie whispered in her ear. 'I have a disclaimer to make.'

'A disclaimer! And what, good sire, is that?'

'That past performance is no guarantee of future results.'

She laughed. 'Oh well, I'll mark your card out of ten in the morning.'

Chapter Thirty-Three

Reggie took the wheel of the Rolls, joining a slow-moving queue of vehicles as they journeyed from Beaufort Towers to link up with the A3052 just outside Sidmouth.

Glancing at Sylvia, Reggie said. 'We're in no hurry this morning, m'dear. According to Mr Lee's little gizmo here, it's only nine miles before we turn off for all the glamour and bright lights of Seaton.'

His comment must have jerked the satnav into life as a female voice, uncannily like Margaret Thatcher's, provided immediate confirmation. *Keep straight on this road for eight miles.*

'There you are,' Reggie beamed, 'Ruddy marvellous, isn't she?'

'Good old Mr Lee,' Sylvia said. 'In my old car, I can never get the gadget to work properly, unless I'm with Ches, of course. Incidentally, Reggie, I can't help noticing that you're wearing glasses today'

'Shhh, keep it a quiet m'dear, it'll ruin my image.'

'Does MI5 know about this?'

'Oh, ha, ha. I have to wear them when driving, or at least supposed to,' he grumbled. 'The ruddy licensing authorities and insurers insist.'

Peering ahead as they crawled up Salcombe Hill, they could just see some large farming machinery which was the most likely cause of their slow progress. Forced to a snail's pace, they continued as light clouds blew in from the Channel with a threat of darker skies to follow.

A slow smile lit up Sylvia's face. 'I enjoyed last night, Reggie. You know ...'

'And by George, I do know, my *petite chérubin*. Just like old times,' he giggled mischievously, 'That's if my memory serves me right, of course.'

She poked him in the ribs, 'Cheeky. For your information, sire, my memory remains crystal clear after engaging in sexual activities. It's one of the nice things about being a woman.'

'Now who's being cheeky.' He tried to return the poke, but the seat strap held him back.

'But if I may turn to a different subject,' Sylvia said. 'When we get to Seaton, have you decided how you are going to, well, enquire about Gertrude Dogberry? See if anyone knows her.'

'Yes, of course. And at the same time, I also want to see who knew the Portia Barton woman. Miles gave us an address for Mistress Barton, so we'll start there.'

'That's not really what I meant, How will you go about it - you know, asking?'

'That's easy. I'll address whoever's there using my natural diplomatic tact. My brilliance will appear effortless and natural.'

'Oh God.'

'And pray, madam, what does "Oh God" mean?'

'Reggie, your style of diplomacy may well have worked in the colonies, but I think it may not be appropriate in rural Devon.'

'Oh really. And what do you suggest? '

'That I do the talking and you stand quietly at my side looking dignified.' Before he had time to protest, she changed the subject by asking, 'Is that a new blazer you're wearing?'

Thrown off his train of thought, he answered in a slightly irritated voice, 'Yes, it is. It was made in Italy but as you can see, I am wearing it with a strong English accent. As to your sudden interest in my attire, I have been assured the colour will not run on my tie should a wee drop of Scotch be spilt, and as you are obviously interested, I'm breaking in a new pair of brogues.'

'Breaking in – I thought that was horses.'

'Oh, very droll. But Foxy, my angel, all that is beyond the point, I'm shocked you ...'

In four hundred yards, take the turning on the right.

'Damn the bloody woman. She doesn't know ...'

In two hundred yards, turn right.

'Ruddy hell,' he yelled. 'It's here already. That's nowhere near two hundred bloody yards you stupid female.'

'Temper, temper, Reggie,' Sylvia smiled. 'Remember your natural diplomatic tact.'

Two guttural grunts were his only response.

Turn now.

'What, now you stupid ... where, for God's sake?'

'There.' Sylvia pointed to the clearly signposted road.

Grumbling to himself, Reggie did as he was told.

Stay on this road for the next one mile.

Sylvia laughed. 'This looks right. We're on Poldark Road where Portia Barton lived. We'll be there in a minute or two.'

You have reached your destination, your destination.

'You can't stop here, Reggie, double yellow lines. Look, there's a side road just further down, turn in there.'

Through gritted teeth, Reggie growled, 'Yes dear, whatever you say dear.'

As Reggie pulled into the kerb, they heard a loud voice yell, 'Oye ya grackle, tha canna put tha can the-er.'

'Who in the blue-blazes?' Someone aping a scarecrow waved vigorously at them. 'Sylvia, m'dear, I can't abide hostile natives, whether British or foreign. Leave it to me.'

She held her breath. 'Please be careful Reggie.'

The native, a raddled ancient with a neck like a Galapagos tortoise and a red lump for a chin, was scruffily dressed, with mounds of grey hair sprouting from under a raggedy hat.

'And a good morning to you, my man,' Reggie boomed. 'We are leaving the automobile in this location for a short while. Pray sir, do not interfere with it.'

'Eh, wa did yon spuddler say?' was said in a Worzelesque accent. He ambled in their direction. The front of his sweater was a record of food that had missed its target, and his threadbare, dirty trousers, were so copiously flared that it made it impossible to see his legs moving as he walked.

A bewildered Reggie didn't know whether to laugh or cry. He mumbled to Sylvia, 'I assume this yokel chappie is trying to converse in a form of local dialect. Any ideas?'

'Leave it to me, Reggie.' Sylvia stood in front of him. 'Hello.' she smiled.

'Alrite me bubber.'

'Yes, thank you. My name's Sylvia and my friend here is Reggie.'

The man raised his cap. His grey bushy hair looked like he'd used an egg whisk instead of a comb. Grinning, he revealed a startling selection of random teeth. 'Wal Grommitt me name. Grommitt bi name, Grommitt bi nature.' This was followed by an old galoot's cackle.

Briefly struck dumb, Sylvia smiled and said, 'Well Mr Grommitt, may we leave our car here for a few minutes. We're going to number sixty-two over there.'

'Nay point me luvver, maid Barton stiffer than an ol' post. Old Tommy Green's combine 'arvester 'smashed er.'

'Yes, we heard the sad news, but we'd like to meet members of her family.'

'Ooh arr. Tha need see ol' Maid Dog Berry then, be at forty-four, Poldark.'

Both Sylvia and Reggie's ears pricked up. 'Did you say Dogberry,' Reggie boomed, leaving the 'g' silent. 'Would that be Gertrude Dogberry?'

'Neh, 'ark at he, not Gertrude, nay, it Maid Dog Berry.'

'Thank you, Mr Grommitt,' Sylvia quickly intervened. 'Forty-four I think you said.'

'Aye, me gert lush. Go see Maid Dog Berry.'

Before Reggie could make things worse, Sylvia grabbed him by the arm and marched him in the right direction.

Unexpectedly the sky that had earlier been picture-postcard perfect, rapidly darkened as a gusty wind drove threatening pillows of clouds from the south, and spots of rain began to dampen the ground. They quickened their pace, hurrying along the pavement.

Number forty-four had a white picket fence and gate, a pre-war semi-detached, set back from the road. They could only glance at the small, unkempt garden as they scurried down a sorry-looking path in the ever-increasing rain. Fortunately, the front door had a weather canopy. A gnarled plum tree flavoured the air with the scent of fermentation.

Pausing briefly to get their breath back, Reggie vigorously used the shiny brass knocker. Sylvia cringed. 'Let me do it.'

Sylvia's gentle knock was followed by footsteps. A bolt and chain rattled before the door opened to reveal a stern looking woman, wearing a brown loose-fitting, ankle length dress. She eyed them warily.

'Good morning, madam,' Reggie raised his hat. 'We are looking for Mrs Dogberry and have been directed to this house by a gentleman named Grommitt.'

'Oh Wal, was it?' The lady was probably in her late seventies with a series of fleshy outcrops beginning with her lips, progressing downwards to three chins, then over a formidable chest to end with swollen ankles overlapping her slippers.

'My name is Reginald Grosvenor Smythe, some know me as Reggie Smythe, and this is my friend, Mrs Sylvia Makepeace. Would you be Mrs Dogberry?' Reggie's courtly ways only brought a one-word response.

'No.'

'Oh,' Reggie hesitated, 'Well in that case, madam, would you happen to know where we might find her.'

'I've been expecting you,' she said severely.

'I beg your pardon,' Reggie frowned. 'You know who I am?'

'Come in and shut door.' She turned her back and accompanied by a jet-black cat, painfully made her way down the corridor before turning into a room at the end. The house smelled of stale cabbage.

She pointed to an old-fashioned chesterfield. 'You'd better sit yerself. Now, what do you want?' She folded her arms, watching them closely. The cat jumped on her knee, purring loudly. 'Alright Cobby, it's alright.'

'If you know who I am, you probably knew my aunt,' Reggie said. 'Cressida Smythe, who died on July 5th.'

'Of course I know. I didn't attend her funeral, but I wrote to Edgar explaining that I approved of it.'

'Would that possibly be Edgar Ormrod?'

She made an impatient gesture. 'Who else?'

'And may I have the pleasure of knowing your name?'

'Ha, Cressida told me you were an arrogant bedswerver,' she said. After a moment's hesitation stroking Cobby, added, 'I'm Mrs Pinch, Stella Pinch.'

Reggie could only guess what a bedswerver was, but she was probably right. 'Pinch?' he said. 'Edgar mentioned Jacob Pinch. He was the solicitor who wrote Cressida's will and was an executor, but, oh dear, didn't he die recently.'

'Yes, one week after Cressida's death. Jacob were run over by a runaway Mr Whippy van. Broke his hipflask, glass pierced his heart. He were carrying bag of sausage rolls at the time.'

Instinctively, Reggie wanted to laugh but managed to contain it. At school, a poo in a circular motion was known as a Mr Whippy. He then realised that runaway vehicles had accounted for the deaths of Redknapp Ormrod, a steamroller, Portia Barton, a combine harvester, and now Jacob Pinch. There seems to be a pattern here. He thought of asking about the sausage rolls but decided not to.

Sylvia spoke for the first time. 'I'm so sorry. It must have been a shock for you. Your husband and Cressida dying within a week of each other.'

Stella gave Cobby another vigorous stroking session. 'Jacob's spirit's in his cat.'

Sylvia hesitated before saying, 'Oh that's nice.'

'I'm suspicious of organised religion. I take my own spiritual path, cats understand that.' She stroked the glossy black fur once again, 'Don't you Cobby? When you die you come back as something else, like an eagle.'

Reggie unkindly thought that Stout Stella would more likely come back as an elephant. But the conversation was not progressing well. 'Cressida left a letter asking me to find Gertrude Dogberry, a lady I've never ever heard of.

'That's because she never told you, or anyone - except us in Seaton.'

'Told me what?'

'Because Cressida didn't want anyone to know she'd got pregnant and given birth.'

'What!' Reggie almost exploded. 'That can't be true, Cressida was not ...'

'Not what, boy?' her mouth thinned immediately. 'Not a human being with feelings?'

'I can't believe it, not my Aunt Cressy, she never would.' Shaking his head in genuine bewilderment, 'I always thought she was ...'

'What, a virgin?' Stella glared at him through narrowing eyes. 'Why would she be? Just because she never married doesn't mean she couldn't enjoy, well, you know. In fact, of all people, Reggie Smythe, you should know. Cressida told me everything about you.' She turned to Sylvia. 'Is he still a bedswerver – even at his age?'

Sylvia wasn't sure what to say. 'I'm not familiar with the term, I'm afraid.'

'You can guess though.'

To save Sylvia from more questions, Reggie intervened. 'I'm guessing, Stella, and I can hardly believe I'm saying this, that Gertrude Dogberry is Cressida's child and that is why she came to Seaton every month, to see her daughter. Am I right?'

Stella raised the back of her hand to her cheek to wipe away a stray hair and nodded.

'So, mystery solved,' Reggie beamed. 'Is she here now?'

'No, she's not. Anyway, she doesn't want to be found.'

'But the highly trained sleuths within the Hampshire Constabulary have been looking for her for ages.'

'Why?' Stella snapped, 'What do they want?'

'I think I'd better tell you something you may not know.'

'Huh, I doubt that but, go on.'

Reggie's parched mouth longed for his favourite tipple but now was not the time. He began with Cressida's letter to him saying that someone had tried to steal her identity and purloin money from her account; but the letter had been misdirected and only arrived after her death. 'Did you know that Cressida was murdered?'

Giving a gasp, Stella stiffened, as though something she'd long dreaded, something terribly disturbing, had come true. 'No, that can't be. Don't be daft.'

'I'm afraid it is true. Your friend Edgar Ormrod will confirm it, she was poisoned.' Reggie wondered why Edgar hadn't told her. 'Tell me, did Edgar know about Cressida's child, and that she was called Gertrude Dogberry?'

'Of course he knew. I didn't ...' was as far as she got before wild thoughts raced through her head and brought her to a standstill. After a moment's silence she sobbed, 'Oh God, I knew it, I've always known it, sooner or later, out pops the cloven hoof.'

'A cloven hoof,' Reggie cried, 'What on earth does that mean?' He thought of asking if devil worship was involved but no, not for the time being at least. 'Are you saying you were expecting something like this, and you're not surprised Cressida was murdered?'

Stella shook her head, her lips clamped together as if glued.

Desperate for clarification, Reggie went on another tack. 'Did you know that in her will, Cressida left sixty percent of her estate to Gertrude?'

'Of course I know,' Stella was back in the present. 'Jacob wrote her will, didn't he? But Gertrude's not interested in sixty percent of nothing.'

'Oh dear,' Reggie sighed, 'Cressida clearly didn't confide in you.'

'What do you mean? Of course she did, Cressida told me everything.'

'Did you know that her estate is in the region of six million pounds and Gertrude is due to get over three and a half million. Call Edgar, he'll confirm it.'

It was now Stella's turn to be flummoxed. 'Surely not, no it can't be. Cressida never had much to speak of, she gambled it away, even here in Seaton.' She stood unsteadily, mumbling incoherently to herself. Unable to settle, she wandered round the room, randomly picking up objects, staring at them as if answers to this confusion were right in front of her eyes, before sighing and putting them down again. 'Please Reggie, be honest with me. Is what you've just told me the truth?' Although she addressed the question to Reggie, she studied Sylvia's face for confirmation.

'It's all true,' Reggie assured her.

Taking a deep, rasping breath, Stella sat down again. 'You see,' she croaked, 'When she got pregnant, Cressida was ashamed and did everything she could to keep it a secret, even up to the end. As soon as she started to show, she first came to live here with Jacob and me – Jacob was unable to sire me a child, and we, well, we did a terrible thing.'

'What was that?'

'We pretended that I was pregnant. We didn't need a doctor or anyone else. Cressida and I went to Norfolk to stay with a mutual friend for the last three months, she be a district nurse you see and a particularly good friend. She delivered the child. Within an hour of her being born, Jacob and me bring her here and we brought her up as our own. Nobody the wiser.'

Sylvia's first impulse was to cluck sympathetically, but checked it.

Reggie, his voice hardly above a whisper asked, 'Do you know who the father is?'

From Stella's stony expression, he knew he wasn't likely to have an answer, and would have to bide his time.

'How was her birth registered,' Sylvia asked gently. 'In what name?'

'Here in Seaton, my daughter, Mary Stephanie Pinch.'

'Mary Pinch?' Reggie questioned. 'Why is she now called Gertrude Dogberry?'

'She changed it by deed poll as soon as she knew the truth, that Cressida was her birth mother. It's not compulsory to register name change by deed poll; it's considered a private matter, not a public or even a government matter.'

'But why?' Reggie asked. 'Why change her name? Why not stay as Mary Pinch?'

Visibly trembling, Stella went over to the sideboard, took out a bottle of Grants Whisky with a shaky hand. 'Gertrude can be, how should I put it? Difficult at times. No, she can be more than difficult, she can be downright nasty.'

'Can you help us find her?' Reggie asked.

'Enough of all the secrecy,' Stella confirmed, 'I know where she is now. I'll write her address down for you. She poured herself a large measure and drank half of it down in one go, grimacing and coughing as she did so. 'You should tell her …' she almost wretched … 'about her inheritance.' Suddenly remembering the others, she swayed unsteadily on her feet before turning to Sylvia. 'Oh, I'm sorry, dear, would you like a drink?'

'Oh, thank you, Stella, just a small one please.'

Stella then turned to Reggie. 'Do you drink … spirits that is?'

'On an occasion like this, yes. Make it a large one please.'

While pouring their drinks, Stella suddenly gave a sharp cry, there was a rattling noise in her throat, the whisky bottle fell from her hand and smashed on the floor. Clutching her chest, she collapsed with a massive thud. Cobby, jumping down off the chair, put its head back giving a piercing, unearthly howl and laid by her mistress's prone body.

Chapter Thirty-Four

After calling the emergency services, Reggie and Sylvia stayed in the house until the paramedics confirmed Stella Pinch's death, and WPC Lusby had taken their details. They agreed to go to Exeter Police Station the following morning to provide statements.

During the short drive to Seaton front, they each took several nips of whisky from Reggie's hipflask. 'I always keep a supply of stimulant handy in case of snakebite, bubonic plague, or any other serious jolts to the system.'

'I thought you might,' the liquor burning the back of her throat.

Parked nose to tail, vehicles lined the promenade. 'Damn, how can any man pursue his goal in life if he can never find a ruddy parking space.'

'Steady on, Reggie,' Sylvia calmed him down. 'Aha, look, you're in luck.' A builder's lorry pulled out in front of them leaving a large space outside *The Crown Arms*.

Parking with surprising ease, Reggie helped Sylvia out of the car. There was a tangy scent of salt in the air, and next to the hotel's canopied entrance, a dog, slumped in a kennel sheltering from the rain.

It was only then that delayed reaction to Stella Pinch's death suddenly hit Sylvia, giving way to floods of tears. 'Oh Reggie, I've never seen anyone drop dead before.'

'No, neither have I, m'dear,' he sympathised. 'I've seen my fair share of dead bodies in Africa, but nothing like poor Stella; one moment she was about to pour our drinks, the next ...well, goodnight Vienna.'

Wiping away the last of her tears, he tenderly kissed her. 'I love you, my *Angelina*.'

Snuggling comfortably in his arms, she kissed him back. 'Yes, I know.'

'Let's go into *The Crown* here for a couple of stiffeners and some victuals.' Needing no persuasion, he gently guided her inside to a table by the window. It was eleven forty-five and the place was quiet. Outside, the sky was full of tumultuous dark, ragged clouds, while a brisk wind sweeping rain across the promenade.

'What a dismal sight, on such a upsetting day,' Sylvia murmured.

'Indeed it is,' Reggie agreed. 'An unseasonable wuthering day. Even the palm trees look as though they want to go home.'

'I need the loo,' Sylvia stood. 'Why don't you order our drinks while I'm away?'

'At your command, m'dear.' Looking out of the window, Reggie saw a tourist coach stop outside. Swearing under his breath, he hastily made his way to the bar, before that herd of the undead with their sticks, wheelchairs and Zimmer frames jammed up the place.

The only one barman in attendance was on the phone arguing about his car insurance. 'Your immediate attention, young man,' Reggie boomed from close range. The poor chap almost had a heart attack. 'Four double Scotch's – malts. Also, bring two bottles of spring water and the menu.' He pushed three twenty-pound notes at him. 'Over at our table if you please – you can keep the change.'

'Yes, of course, immediately, sir.'

Sylvia was smiling when she returned to their table. 'The things one overhears in The Ladies can be quite amusing at times.'

'Really, and what girly gem did you overhear just now? Whatever it was, it's brought a welcome smile to your face.'

'It was two ladies. They were discussing the sexual protocol of their husbands and one of them confided that her man was well brought up, and always asked first and said thank you after.'

'A true gentleman, me thinks. Did you enquire how often the polite but lascivious request was made?'

She laughed. 'Don't be silly, Reggie.'

Their feet hooked together under the table as their order arrived. 'Why four? Ah,' she smiled, 'Of course, silly question.'

Glancing at the menu, Reggie sighed. 'Oh dear, not quite Heston Blumenthal, I'm afraid. And what in God's creation is Today's Special? *Steak bouquet en croute drizzled with jus.* Drizzled with jus! This is an English pub, not a poofy French gastro joint.'

Sylvia laughed. 'At a guess, my love, I'd say it's a meat pie, microwaved from the freezer, with not enough gravy. But it'll do. I need something to settle my churning guts.'

Her guess proved to be correct. By the time they'd picked despondently through the sad excuse for the *Special*, they were more fortunate with some fine stilton and cheddar which followed. Three empty glasses stood in front of Reggie whilst Sylvia kept topping-up her glass with water. 'Waiter,' Reggie called, 'two doubles and decent coffee for both of us.'

'You can't drive after all that booze, Reggie.'

'Yes, I know. I'll call Mr Lee to come by taxi and he can drive us back to Sidmouth.' It was then that Reggie realised his mobile had been switched off since they left Kingston. As soon as he switched it on, it rang. It was D I Farthing.

'Where are you, Smythe?' he asked aggressively.

'Here.'

'What do you mean, here? I've been trying to get you for two days.'

'D I Farthing,' Reggie articulated calmly. 'If you'd do me the grace of addressing me politely using my full name, then I may be prepared to continue with this conversation.'

A moment's silence followed. 'Of course,' came a restrained reply. 'But you and Mrs Makepeace must complete your police statements. Mrs Makepeace's son, Chester, has already done so and been cooperative. Kindly go to Lymington tomorrow, it's important. And one other thing, sir,' Reggie wasn't sure if he was being sarcastic, but let it pass. 'Do you know where your late Aunt's housekeeper is, Miss Dorothy Smerdal? She's been missing for a few days.'

'I've no idea where she might be.' He handed the phone to Sylvia.

'Have you tried her relation in Scotland? That's where she went before.'

'Thank you, Mrs Makepeace, we've tried all her known contacts; there's no trace.'

Reggie took over. 'For your information, Inspector, I'd like to make something absolutely clear. We have no intention of being in Lymington tomorrow. We will only go there when it suits us, maybe in a few days' time.'

'But as I said, Mr Grosvenor Smythe, it's important. Why can't you be there?'

'Because we have to be at Exeter Police Station tomorrow, to give statements.'

'What! To give statements in Exeter! Why Exeter, what's going on?'

'Because Inspector, unlike the Hampshire Constabulary, we have traced ... well, almost traced, the elusive Gertrude Dogberry.'

Farthing hesitated. 'I need to see her urgently. What do you mean, almost traced?'

'A friend was able to locate her through a lady called Portia Barton.'

'Well, is the Portia Barton woman there now? Let me speak to her.'

'You can't, she was killed last week. Crushed to death by a combine harvester.'

'She was what?'

'But we were able to contact her neighbour Mrs Stella Pinch who, interestingly, is the widow of Jacob Pinch, and Jacob Pinch was the solicitor who wrote Cressida Smythe's will. You will obviously recall, Inspector, that Mr Pinch tragically died five days after Cressida, killed by a runaway Mr Whippy van whilst carrying a bag of sausage rolls.'

'Mr Whippy ... sausage rolls. Are you serious?'

Reggie was enjoying himself. 'Of course I'm serious, Inspector.'

'Well, where can I contact Mrs Pinch?'

'You could try the mortuary in Exeter. She dropped dead after drinking a glass of whisky a couple of hours ago, just as she was going to give us Gertrude Dogberry's address.'

'What, she's dead as well?' Farthing was rapidly becoming hysterical.

'It rather looked like it when we left. By the way, when you speak to your counterpart in the Devon Constabulary, ask him, or in these modern times, her, to check the contents of the whisky Mrs Pinch drank before she collapsed, just in case it was poison.' With that, Reggie had had enough, disconnected Farthing and phoned Mr Lee.

CHAPTER THIRTY-FIVE

'Have you enjoyed your brief sojourn here in this glamorous resort of Sidmouth, Mrs Kim?' Smiling benignly, Reggie admired her ankle length scarlet dress with matching headscarf. Her companion, himself dapperly attired in a grey suit, white shirt and tie, grinned with pleasure.

Like Mr Lee, Mrs Kim had given up trying to understand Reggie's flowery language, but knew that whatever was said, was well meant. 'Oh yes, *Weggie*, Sidmouth *wovewy pwace* and the hotel also *vewy wovewy. Ee wook* after me *vewy* well.'

'We're so pleased you enjoyed your stay, aren't we Sylvia? And well done to you Mr Lee, you old charmer. But alas, we must be on our way to our domicile in the Royal Borough of Kingston upon Thames.' Handing over the car keys, he gave Mr Lee the postcode he had written down. 'First stop, however, is Exeter Police Station.'

'*Powice!*' Mr Lee exclaimed, shaking his head. 'They *awest* you again?'

'No, not *awested* Mr Lee, nothing like that. It's just that Sylvia and I witnessed an unfortunate incident yesterday; a lady died, but all we have to do is hand in these statements we've already prepared.'

'Ooo, *wady* died. You make her died?'

213

'No, Mr Lee, we did not. She just, collapsed and shuffled off this mortal coil.'

'Ah so, she shuffle and die,' he nodded, 'We have saying in my *countwy*.'

'I thought you might.'

'When eagles *dwessed* in *bwack* are silent, *wady* die with bite of big moon. You have the same saying in your *countwy*?'

Reggie turned to Sylvia. 'Are you familiar with that one, m'dear?'

Jabbing him in the ribs, she answered, 'No, Mr Lee, we don't, but mores' the pity, it's an excellent saying.'

'Thank you, *Sywvia*.'

Stopping in a no-parking zone outside Exeter Police Station, Reggie told Mr Lee to wait. As he and Sylvia entered, a group of squabbling European tourists suddenly became silent, standing aside as the commanding figure of Reggie, striding in majestically, loudly demanded attention. The desk sergeant was expecting them and duly witnessed their statements. He then asked them to stay to be interviewed with D I Spratt of the Devonshire Constabulary, who would be able to see them in ten minutes or so.

'Definitely not,' Reggie responded. 'We wait for no man nor beast ... or even a sprat for that matter. You have our statements, Sergeant, and my address. You may contact me there, only if absolutely necessary.' And with two of the impressed foreigners bowing respectively, Reggie took Sylvia's arm and strolled out to the waiting car.

'Are you sure about that, Reggie?' Sylvia was concerned. 'We could wait.'

'No, my dear. Knowing the soporific pace at which law enforcers' work, we could be here all day. They know where to find us.'

Entering the apartment, they were greeted by Aida with plates of sandwiches and cakes. She scurried around making tea for Sylvia, whilst Reggie poured himself a gentle anaesthetic from his crystal decanter.

Sylvia went on the balcony to take in the view of the Thames. 'It's nice to be here again.'

Reggie joined her. 'Marvellous, isn't it? Old Father Thames, an avenue of history. In that direction,' he pointed to the left, 'is the town of Kingston followed by Hampton Court then Windsor, and in the other, is Teddington, London and the world. Are you tempted to forego the excitement of Ringwood for this?'

She laughed. 'Tempted? Of course I'm tempted.'

Aida was about to carry their respective bags into the bedrooms. 'Put them all in my room for now, Aida.'

'Oh,' she stopped in mid-step, looking for Sylvia's reaction.

'Thank you, Aida. You can do that. We will go and unpack in a few minutes.'

'Yes madam, I do that for you.'

After finishing their refreshments, they went through to Reggie's bedroom.

'I'm sorry to dash any hopes you may be holding, m'dear, but an afternoon's fornication on my part has become an extinct activity, like clog-dancing, if you see what I mean.'

Sylvia sighed theatrically. 'Am I not a sex object anymore?'

'Sylvia, my Carino, you are, and always will be. But my rusty old boiler takes time to build up pressure, and hopefully will be ready to rumble into action later.'

'I can assure you, sire, that I've had much better propositions than that before.'

'I'm sorry, but you know that I love you.' Kneeling in front of her, his knee locked. 'Ow, ruddy thing.' Painfully, with bones clicking, he managed to stand. 'If the international postal services hadn't conspired to lose our letters, I'd have done this years ago. Let's move in together, make it permanent.' He took her in his arms, and they kissed.

'I was planning to be hard to get, but your charm and, not forgetting your splendid apartment and fat wallet, has won me over. The only other offer I had of living in sin – that was after dear Freddie had died of course, was from a chap called Amos Scrum – as in rugby.'

'And what, pray, was wrong with old Amos Scrum – as in rugby?'

She pulled a face. 'He snored like a warthog in labour. In fact, I've never known anybody who could snore and fart at the same time.'

'So, you cut poor Amos adrift – quite understandable on your part.'

'Yes, I did. I was lonely after Freddie died. I felt I couldn't love again that nobody would be able to fill the void in my heart. But all that changed when my first, and yes, only true love, came back into my life.'

'And here I am,' Reggie grabbed her and playfully pulled her down on the bed. 'Your knight without a personal wind problem. Aren't you the lucky one?'

CHAPTER THIRTY-FIVE

As they lay cuddling on the bed, Reggie's phone rang. 'Damn the thing.'

It was D I Farthing. 'Where are you now, Mr Grosvenor Smythe? You are very difficult to get hold of.'

'At my residence in Kingston. What do you want, Inspector, as I'm busy?'

'There has been another development – another death.'

'Oh my God, who is it this time?'

'Your late aunt's housekeeper, Miss Dorothy Smerdal. She was found dead last night, impaled on the Bournemouth Pier Zip wire.'

Chapter Thirty-Six

Standing at the foot of the bed, Reggie held a tray containing tea, orange juice and a plate of toast and marmalade. He gave a light cough to ease Sylvia awake, 'Good morning, Cara Mia, I stand here, your humble minstrel delivering your morning repast.'

One of Sylvia's eyes slowly opened. She gave a sleepy murmur.

Seeing her slowly coming to, Reggie, using his most lyrical voice, said, *"Shall I compare thee to a summer's day? Thou art more lovely and thy eternal summer shall ne'er fade."*

'What the hell!' she groaned, sitting up and rubbing sleep from her eyes, 'Were you reciting something?'

'Indeed I was, but even the Bard of Avon's finest sonnets do not do thee justice.'

'My dear Reggie, you are so full of bullshit at times. But hey, breakfast in bed is rather good. Is this what I can expect every day from now on? Because I can tolerate, without any discomfort, being waited on hand and foot.'

'Ah well now,' he paused for a moment. 'Let's say that on all special occasions, like today for example, then yes, *petit-déjeuner* will be yours, accompanied by a romantic verse or two.'

'A verse or two, eh? Well in that case, my own laureate, let me think of a poetic response.' She drank the juice and poised, holding a piece of toast aloft. 'Yes, I know.'

"There was a young fellow called Reggie,

Who er ... mmm, certainly wasn't a veggie," No, veggie's not right.' She wrinkled her nose. 'I can improve on that.' She took a bite of toast for inspiration. 'I've got it.'

"There was a young fellow called Reggie,
Who's standing right here looking edgy,
His passion is malt,
But nothing will halt,
Him from having a drink ...when he's ready."

'Absolutely brilliant,' Reggie laughed and applauded. 'My God, you're so talented.'

She took another bite of toast.

He opened the curtains to reveal rain-splattered windows, the branches of the large cedar tree outside waved vigorously in what appeared to be a gale-force wind. 'Me thinks today is ideal to remain indoors, m'dear. And do not forget, Miles will be here for lunch at noon.'

She pulled a face. 'I didn't take to Miles. I found him to be … I don't know, something of a snob, whereas you, my dear, may be posh, but you are no snob.'

'Thank you for that, but I do know what you mean about Miles, he can be a little difficult at times.'

'Oh, and one more thing whilst I remember,' she added, 'Don't forget to call D I Farthing today, and maybe you should phone Edgar Ormrod as well.'

Reggie sat on the edge of the bed as Sylvia finished her breakfast. 'I'll certainly call Farthing, but I'm not sure about Edgar. He certainly knows more than he's let on so far, like knowing Gertrude Dogberry could be contacted through Stella Pinch. I think I'll leave his cross examination to Farthing.'

'Yes, you're probably right.'

'Do I look alright in this?' Sylvia questioned as she was getting ready.

'Of course.'

'There's no "of course" about it. This body-shaping underwear lets bits of me pop out at one end or the other, but I guess it all has to go somewhere.'

'I think you look lovely, including all your bits.'

'Huh.' She took a sweater out of the wardrobe. 'I think I'll put this on. A good polo-neck is supposed to be equivalent to eight hours' sleep – hides all manner of things.'

Reggie smiled. 'We're being very domestic, aren't we, like an old married couple.'

She smiled, 'Yes, I guess we are,'

'Don't forget Aida is making a special lunch for us. Don't wear anything too tight.'

'Tights! And that's another thing,' Sylvia complained irritably. 'I hate the claustrophobia of tights, but can I have bare legs? No way. You can probably see them from space, but how much fake tan to use? And to cap it all, I'm getting a hot flush. Men are so lucky.'

Reggie was saved from more 'womens' woes' by the doorbell. 'That'll be Miles. I'll go and let him in.'

A sodden Miles brusquely thrust his coat and umbrella at Aida, which she took with sullen grace. He smiled at Reggie. 'I see our summer has set in with its usual severity.'

'Yes indeed.' Reggie acknowledged. 'Anyway Miles, how about a drink?'

'One of your specialities would go down very nicely. Thank you, squire.'

Sylvia entered the room and Miles made a show of kissing the back of her hand, adding in his faux-humble voice how extremely attractive she looked.

She cringed inwardly.

Turning back to Reggie, he asked, 'Was your trip to Seaton successful?'

'In a way, yes. But thanks to your research, we learnt more about Gertrude Dogberry. Unfortunately, we didn't actually see her. However, I have spoken with Inspector Farthing and filled him in on all we learnt, including the sudden demise of Cressida's close contact in Seaton.'

'Demise?' Miles exclaimed. 'Another death! What next for goodness sake? If God is in his heaven and all is well with the world, then he has a peculiar blind-spot when it comes to your aunt's murder and its consequences. How many is that?'

'Two more since we last met.' Reggie told him of the latest fatalities being Stella Pinch after downing a glass full of whisky, and Cressida's housekeeper Dorothy Smerdal, impaled on Bournemouth pier's zip wire.

Open mouthed, Miles shook his head.

'The police are making enquiries,' Sylvia added, 'They're still unsure if they were accidental or not.'

'The police, God bless them, are always making enquiries,' Miles railed. 'At some defining moment in time, a sea-change seemed to happen when the police force became a police service. A downhill moment I fear. Have they made any arrests?'

'No, not yet.' Reggie refilled their glasses.' But as we speak, Farthing, after what I've told him, is hot-footing it to see Edgar Ormrod.'

'Ha, that's an interesting saying I've not heard for ages,' Miles said. 'Hot-footing. I wonder where that comes from.'

'I'm not sure,' Sylvia ran a hand through her hair. 'But like all sayings, it interests me. English language, being my subject at Uni, can still excite from time to time. Language changes, doesn't it? Even I get lost with modern-day parlance. And how do we decide what is correct? In my opinion, grammatical rules should merely reflect what people use, because that's where they come from in the first place. No *Acadiéne François* to authorise words we use in this country.'

Miles was impressed. 'And quite right too, dear lady. Language is a runaway train and trying to stop it is a waste of time, like trying to mend your children's ripped jeans,' he smiled. 'Yes, I tried it,'

Sylvia tilted her head. 'Oh dear.'

'Yes, oh dear, indeed, my daughter was furious. So, you two harbingers of death and destruction, what's your next move?'

'Sylvia and I will spend a few days here, much to Farthing's annoyance,' he laughed. 'Then we'll head back to Ringwood to make our statements.'

Aida was just about to serve lunch when Reggie's mobile rang. A female voice spoke in almost a whisper. 'Is that Reginald Smythe?'

'Reginald Grosvenor Smythe, yes. Who is that?'

'My name's Gertrude Dogberry. I believe you're looking for me.'

CHAPTER THIRTY-SEVEN

'Great Jupiter, woman,' Reggie cried, 'the brave boys in blue of the Hampshire Constabulary have been trying to find you for weeks. Where on earth are you?'

'But why - why do you want to find me?'

'Because, young lady, the late Cressida Smythe instructed me to find you.'

'Well, I'm not ready to be found. Anyway, Cressida was broke – she lost all her money gambling. I'm sending you a package – open it and use it.' Abruptly, the line went dead.

'Damn the woman.' He turned to the others. 'You probably gathered that that was the elusive Gertrude Dogberry. But she said she doesn't want to be found.'

'Did she seem a bit strange?' Sylvia asked.

He thought for a moment. 'No, I don't think so, more troubled than strange, I would say. I don't really know why she phoned, except she probably wanted confirmation that I am who I say I am. Oh, and she's sending me a package.'

'A package?' questioned Miles. 'Containing what?'

'I've absolutely no idea. She said, "*You must use it*" when it arrives.'

'Use it, use what?' Sylvia pulled a face. 'That does sound weird.'

Giving her usual gentle cough, Aida hesitated at the kitchen door. 'Excuse madam, I shall serve meal now?'

'Oh yes, please, Aida. Reggie, you can get the drinks. I'll have white wine.'

'You want salad first, or with meal? Aida asked.

'I can't bear salad,' Miles boorishly butted in. 'It grows while you're eating it. You start at one side of your plate and by the time you've got to the other, there's a fresh crop of lettuce taken root.'

Sylvia fumed; she was not amused. To show she was the host and set the rules, she smiled at Aida, 'Reggie and I will have salad first and Mr Miles will wait until we've finished.'

'Thank you, madam. I do that.'

Unfazed, Miles continued. 'Take cucumber for example. It should be sliced, dressed with pepper and vinegar, and then thrown out as good for nothing.'

'That's ridiculous, I love cucumber.' A defiant Sylvia held a wedge of it on her fork before devouring it.

Tension prickled the hairs on Reggie's neck. Whilst he'd always considered Miles to be entertaining, he was now being tiresome.

After deliberately lingering with her salad, Sylvia told Aida to serve the rest of the meal. 'It's a new recipe she's been practising whilst we were away in Devon.'

'I'm looking forward to this,' Reggie said. 'The discovery of a new dish from her does more for the happiness of mankind than the discovery of a new star.'

Sylvia laughed, relaxing in Reggie's timely humour.

Feeling more confident, Aida said, 'In English language, it called, Fowl Red Fly. It made from Luzon duck, hot fry with Asian spice, batter red rice and something we call tagalty, it like you call dumpling in dead red sauce – but it not.' She brought the meal out on two separate platters.

'A wonderful description, Aida, and I can already savour its glorious oriental origins. In addition, it looks amazing.'

Aida smiled and returned to the kitchen.

Nearing the end of the feast, Reggie's mobile rang. 'Whoever it is can wait, until we've finished the meal. Five minutes later, it rang again.

'You'd better take it, Reggie, we've pretty well finished. It could be Gertrude again.'

It wasn't Gertrude but D I Farthing. 'What is it, inspector? We're in the middle of an extended luncheon.'

'It won't take long, sir. The whisky Mrs Stella Pinch drank was loaded with cyanide.'

'But who would want to kill her - a harmless old lady?'

'The Devonshire police are making enquiries.'

'Well, that's a relief,' Reggie's sarcasm all too clear. He decided not to tell Farthing about his call from Gertrude Dogberry - for the moment at least. 'Inspector, have you questioned Edgar Ormrod about the information I gave you yesterday?'

'He's not at his house or his office or answering his phone. However, I can reveal that the death of Miss Dorothy Smerdal on the Bournemouth pier zip wire was not accidental, and we've launched a murder enquiry. The press have not picked up on this so far.'

'And who are the suspects?'

'Confidentially, we have interviewed all the staff working there, and we're presently checking their alibis. We hope to make an arrest imminently.'

'I'll wait with bated breath,' Reggie sighed. 'And Redknapp Ormrod's death, what is happening there, and please don't say you're making enquiries.'

'I am not at liberty to give you that information, but we're making ... er, we're interviewing some people, and that's all I can tell you.' He ended the call.

'Are you any further forward?' Miles asked. 'It's an excellent murder mystery, by the way. If dear Agatha was alive today, she'd have had a field day with this.'

Reggie shook his head. 'More backward than forward I think, although Edgar Ormrod has now gone missing – whether that's relevant or not, I can't say, and neither can Farthing.'

Just then, Aida came in to clear away the dishes.

'Thank you, Aida,' Reggie beamed. 'We could not have had a better dinner had there been a Synod of chefs beavering away all morning. I, for one, feel some light exercise would not come amiss.' Turning to Sylvia, 'If we dine like this every day, m'dear, we should probably join a gym.'

'In my day,' Miles spoke in his light, bantering tone, 'We didn't go to a gym, we went to the tobacconist and pub instead.'

'Ah, and speaking of pubs,' Reggie added, 'How about a new round of drinks?'

'Not for me, dear,' Sylvia rose from the table to go through to the kitchen. 'I'm going to help Aida. She needs it after all she's done.'

Miles watched her leave. 'Your lady friend is an attractive and formidable woman, young Reginald. I envy you. If I hadn't known that you'd just got back together after forty years, I would have thought you had never been apart. You are so relaxed in each other's company.'

'Well thank you Miles. But surely you're happy with your wife.'

'Huh – if only. If the Elephant Man had a sister ...' he was lost in thought for a moment. 'A comfortable estate of widowhood is the only hope that keeps her spirits up.'

'Oh Miles, but I'm sure you're just joshing. Go home rekindle your desire for each other and give her a present, something exciting.'

'I think we're well passed that stage, I'm afraid, but I did read that there are a number of mechanical devices which increase desire in women. Chief among them is a from those wonderful folk who gave us the holocaust, a Mercedes convertible. And that, old chap, is out of the question.'

Chapter Thirty-Eight

'I need a drink.' Reggie reached for the bottle of whisky.
'You can pour me one of those,' Sylvia said. Taking a
significant sip, she coughed as the liquor caught the back of
her throat, then giggled, and gave Reggie a kiss on the cheek.
'I'm really sorry if I was offhand, but Miles can be a pain in
the butt at times.'

'It's only a friendship of sorts.' He removed his monocle
and wiped his eye with a handkerchief. 'It's like I know Miles
well enough to borrow from, but not well enough to lend to,
if you see what I mean. And he can be a tad on the arrogant
side at times.'

'Nicely put, sire. Let's take our drinks onto the balcony
before the sun is blotted out by those dark clouds on the
horizon.'

'Splendid idea. Happily, the clouds in question are in the
east so they'll miss us. Maybe they'll piss down on France
instead.'

'We can but hope.'

Across the river, the sun's reflections on the boat sheds and
building windows gleamed like brilliant jewels on the river.
Sylvia took his hand and gave it an affectionate squeeze. 'By
the way, your phone call with Farthing during dinner; is there

anything we need to discuss? I am still concerned that Chester was questioned over Redknapp's death. Did he mention him or the steamroller at all?'

'No, he didn't. But he did confirm that Stella's whisky contained cyanide but doesn't know who it was intended for. However, you may sleep easy abed tonight,' he mocked, 'because the police are making enquiries.'

The entry phone buzzed. Reggie checked the monitor screen and saw it was Wallace String, the resident caretaker. 'Hello Wallace.'

He was holding a bulky, brown envelope. 'This has come for you. Shall I bring it up?'

'No, that's alright Wallace, I'll come and collect it.' Reggie Hurried to the lift. 'It could be Gertrude's package. I'll see if she's still there.'

It was five minutes before an out of breath Reggie returned holding the envelope and gasped, 'According to Wallace, a taxi pulled up and gave it to him.'

'You're out of puff, Reggie, you'd better sit down before you have a heart attack.'

'I'll be alright. There was only the driver and no message. I ran after it, hoping it would be held up at the gates, but I was too late. Pour me another drink, will you m'dear?'

'I'll get your drink in a minute, but first, open the package.'

Carefully using a letter opener, he gently tipped the contents on to the table. Looking questioningly at Sylvia, he said, 'Three mobile phones!'

Similarly mystified, Sylvia pointed to the envelope. 'Is there a note?'

Taking out a piece of paper, he straightened his monocle. It read. *"I will call you on phone A at seven-thirty tonight. Do not use it before then. Do not use phones B and C until I tell you. Gertrude Dogberry".*

'What in God's name is all this about?' Picking up the phones, there were large stickers on each one, A, B and C. 'It looks like childish nonsense to me.'

'They are just cheap 'pay-as-you-go' phones,' Sylvia said. 'Maybe she has a reason - a good reason. She must be too frightened using registered phones or landlines.'

'But who is she frightened of?' an exasperated Reggie shook his head.

'Probably being added to the list of deaths, but you'll probably find out when she calls at seven thirty.'

'Time to get changed and have another snifter or two.'

'Don't have any more, Reggie, you should be fully compos mentis when she calls.'

'For your information, my angel, there is medical evidence to show whisky prevents heart attacks, blood clots and keeps me alert. It helps to fight cancer and dementia and keeps blood sugar levels in check.' Reggie's voice and body language made it pretty obvious that he did not like being lectured to on the subject of his favourite pastime.

Tactfully, she didn't reply. Drinking whisky was clearly a subject Reggie would not be challenged on, so she held her tongue - for now at least. 'You know, Reggie, with all these deaths over the past month, I think we should be concerned – I know I am.'

'Concerned!' Reggie cried. 'No, not at all. I don't see us impaled on a zip wire or flattened by steamrollers. No, we're perfectly safe.'

Sylvia was not reassured. 'By the way, Aida has invited me round to see her flat and meet her daughter, so I'll go now. I'll be back in plenty of time before seven-thirty.'

'Excellent.' Reggie smiled as the tension between them moderated.

Sylvia was back just before seven. 'Aida has an amazing two-bedroom flat with the same views as we have, and her daughter, Tala, is delightful. Aida is so grateful to you, but worried you'll let her go.'

'Why would I do that?'

'Firstly, because I'm here, your new woman, and secondly because she overheard us talking about moving to Ringwood.'

'Oh dear, I'll speak to her. I made a commitment to keep her on for er ... what was it? I think it was a year.'

'Yes, that's what she told me, but she's not sure how things work in this country. She said in the Philippines, it's easy to break any agreement.'

'Oh poor lady, I won't break any agreement.' Just then, mobile phone 'A' rang.

Reggie checked his watch. 'At least she's on time.' The events of the day had not left him in the best of moods. First, there was Miles behaving badly, then the ominous phone call from Farthing, followed by the weird call from Gertrude Dogberry, and then the package. He let it ring several times before picking it up. 'Good evening to you, caller,' he spoke forcefully. 'May I assume that you are a certain Gertrude Dogberry, calling in this bizarre manner?'

'Yes, it is.' He recognized the voice from her earlier call.

'Well then, Gertrude Dogberry, or whatever your real name is, this is becoming a bit of a mare's nest. Pray enlighten me as to what in the blue-blazes you are playing at with all these mobile phones. It's like a juvenile plot from Enid Blyton's *Famous Five* … or was it seven, I forget? It's certainly not John Le Carré, is it?'

'I have to be careful.'

'Careful of what, for God's sake?' Reggie's powerful voice did not moderate in the slightest. Sylvia stood at his side, gesturing vainly for him to calm down. But she knew that being *old school*, Reggie excelled at being irritated.

'I have some information,' Gertrude paused for a moment, 'For the police.'

'Information for the police!' Reggie's exasperation was clear. 'Then, by the blood of our sainted martyrs, tell them yourself. I'll give you Inspector Farthing's number.'

'I already have it,' she hesitated. 'Did you hear that click?'

'Click! What ruddy click?'

'There was a click on the line, I think this phone's being tapped. I am begging you, please do as I say. When I hang up, remove the SIM card, break it up and flush it down the toilet, then throw the phone away.'

'Oh, for God's sake, woman, give me strength. I'm not …'

The phone went dead.

'Damn the woman.' In a mixture of annoyance and frustration, he sought solace with Sylvia. 'Did you hear all that damned nonsense?'

'Most of it. She sounded genuinely worried. Anyway, whether the line was hacked or not, please do as she says.'

Sighing loudly, he handed the handset over. 'To please you, but I've no idea about how to get a damn SIM card out.'

'Here, I'll do it.' Using a nail file, she opened the back and removed the SIM, cutting it with her manicure scissors. 'So, what happens now?'

'I don't know. Maybe she'll call on 'B' or 'C'. Or maybe the place will suddenly be surrounded by heavily armed military, creeping down from the roof with those laser beams targeted on our chests. That's what happens on TV police dramas, and that's probably where she gets it all from.'

As they were preparing to settle in their armchairs, Sylvia closed the balcony doors. The heat of the day had faded as the evening had worn on. 'This is a magnificent view, Reggie,' she looked down at the river and smiled. 'I love it. My humble abode in Ringwood can't compete with this.'

'It is nice, isn't it? It helps me to un-ruffle after a day of turmoil.' He was savouring the last of his whisky when phone 'B' rang. 'Damn, that must be her again.'

'You'd better answer it.' Sylvia passed it over.

'What now Miss Dogberry?'

'Please Reggie, bear with me.'

'Why?'

'I'm in danger, that's why. Somebody has tried to kill me on at least two occasions.'

'Really?' His voice questioning. 'Kill you - are you sure?'

'I'm very sure. My friend, Portia Barton, was driving my car when she was crushed by this, so-called, runaway combine harvester. I assume you heard about it.'

'Yes, we did. Go ahead.'

'Well, it wasn't a runaway at all, it was deliberately crashed into the car. I was supposed to be driving it to Exeter to collect a parcel from the central post office. I had told several people

I was going, but at the very last second, I had a bad headache and pulled out. Portia agreed to do it for me.'

'That's hardly proof though, is it? I'm sorry for your friend but ... you said there was a second attempt, what was that?'

'You were with Stella Pinch when she died, weren't you?'

'Yes, we were there.'

'She drank whisky which she almost never did. And we now know the drink was poisoned. That was my bottle of whisky, I was the only one who drank it. That poison was meant for me.'

'Hell's fury,' Reggie cried, beginning to take Gertrude seriously. 'That could have been us. Stella was about to pour our drinks when she ... well, you know.'

'So now you realise why I'm scared.'

'Well ...yes, I do understand. But how did you get this information? I only heard about the poisoned whisky from the police earlier today.'

'I have my sources - I'll explain later. Now Reggie, will you meet me? There's a lot we need to talk about, starting with Cressida's murder.'

'I will. Say where and when. I'll bring Sylvia Makepeace with me.'

'That's fine. I'll call you on the other mobile tomorrow morning at nine-thirty. Do the same again with the SIM card in 'B' and throw the phone away.'

'One thing, Gertrude, and this is important. When we meet, I'll need to see proof of ...' The line went dead.

CHAPTER THIRTY-NINE

The bedside lamp cast a pool of yellow light on the ceiling, reflecting down across the carpeted floor. Stretching luxuriously, Sylvia placed her arms above her head. 'How was your night, Reggie?'

'A tad on the restless side if you must know, m'dear.' Reaching across, he gave her a gentle kiss. 'I was thinking of the poisoned whisky in Seaton. I know it wasn't meant for us; wrong place - wrong time, so to speak, but these things can happen. And how on earth did Gertrude know about Portia Barton's death and the poisoned whisky, she seems to have access to the inner dealings of the police.'

'That is a puzzle, but I think you're right. She must have a contact there, but who?'

'Who indeed. It reinforces my distrust of the boys in blue so we should be selective on what we tell them. Hopefully we'll get an answer when we eventually meet Miss Dogberry.'

'But with all these deaths, I'm not worried for myself as long as you, my noble protector, are by my side.'

'Noble protector, indeed? I like that' He kissed her again. 'And, of course, will the mysterious Gertrude Dogberry call as promised?'

'I think she will, and then we may be able to fathom out what on earth is going on.'

'You're right. Anyway, bad night or not,' Reggie announced, 'I'm hungry.'

As had become the custom, Aida made their breakfasts to order. 'Today Aida, I'll have fried bacon, sausage and eggs, followed by your delicious crispy toast and Coopers thick-cut Old English marmalade.' He gave her a warm smile.

Sylvia gave him a look of mock-distaste. 'Today! My God, Reggie, you have the same thing every day.' She ordered fruit and cereal with almond milk.

He raised his eyebrows in wry humour. 'Are you on a health kick, m'dear?'

'Yes, and so should you. That greasy stuff will clog your arteries.'

'My arteries, young lady, are thoroughly cleansed every day.'

'Oh Reggie.' She couldn't argue with his logic. His energy during the day was formidable and his nightly activities were impressive. She would not describe it as throbbing, passionate lust, but nevertheless, it was very enjoyable, especially after many years of almost total celibacy. Being a kept, loose woman in this ritzy apartment, with Aida doing all the meal preparations and domestic chores, was definitely very appealing.

'And now,' Reggie said as Aida cleared away their dishes, 'We're ready to take on the world. Thank you, Aida, that was excellent.'

'I happy you say it good, sir.'

'Aida, we're expecting a phone call at nine-thirty, and after that I wonder, if it's convenient of course, for me, that is us, to come and see your flat.'

Aida looked pleased. 'I glad for you to come, sir, Tala will be at school. You want that I keep her home for you to inspect?'

'No, no, I'll inspect ... I mean, I'll see her another time.'

'Thank you, sir. I see you at my door after thirty minutes passed the nine o'clock.'

'That was nice,' They went onto the balcony to take in the morning air, listening to the birds and watching the ever-changing activity on the river.

'It's nine-fifteen, Reggie, I wonder if Gertrude will call on time again?'

She did. Right on the dot, mobile "C" rang. 'Good morning,' Reggie said.

'I want to meet you outside; less chance of being overheard.' Her voice abrupt.

'If you say so.' He wanted to add that this cloak and dagger pantomime was getting ridiculous but decided to keep his counsel for the time being.

'Go into Canbury Gardens, walk past the Rowers Inn, and sit on any vacant bench facing the river. I will join you there at ten.'

'At ten?' he cried. 'Can't you make it later?'

'No, at ten, Reggie, it has to be then.'

Shrugging, he gestured questioningly at Sylvia. She nodded.

'Okay Miss Dogberry. We will do as you say, but ...'

The line went dead. 'Ruddy woman. I hate it when she does that.'

Sylvia looked at her watch. 'I'll tell Aida we'll have to see her later, and then we'll have to go,' She went through to the bedroom to get ready.

Chapter Thirty-Nine

Reggie decided to take with him mobile "C" and his own phone - just in case.

On the way out, the lift stopped on the ninth floor, where Mr Lee and flamboyantly dressed, Mrs Kim, stepped in.

'Ah, *Weggie* and *Sywia*, we go *walky* in park. You *arso go walky*?'

'Indeed, we are, Mr Lee. We are meeting a lady at ten o'clock in Canbury Gardens.'

Walking along the Thames towpath, Reggie and Sylvia passed the Rowers Inn and found an empty bench a little further on. As they sat down, he checked his watch - three minutes before ten. Slightly puffed, they waited. 'From her tone and mannerism,' Reggie said, 'I wouldn't be surprised if she turns up wearing jackboots.'

Sylvia laughed.

'And I will finally fulfil my obligation to Aunt Cressy. Not since the Queen of Sheba descended on Jerusalem with a retinue of eunuchs and camels, has a meeting been more anticipated.'

'My God, Reggie, will I ever get used to your ... your hyperbole?'

'In time, my angel, in time.' They waited a further ten minutes. Although many people walked past in each direction, some of whom did a double-take at the Panama-hatted, tropical-suited toff, with a silver topped cane. Nobody stopped or spoke.

'I think we've been stood up,' Sylvia said. 'How long do we wait?'

'Damn the woman. We'll wait until quarter past ten, and then seek refuge in the Rowers. They have an excellent selection of malts.'

Just then, mobile "C" rang. 'Where the hell are you?' Reggie yelled.

'I was held up.'

'What, with a gun?'

'No, in a traffic jam. I'll be with you in a minute.'

'*Hewwo.*' Reggie's heart sank as Mr Lee and Mrs Kim arrived. Mrs Kim sat next to them. 'I have *vewy* important thing to tell you.' Beetling her brow, she looked nervous. 'It *Ee* and me ... we *wovers.*'

'*We wovers*!' Reggie cried, 'What in holy Christendom is *we wovers*?'

Shrinking back, Mrs Kim looked at Mr Lee for support. Seemingly unaware of the confusion, he sat happily swinging his legs to and fro under the bench seat. Smiling he said, 'We have saying in my *countwy.*'

Oh, God help me, Reggie looked at his watch hoping Sylvia would help.

'The saying that *wady with wapture, pweases* the god of *wove.*' Turning hopefully to Reggie and Sylvia. 'You have same saying in your *countwy*?'

'Nothing bloody well like it.' Reggie barked just when mobile C rang. Turning his back on the others, he placed it to his ear. 'What in heaven's name is going on? You're late.'

There was a moment's silence. 'Who are those people?'

'They happen to be friends of ours, stopping for a chinwag on their way into Kingston.' He had a picture in his mind of Gertrude, wearing a Gestapo uniform and carrying a large whip. 'Where are you?'

'I'm over by the bowling green. Get rid of them and then walk slowly over past the tennis courts. Then I can see if you're followed.'

'We will, but this hocus-pocus load of bunkum has got to end.' He turned to face the others and was about to politely tell his Korean friends to bugger off.

Sylvia's expression had cleared. 'It was a misunderstanding, Reggie. Mr Lee and Mrs Kim are lovers?' putting extra emphasis on the "L". 'They are going to live together.'

'That's what we say, *wovers*.' Mr Lee said. 'That is the *vewy* important news we have. Me and Mrs Kim *wiw wive* in same *pwace wike mawwy* couple.'

'Oh my God,' Reggie relaxed. 'Well, our heartiest congratulations,' he smiled, and was about to embrace them, but before he could, they both bowed deeply to him, and stayed there until Sylvia asked them to straighten.

'Come up to our flat at five o'clock and we'll celebrate. But for now, we are going to meet the *wady*.'

'Ha,' Mr Lee laughed, 'no, not *wady* but *wady*.'

Sylvia laughed. 'That's correct Mr Lee.'

'Well that's clear, we'll see you both later. Goodbye for now.'

As they walked away, Reggie took Sylvia's arm. 'Come on now, the lady awaits by the bowling green.'

'Please Reggie, you must take Gertrude seriously. She says she's already had two attempts on her life and, don't forget, we were almost poisoned ourselves.'

'Of course, my little flower of Absalom, I am all too aware of the danger we were in. But remember, we were never the target of the would-be assassin. Once Gertrude stops this cloak and dagger behaviour and gets serious, I promise, on scout's honour, to comport myself in a becoming manner.'

Sylvia sighed. 'Reggie, if it was you who felt someone was trying to kill you, you'd take precautions – and that's what's she's doing.'

He nodded, accepting her female logic. They made their way unhurriedly towards the bowling green, blowing away some stray dandelion clocks which floated around them in the morning air. Hurriedly taking a tissue from her pocket, Sylvia sneezed a couple of times. 'A touch of hay-fever, I'm afraid,' she snuffled. 'I forgot my antihistamine after breakfast.'

'Strange, isn't it?' Reggie mused as they continued their stroll. 'Did God, who gave us these glorious flowers and trees, also provide the allergies that come with them?'

'I'll ask him next time I'm in church,' Sylvia coolly responded. 'Until then, I'll keep taking the pills.'

After passing two tennis courts, full of sweaty individuals, shouting it's "Out" to their doubting, red faced opponents, they came to the bowling green. The manicured lawn was surprisingly empty of bowlers.

'So, here we are,' Reggie announced to no-one in particular. 'And more to the point, where is the damned elusive pimpernel?' They looked around for any woman making a sign that she was the one. Nothing. There were lots of other people in the park; groups of families with noisy children, struggling to eat ice cream that was melting quicker than they could consume. Dogs of varying shapes, tugged on leads to sniff other canine posteriors, and couples of all ages leisurely meandered here and there. The handful of park benches near them were all taken.

'Damn the woman, where the hell is she? If she doesn't show herself within the next minute or two, we're bloody well going to ...' His rant was interrupted by mobile 'C' ringing.

'Yes,' he yelled.

'I can see you.' Her voice firm and under control.

'But we can't see you.'

'You will. Walk in the direction of Albany Park Road. Stop by the red-letter box and I'll call you again.' Before he could respond, the phone went dead.

'She's done it again,' he cried, staring malevolently at the mobile. 'She wants us to walk back towards the apartment, and stop by the post box.'

'Just do as she says, Reggie,' Sylvia tried to sooth him. 'Ignore all her drama and if we do as she says, we'll eventually meet her. That is what you want, isn't it? You want to fulfil the task Cressida set you, and this is your chance.'

He let out a deep sigh before taking Sylvia's arm to continue their stroll to the new meeting point. He felt no necessity to hurry, but peculiarly, he felt a spasm of anxiety in the pit of his stomach – Gertrude Dogberry's charade must be having an effect. When they arrived, he leant against the post box, holding the mobile, weighing it in his palm and willing it to ring again, wondering if he should have said something earlier.

'Don't turn round.' A voice directly behind them made them jump, 'Keep walking along the towpath towards Teddington.'

'Oh no we jolly-well won't,' Reggie dismissed the instruction out of hand. 'We'll stop right here and sort a few things out first.' He turned to face the woman. 'By the Great Gods of Laki, you certainly have Cressida's looks.'

CHAPTER FORTY

'Oh really.' There was no flicker of pleasure on Gertrude Dogberry's plain face, devoid, as it was, of any makeup. But her features registered tension, making her look as alert as a fox sniffing the air. She was big-boned with a stretched-out neck and secretive eyes. Her greying shoulder-length hair was set in the same style as Aunt Cressy, even using the same kind of lacquer to keep it in place – it had always reminded Reggie of Bovril.

'I'm Gertrude Dogberry.'

'Well, yes of course you are.' Reggie agreed. 'There's no mistaking your pedigree.' Looking at her closely, he thought there was an air of a geography teacher about her – or worse still, a Liberal Democrat.

'And there's no mistaking you, Reginald Grosvenor Smythe OBE,' she responded forcefully. 'What with your thundering, upper-class voice and monocle, and your over-the-top dress sense, you are exactly as Cressida described you.'

Reggie wasn't sure what to make of that, so let it pass. 'And this is my lady friend, Sylvia Makepeace, who is totally in my confidence.'

Gertrude faced Sylvia. 'Yes, I know who you are. I've seen you in Ringwood a few times over the years. How's your son, Chester.'

'He's very well – do you know him?'

'Hardly at all. He was with Redknapp Ormrod when he was flattened by a steamroller. Is he still a suspect?'

Sylvia scowled, 'How did you know that? Anyway, I'm sure he's not.'

Gertrude nodded. 'The reason I'm asking is I don't trust them - the police that is. They begin with their preferred conclusion and then cast around for evidence to support it.'

'Well, you may be right,' Sylvia acknowledged. 'By the way, were you there when the accident happened?'

'No. Can I ask you both to walk with me towards Teddington. I don't like being out in the open like this - a target.'

'A target,' Reggie boomed. 'Are there a number of snipers with high-powered rifles poised to open fire at any moment?'

Gertrude didn't answer but impatiently gestured them to follow her along the towpath.

'And what else did my dear Aunt say about me, or daren't I ask?'

'That you were a pompous, snotty-nosed drunk who smoked marijuana, and that you were no slouch in the 'leg-over' department.'

'Oh, that was extremely nice of the old bat. Sorry if that offends you.'

'Don't worry, I used to call her much worse. Can we keep on walking please?'

'There's an excellent hostelry in Teddington over a pedestrian bridge. It's a bit of a trek though.'

'Yes, I know it,' Gertrude answered. 'But I want to know why you've been trying to find me. You were even looking for me in Seaton when dear Stella was poisoned.'

'Yes, we were. I have been trying to find you because Aunt Cressy left me a letter attached to her will, asking me to do so. That was it. No reason why, no message to pass on, only to find you. At the time, I had no idea who Gertrude Dogberry was until it gradually came to light that you were her illegitimate daughter. That was one hell of a shock, I can tell you. Puritanical Cressida Smythe having a child out of wedlock. I couldn't believe it.'

'Well, you've found me. What now? Why are you sticking your nose into my business?'

'Madam. Noses, and, for that matter, any other protuberances have not really entered the picture to any great degree. I can only guess she wanted me to find you to tell you about your inheritance.'

'What inheritance?' she mocked. 'She lived hand-to-mouth, having no money because she was addicted to gambling.'

Reggie gently grabbed her arm and brought her to a stop. 'That is where you are completely wrong, young lady. Your inheritance is in the region of four million pounds.'

'Don't be ... whatever gave you that idea? She was broke.'

'Gertrude Dogberry, I have seen all the evidence with my own eyes. Now, carefully read my lips.' Articulating each word slowly, he said, 'You will inherit a sum close to four million pounds.'

Sylvia thought Gertrude's reaction to such a large inheritance was disbelief.

Arriving at the *Queens Arms Hotel* near Teddington Lock, Gertrude chose a table at the far end of the bar. Immediately, she caught the barman's attention. She was clearly no shrinking violet; her authoritative persona must be in the family genes.

'I'll have cold lager and would you like the same, it'll help cool us down after that long walk.'

'I'd love a lager,' Sylvia replied. 'I enjoyed the walk along the towpath. It's far enough away from noisy traffic and houses and felt quite countrified.'

'Yes, it did.?'

Reggie questioned the cosy rapport that seemed to have developed between the two of them. Gertrude was still a stranger to him, and a very strange stranger at that.

'And you, Reggie,' Gertrude enquired, 'Can I get you a lager? I guess now I'm a millionairess, I can afford to be generous, but it'll take some getting used to.'

'No lager or anything of its *ipsissima verba* for me. I'm happy to state that I'm a beer and lager teetotaller, an abstainer, but fear not, I'm not a whisky teetotaller.' He addressed the waiter directly. 'Young man, I'll have a double of your finest twelve-year-old malt whisky, there's a good fellow. Oh, and make sure it's from the top shelf.'

Slightly puzzled by this last remark, the waiter rushed off to fulfil their order, clutching two twenty-pound notes Gertrude had slipped him.

'Do you feel relaxed now, Gertrude?' Sylvia asked, settling in the chair next to her.

'Not entirely, no. That's why I'm sitting here – back to the wall. Nobody can enter the pub without me seeing them.'

'And will you recognise whoever it is that's trying to kill you?'

She shook her head. 'I don't know. I hope I will.'

'And do you know why you're a target?'

'No. Well actually yes, I do now - now that I know my mother left me a fortune. I had no idea before, and that is probably the motive.'

Carefully examining the drink placed in front of him, Reggie placed it under his nose before taking a sip. 'Mmm, not bad.' Turning to Gertrude he raised his glass. 'I'm glad we've finally met despite all the shenanigans with three mobile phones and your bizarre telegraphic techniques.' He took a drink. 'But yes, I think you could be right about the motive. When I met the police in the personages of the unflagging D S Clapp and pertinacious D I Farthing, they both thought that the likely murderer of Cressida would probably be homicidal desperados, on behalf of one of the beneficiaries. But, indeed, which one?'

'Since the attempts on my life, I've become suspicious of everything and everybody. A touch of paranoia.'

'I would imagine that you may well be top of their *most wanted* list, being by far the largest legatee at sixty percent. The others to benefit are, or in two cases, were, Redknapp Ormrod, now deceased; Dorothy Smerdal, similarly deceased, Edgar Ormrod, and finally Ringwood Parish Church. Each was to have received ten percent.'

'So, what happens to the money that Redknapp and Mrs Smerdal would have got?'

'According to the fine print in the will, written in tiny script that only an ant could read, it's added to the pot. So, every time one of them pops their clogs, the remainders' share goes up. Like yours for example.'

'I didn't know Miss Smerdal very well, but she had a lot to put up with as housekeeper for my mother.' She frowned. 'But I feel sorry for Redknapp, not one of nature's intellects.'

'And his father didn't do anything to boost his morale,' Reggie added. 'He said he was only slightly more eloquent than a speak-your-weight machine. And speaking of Edgar Ormrod, I think he may be implicated.'

She arched one eyebrow in disbelief. 'Why do you say that?'

'When I first met him, he told me and the police that he'd never heard of you, Gertrude Dogberry that is. But all along, he did know of your existence and your connection with the Pinches. So, why would he lie? And you changed your name from Mary Pinch. Why did you do it?'

'It's a long story so we'd better get more refreshments before I start.' She raised her arm and quickly drew the attention of the same waiter. 'We'll have the same again and three ploughman's,' she looked at Reggie and Sylvia, 'Is that alright?'

'Yes, thank you,' Sylvia replied for both of them. The only response from Reggie was a grunt; being in charge of ordering refreshments, or anything else for that matter, was normally his prerogative.

'I'd like you to know my story, Reggie, as I believe you are my closest relative.' She told them that up to the age of twenty-one, she hadn't doubted her parentage for one second. She was Mary Pinch, and her mum and dad were Stella and Jacob. Her childhood was happy, did well at school and university and had a good position lined up after she'd graduated. Then, completely out of the blue, on her twenty-first birthday, they had sat her down and told her she wasn't their biological daughter – they felt it their duty to tell her.

'A bit of a shock, eh?'

'Shock! More of a bloody thunderbolt. I felt my life had been one big lie. I went bananas. I yelled and screamed, called them terrible names, packed a few things, and left.'

'Oh dear. Did you ask them who your biological parents were?'

'No, it didn't seem to register at the time, only in hindsight.'

'So, what did you do?'

'Well, the next few years are a bit of a blur. I lived with my friend, Portia Barton, off and on, lived in squats, begged or stole food, mixed with the wrong crowd. You name it, I did it.'

'Didn't your parents try to find you?'

'When you're underground, moving from squat to squat, it's hard for anyone to find you. But when they did, through a private detective, I changed my name by deed poll, and went missing again. I kind of liked the name, Gertrude Dogberry – I played the part of Dogberry in a Shakespeare play at school.'

'But you were eventually reunited with your family, the Pinches.'

'Yes, on the tenth anniversary of my walking out on them, I phoned my mum, Stella. She asked me to come back, so I did. It took time but, in the end, we became a family again.'

'Was it then you found out who your biological mother was?'

'Yes, but they didn't know who my father was. Cressida never told them.'

'And how soon was it before you met Cressida?'

'At first, I wasn't sure I wanted to. Why should I? She'd abandoned me at birth so what right did she have? And by the time we did meet, she was a stranger. She said she wanted to make amends. Ha, I never forgave her. Never.'

Sylvia gently took her arm. 'What about in hindsight? Do you wish you'd given her another chance?'

Gritting her teeth, she nodded. 'Yes,'

Chapter Forty-One

Arriving back in their flat, Reggie had just poured drinks when Aida knocked on the door and peeped round. 'Sir, Madam, this arrive.' She held up two large bouquets of flowers. 'The note say one for you, Sylvia. It from Mr Miles Elderbeck, he say sorry.'

'And who are the other flowers for?' Reggie asked.

Aida looked embarrassed. 'The note say for Aida, that me, he say sorry.'

'Mr Elderbeck was rather rude yesterday, Aida. It looks as if he's trying to make amends.'

'Thank you, sir,' Aida smiled. 'I ask what you like for dinner tonight?'

Sylvia stood. 'I'll come through to the kitchen with you, and we'll choose something together. And by the way, Mr Lee and Mrs Kim are coming for drinks at five o'clock, to celebrate that they are going to live together.'

'Live together, like marry together?'

'Of that, Aida, I am not certain, but make sure there's a chilled bottle of champagne ready, and we'll serve some light snacks. What would they like?'

Aida smiled. 'I know what Korean peoples like, I make small, small hot, spicy eats.'

Sylvia raised an eyebrow. 'You'd better make something milder for us.'

'Yes madam, I do that thing.'

'And Aida,' Reggie called out, 'if they haven't left by six thirty, come in and say I'm wanted urgently on the telephone - say it's the police. That should get rid of them.'

Puzzled, Aida wrinkled her brow. 'You getting urgent police phone call at thirty past six tonight? It only three past the hour now, already, I not understand, sir.'

Taking her arm as they went into the kitchen, Sylvia smiled, 'It's alright, Aida, I'll explain.'

Reggie poured a whisky, and an amontillado sherry for Sylvia, and they settled comfortably in the armchairs. 'Now then Sylvia, *mon trèscor*, tell me what you think of Gertrude Dogberry. I would like a woman's point of view. I noticed when you were walking ahead of me just now, you talked a lot together – what about? Oh, and by the way, people of our age shouldn't walk but stroll.'

'Reggie, we did stroll, but quicker than your languorous plodding.'

'Languorous plodding, madam!' putting on an injured expression, 'I've never plodded in my life, languorously or otherwise. Anyway, I want to know what you said to each other.'

'Well firstly, she's convinced someone is trying to kill her. Unfortunately, she doesn't have any concrete evidence to take to the police.'

'You don't think it's all in her vivid imagination then?'

'Difficult to say. I made a point of looking directly into her eyes, the windows of the soul, and the glass was somewhat smudged, so she is holding something back. She said her life went belly-up on the day she learnt she was somebody else's child, and now some unknown person wants her dead.'

'Tell me more.'

'It seems that Cressida, Stella Pinch and another lady she called Fran - she didn't say her last name, were best friends from nurses' college. When Cressida got pregnant, the three of them came up with a plan. Stella, who hadn't been able to conceive, went with Cressida to stay with Fran in a remote hamlet somewhere in Norfolk. Fran was a qualified midwife and single. Before leaving Seaton, Stella told everyone, including the doctors' surgery, that she was pregnant and going away to have the baby. When the baby was born, they pretended it was Stella who had given birth and registered her accordingly. Jacob Pinch was happy to go along with it. They all swore that this would remain a secret, never to be revealed. So, Cressida was able to return to her normal life in Ringwood saying she'd been looking after a sick friend in Norfolk.'

'Well, well, what a clever wheeze, an illegal wheeze at that. So, which of them squealed and broke the oath?'

'Yes, I wonder,' Sylvia reflected. 'Gertrude knew, of course, on her twenty-first birthday but she swears she told no-one else.'

Refilling his glass, Reggie frowned, 'But I can't think how knowing that would make anyone seek revenge. What they did was against the law but pretty harmless, the only injured party is Gertrude herself. The Pinches and Cressida are already dead but, ah, I wonder if this Fran woman is still alive? Did Gertrude say anything about her?'

'No, she didn't.'

Reggie took a drink to sharpen his brain. 'And here's another thought, did Edgar Ormrod know? He was very close to Cressida.'

'Yes, I wonder. But there is still another avenue to consider, isn't there? Who was the father? Gertrude says she doesn't know. But the father may well be aware of what they did, the subterfuge. If he is still alive, could he be involved?'

'Spot on, Miss Marple. But I keep coming round to the inheritance. Her total estate is over six million quid, a huge temptation for anyone and the main reason to kill her.'

Sylvia nodded. 'And the birth father may feel he has a right to the money, and it would be a lot easier to get hold of it all if the beneficiaries were dead.'

'Yes, and I keep coming back to Edgar. With the information I gave Farthing about him, I think the fuzz will have thumb screws on him by now. I certainly would. I would also want to know if he's ever used the services of villains, or enforcers, or whatever they're called. Hiring assassins won't come cheap and Edgar was sobbing into his whisky the other day saying how broke he was. So, my cherub, to try and clarify everything, we'll put our combined grey cells together like Inspector Clouseau.'

'Inspector Clouseau is the wrong *main*. You mean Hercule Poirot.'

'Wrong *main*! - whatever. The suspects are - I think we can leave out the Parish Church for the moment. Number one, Edgar Ormrod. If Gertrude dies, he gets half of the pot. Then there's Fran the midwife – if she is still alive, she knows everything about the baby swap and, maybe, the name of the real father. How am I doing?'

'Pretty good so far but you're forgetting something here.'

Reggie frowned. 'Am I indeed?'

'The only people who can financially benefit from Gertrude's estate are the ones listed in her will, so the birth father or Fran would have to be in cahoots with either Gertrude, Edgar Ormrod or the Parish Church.'

'Spot on once again Miss Marple, and my bet would be Edgar Ormrod. I think we should return to Ringwood tomorrow and see Farthing.

CHAPTER FORTY-TWO

'Thank you, *Weggie* and *Sywvia*,' piped Mr Lee as he brought the Rolls to a halt outside the Massage Parlour on West Street. 'We get out.'

'We are now going to Sylvia's house,' Reggie explained, 'located in the Sodom and Gomorrah area of Poulner in Ringwood.'

They both looked blank. 'You *wive* in a *pwace Sodomorah*?'

Sylvia smiled. 'Reggie was only making a joke.'

'Oooh.' Mr Lee dutifully laughed. 'I think a good joke.'

'So, Sodom and Gomorrah, eh?' Sylvia said as their Korean friends said their farewells.

'Maybe a slight exaggeration, but if your lascivious neighbour, the ever-lovely Grace Pluck has seductively draped herself over the threshold for my benefit, I promise to keep my rampant loins well under control.'

'Rampant loins or otherwise, l want to find out from Grace whether the police have been to see Edgar.'

'All in good time – *tempora mutantur nos et mutanur in illis.*'

'I do wish you'd speak English. By the way, Chester said he will be home this afternoon, so we'll catch up on his news, especially Pandora.'

On arriving at Shady Grove, Chester's car was parked in the drive and the voluptuous Grace Pluck was noticeable by her absence.

'Hello Mum,' Chester greeted Sylvia with a warm embrace and kiss on the cheek. 'And you, Reggie, have you had a nice break.'

'Yes, thank you, Ches,' Sylvia murmured. 'Reggie's flat is exceptional and from what I've seen of Kingston, it all looks very nice. Is Pandora with you?'

'No. She's still having medical treatment and staying in my flat. I'm happier here at the moment. And I want to know about you – still together I see.'

'It's more than that, Ches, it's permanent. Before I met Reggie this time, I felt I couldn't love again, that nobody would be able to fill the void in my heart.' Almost in tears, she added, 'But that's changed.' Reggie lovingly placed his arms around her.

Chester chipped in. 'I'm pleased. My mother and father together at last. It makes me feel, I don't know, whole, if you see what I mean.'

'Yes, of course we do, son.' Reggie experienced a strange feeling; Fatherhood was pumping a curious liquid around his veins.

'And Pandora, what's wrong with her?' Sylvia asked.

Chester pulled a face. 'If I was to say, *gender realignment*, could we leave it at that?'

'Oh my gosh, yes, with pleasure.' Sylvia made her way into the kitchen. 'Do we have anything in for lunch?'

'There's ham, cold chicken, salad and fresh bread. Is that okay?'

'Sounds perfect. I'll put the kettle on. Tea for you, Reggie, or ...'

'I'd rather have the "or" if you don't mind. After driving from Kingston listening to the chatter of Korean lovers for nearly two hours, I need a Scottish tonic for sure.'

'You'd better make it a double,' Chester laughed, 'D I Farthing is coming here at two o'clock.'

'To see us or you?'

'No, he's finished with me for the time being. I think he must be related to Vlad the Impaler the grief he gave me. There was a coroner's inquest on Redknapp Ormrod yesterday. Tiffany Golightly and I gave witness statements, the police gave their pennyworth but, until there's more evidence, an open verdict was given.'

It was almost half past two when Farthing arrived. He was dressed casually and looked a little downcast. 'I'm off duty and I want to talk to you off the record, Mr Grosvenor Smythe. Will you give me your assurance?'

'If that's what you want, Farthing, then yes. Come in and take a chair.' Reggie held up a bottle of malt. 'As you're off duty, would you care for a tincture or two?'

It was a couple of wistful seconds before he nodded. 'That would be nice, thank you sir. To be brutally honest with you, sir, er, madam,' nodding in Sylvia's direction, 'I'm getting stick from the Chief Constable about Miss Smythe's murder and the growing number of deaths which seem to be either directly or indirectly connected, whether accidental or otherwise. In cases like this, I like to get inside the murderer's skin – walk around in it – wear it, if you see what I mean?'

Fighting back a grin, Reggie glanced at Sylvia's blank expression before replying. 'No Inspector, I don't have a clue what you mean. Although, as Edgar Ormrod is at the top of my list of potential truculences, you could probably try getting inside his skin – but it would be a tight fit.'

Farthing frowned, wondering if public school boy, Grosvenor Smythe, was taking the piss of a mere grammar schoolboy. 'Ormrod is being extremely obstinate with his "no comment" replies.'

'I see.' Reggie thought thumb screws would be a good idea but kept quiet. He had teased poor Farthing enough for one afternoon.

Feeling sorry for the Inspector, Sylvia asked, 'Have there been any developments since we last spoke.'

'Yes, there has. A female body was found yesterday. She's been identified as Gertrude Dogberry.'

'Gertrude Dogberry - dead!' Reggie bellowed. 'By the Hallowed Gods of Rippet, when in the blue-blazes did this happen?'

Farthing looked apprehensive, 'Her body was found by cleaners yesterday morning.'

'Cleaners, for God's sake, what cleaners?'

Farthing was not enjoying this encounter. 'It is still off the record. I'm only telling you because of your connection with the deceased, and I'd appreciate you not passing this private information on to anyone.'

'Yes, yes,' Reggie was about to explode. 'It's off the bloody record, now get on with it, man. Precisely when and where was she found?'

'She was found at 08.30 hours, semi-immersed in a barrel of Dorset Best Bitter, in the Razzle Dazzle nightclub at Friday's Cross.'

'Great God, man.' Reggie's voice had become a roar. 'You must be joking.'

'It's no joke, sir. I was hoping you would understand my position here.'

'Understand! If I understand anything in this world, it is the use of my vernacular tongue to relate matters of fact, followed by some suitable epithets like the load of clap-trap you've just told us.'

'There's no need to be abusive, Mr Grosvenor Smythe. I'm only relaying information which is confidential to you and Mrs Makepeace.'

'I'll tell you why you are a complete hoddy-doddy, Detective Inspector Farthing, because Mrs Makepeace and I entertained the one and only Gertrude Dogberry for lunch yesterday in Kingston upon Thames. She was alone and alive at that time, and not polluting a barrel of Dorset Best Bitter.'

'But she ...' was as far as Farthing got. Slowly, he sat in a chair, scratching his chin. 'That cannot be, can it?' He looked stunned. 'Are you ... well of course you are.' He continued to rub his chin. 'I think I need another drink.'

'By all means, Inspector. It'll clear out that fogged-up head of yours. Perhaps you will then be able to relate to us, the name of the person who provided you with the inaccurate information, followed by the idiot who identified the corpse? Have you actually seen the body yourself?'

Taking a large drink made the pupils in his eyes contract. 'No, I haven't.' Coughing a couple of times, he slowly took a smaller drink without asphyxiating himself. 'The body is presently in the morgue at Southampton Hospital. I suggest we go together if you agree to see if there are any ...'

'But you haven't answered the question of who identified the body?'

'It was Mr Edgar Ormrod.'

'Ah, the purveyor of this false information came from the number one suspect on my list of Cressida's potential murderers, Edgar Ormrod. How did he look when he saw the body?'

'Traumatized.'

'Did he now? It was only two weeks ago when the charlatan swore, he had never even heard of anyone called Gertrude Dogberry, and now, all of a sudden, he is able to identify her dead body. Have you taken him in for questioning yet, Inspector?'

'With respect, sir, that's not your business.' Farthing had regained some of his composure. 'I acknowledge that you have helped with our enquiries, providing a lot of information that we had failed to gather ourselves, but the investigation of this case is my responsibility.'

'Point taken and accepted, inspector. Now let us go to the morgue to see the body.'

The strong smell of antiseptic and other pungent hospital aromas met them as they entered the outer room of the mortuary. Farthing introduced them to Dr Sidney Thrasher, the senior pathologist. He explained to Thrasher that there was some doubt about the identity of the corpse, and that they were only here to help with the recognition.

'I was just about to conduct the post-mortem,' Thrasher said testily as he led them into the lab where the smell was even stronger. Looking at Sylvia, who had turned a pale shade of grey, he asked if she would prefer to remain in his office.

'It would be best if she stayed,' Farthing said. 'Only Mrs Makepeace amongst us is a native of Ringwood. Will you be alright, madam?'

'Yes, thank you. I'll be fine.'

'Good,' Thrasher said, 'Are there any unique body marks you are aware of?'

'I think the face will be enough for now,' Farthing said.

They solemnly walked over to the body covered in a white sheet. Thrasher gently pulled the cover back off her face.

Securing his monocle firmly in place, Reggie stepped forward and stared at the exposed face. His mouth gaped open. 'Oh my God,' he faltered, 'it's her.'

'You are certain it's Gertrude Dogberry, then sir?' Farthing stood alongside Reggie looking at the exposed face.

Reggie shrugged and held his palms up in a gesture of utter bewilderment. 'It's her, but ... how can it be?' Momentarily lost for words, he wondered if he was losing his marbles. 'How can it be her? We had luncheon together only yesterday.'

Suddenly, Reggie had a thought. 'It can't have been the morning when she was found. Surely it was eight-thirty in the evening.'

Smiles did not come naturally to D I Farthing, but he was starting to enjoy himself having caught out the pompous buffoon. 'It was definitely yesterday morning at 08.30 hours the cleaners ....'

'It's not her.' Sylvia, swaying back and forth on the balls of her feet to the flat of her heels, kept the rocking movement going for a few seconds.

'What?' Reggie exclaimed. 'It's her, look at her face.'

'No, it's not the woman we saw yesterday.'

'Why is that madam,' Farthing's voice, heavy with doubt.

'The lady we saw yesterday had a slight scar above her right eye. This person has no such scar.'

'I didn't notice any scar,' Reggie said.

'It was there alright. Secondly, this woman has plucked eyebrows, the lady we met didn't.'

'Are you sure?'

She turned to Dr Thrasher. 'Could I see her hands please – and feet.'

He lifted the sheet at the side and the bottom. Old reddish polish was on her nails, which had peeled off in places.

'The lady we met had fingernails bitten down to the quick and no varnish. She wore open-toed sandals and had no polish on her toenails either. This is a different woman.'

Reggie stared at the face once again. 'Well, I'm blowed. '

'Can I take it then, sir,' Farthing smiled derisively, 'that you have changed your mind, and that contrary to your first statement, the lady purporting to be Gertrude Dogberry you met yesterday is not the same as the person we have here.'

Reggie was too perplexed to pick up the sarcasm in Farthing's voice. 'But who is she then?'

'Maybe she's an identical twin.' Reggie turned to Thrasher. 'How old would you think she is?'

He thought for a moment. 'At this early stage, I'd put her at say late thirties.'

'The lady we met yesterday told us she was thirty-six,' Sylvia said.

Still feeling he had the upper hand, Farthing told them that details, including the photo, DNA and fingerprints of the deceased, had been circulated to all forces in the UK. They hoped that she would be identified very soon.

'How soon?'

Farthing faltered. 'It's Saturday afternoon. The circulation could not be posted as top priority, so maybe Wednesday or Thursday.'

'Is that the best you can do?' Reggie questioned. 'My good fellow, it is a priority as far as the investigation into all these deaths is concerned. Getting her ID may prevent further deaths, including Mrs Makepeace's and mine.'

'Police numbers – I'm afraid, sir. Every station is short-handed.'

'Blah and poppycock with knobs on,' was Reggie's verbal rebuke.

Arriving back at Shady Grove, Reggie poured himself a desperately needed double before phoning Edgar Ormrod's office. There was no reply, or even the facility to leave a message. Sylvia went next door and asked Grace Pluck if she knew where Edgar might be. She didn't, nor did she have a clue as to his whereabouts.

'I think Edgar would know if Gertrude had a twin, don't you?' Sylvia asked.

'Yes, it seems that Edgar knows an awful lot more than he's revealed so far. My question is, why has Farthing not taken him in for interrogation?'

Sylvia shook her head. 'We probably won't find out anything new over the weekend. Fancy going to church in the morning?'

'Church! Yes, why not. At school, I grew to love church-going.'

'Did you really?'

'Yes, it is ritual, its poetry, the dismal chanting. But I cannot abide these latest translations that have replaced the King James Bible. Why-oh-why change the wonderful language that our faith has hinged on since the seventeenth century? The padre in Africa told me the latest version of the Lord's Prayer has ten alterations from the version I was taught. Like trespass is now sin. Also, the passage *"Mary took those things and pondered them in her heart"*. Do you know what replaced it?'

'Not offhand, no.'

'It is now *"Mary thought about it often"*. And to cap it all, "swaddling clothes" are now *"strips of cloth"*.

'The bible I use belonged to my grandmother,' Sylvia said. 'Even though the church is trying to modernize, they must be suffering though as the size of the congregation has dramatically gone down since I was a girl. I think Sundays have become more B and Q than C of E.'

'Well put, m'dear, I'll ask the vicar tomorrow what his thoughts are on the new translation. What was his name again?'

'The Reverend Marmaduke FitzPeter, or Duke to his friends.'

'Ah, I remember now, Duke FitzPeter. And that sneeze of his; my God, it was something between a vomiting donkey and an explosion in a snot factory. He sweats and his body odour is none too appealing,, not to mention his shifty eyes and dramatic gestures of a would-be thespian. Does he know about Cressida's will?'

'I'm sure he does, Edgar would have told him.'

'His prayers to rebuild the church roof will be answered once probate is granted. And if Gertrude Dogberry were to die before that, then ... *summum bonum*, bonanza.'

CHAPTER FORTY-THREE

Standing in front of a full-length bedroom mirror, Sylvia held a designer dress with matching jacket, against her. 'I think I'll wear my new outfit for church today. It's the light fuchsia outfit you spent a fortune on in Bentalls. Is the colour alright, do you think?'

Reggie nodded sagely. 'The effect looks perfectly appropriate for a lady of your standing.'

'Well, that's reassuring ... I think. Although I'm not sure that Ringwood is quite ready for high fashion, to say nothing of Poulner. Oh, and I'll also wear my new high-heels which also cost a ridiculous amount.' She slipped them on for the fourth time. 'They are nice though. Now that I'm a *kept woman,* I want to detox my *wardrobe of shame,* including underwear. Satan himself can't save a woman who wears a five-pound bra and knickers set beneath a four hundred quid outfit.'

'On that, m'dear, I'll have to take your word. However, fear not, for as soon as we are in God's house, Lucifer, the Prince of Darkness himself, will be prohibited from inspecting ladies' unmentionables and despatching them to the furnace of eternal damnation.'

She laughed. 'I feel better already. Now Reggie, I'll be ready in half an hour -will you be wearing something more ...

how can I put this delicately? Appropriate up-to-date fashion, instead of the old-school-tie garb you usually sport.'

'How dare you, madam,' Reggie gave her a mock scolding, 'Fashion s what I wear – what is unfashionable is what other people wear.'

Laughing to herself, Sylvia overdramatically bowed. 'I stand corrected and humbly beg your forgiveness, sir.'

Feeling rather grand in her new outfit, Sylvia whispered to Reggie that she was getting used to the stares and whispered comments as they left the gleaming Rolls Royce outside the *Star Tavern*. Shoulders back and head held high, she took the arm of the stately Reginald Grosvenor Smythe OBE, resplendent in a light beige, three-piece suit, striped tie, Panama hat and carrying his silver topped cane. 'You will obviously note, my dear, that the tip of my tie rests at a respectful position befitting a gentleman, level with the belt buckle, unlike the proletariat who let it coil round their thighs like a python.'

'All well brought up gals know that instinctively.' Sylvia wore a smile, tinged with satisfaction, as they made their way along Market Square to the church. She sang quietly to Reggie, 'We're a couple of swells.'

He must have been on top form as he sang back, 'We stay in the best hotels.'

'I wasn't expecting that, you romantic charmer,' Sylvia chuckled. 'Fancy doing a duet?'

'Probably not at this precise moment.' Reggie had an urge to dance their way into the house of the Lord, but on reflection, decided to stroll as elegantly as possible.

'It's you *agin, ain't* it.' The faces of two ladies were unceremoniously thrust in front of them bringing their gaiety to a halt. 'It's you, *aint* it, with widow Makepeace.'

The appearance of these ghastly creatures dashed Reggie's feeling of euphoria. 'Now then madam, I seem to remember we have been through this charade before. Your formidable powers of recognition are remarkable, second only to that of GCHQ. But as before, your failure of adding a proper noun after the pronoun diminishes the authority of your question.'

Opened-mouthed, neither could come up with a suitable response.

'From memory, however, you are the redoubtable Miss Snout, spinster of this parish, and your faithful, but blissfully silent companion, Mrs Golightly, mother of the wondrous Tiffany, Ringwood's undisputed queen of all things flattening.'

'But er …Tiffany that it … she drives a small steamroller.'

'And with great skill and dexterity, I'm sure. After a short pause, Reggie continued his burst of eloquence. 'For your information, which you are at liberty to broadcast to your bewitchery *diablerie*, I have recently become a widower. I have not caught leprosy so I won't be carrying a bell, and Mrs Makepeace and I shall continue to be seen in each other's company. Now, good day to you both.'

Miss Snout's lips moved; no words were forthcoming. Sylvia nodded curtly to them as they made their way into church.

Hovering in the porch was the Reverend Marmaduke FitzPeter, who greeted them appreciatively. 'Welcome, I'm pleased to see you both again.' He shook their hands with a damp, limp grip, which made Reggie recoil. He felt one could test a man's mettle by the force of his handshake and, alas, there was no mettle inside this holy man.

'Thank you, Vicar ... er Duke, isn't it?' Reggie responded as cordially as he felt appropriate. 'What's on the *carte du jour* for today's epistle? Fire and brimstone, a good dose of damnation followed by the curse of a plague of boils and pestilence.'

Raising his neatly trimmed eyebrows, FitzPeter clasped his hands together in mock disapproval, a pulsing vein throbbing on his right temple. 'Oh no, that would not go down well with some members of our congregation and might even reduce the amount on the collection plates. We need every penny we can get.'

'From my memory of the scriptures, Duke,' Reggie intoned, 'there seems to be much more in the New Testament in praise of poverty than you care to acknowledge.'

Duke's mouth opened, but without saying a word he closed it again.

'I've read your appeal for roof repairs,' Sylvia asked whilst giving Reggie an admonitory kick on his ankle. 'How's it going?'

'Not very well at the moment, Mrs Makepeace. My bishop is convinced God will provide. I'm praying he's got holier contacts than I – an inside track, so to speak.' Using a handkerchief to wipe his brow, he gave a brittle smile. 'By the way, would you mind staying behind for a while after the service, there are a few things I'd like to discuss with you both.'

Reggie looked at Sylvia. 'I'm sure we could give you half an hour. Don't you, darling?'

'Yes, we could delay luncheon if necessary.'

'That's settled then,' Duke responded. 'I'll see you both later.'

A sidesman guided them to a pew near the front.

'What's all that about?'

'I warrant he wants to see us about Cressida's will, hoping for a windfall to fix his sacellum.'

'His what?'

'Sacellum, a church without a roof.'

'Now, how on earth would you know that?'

Reggie smiled. 'My years at Rymers were not completely wasted.'

Unfortunately, his fond memory of boarding school Sunday worship was somewhat ruined by the service that followed. Sylvia nudged his elbow. 'Your eyes are glazing over.'

'Oh dear, you see I never sleep comfortably, except during a sermon.'

'Well not today, and not so loud,' she whispered.

Two dull hymns followed, and Duke, today's pulpiteer, threw a meaningful glance directly at him and preached, *"If you want to be perfect in this life, go and sell your possessions and give to the church, and you will have treasures in heaven – honour the Lord with your wealth."*

Reggie let out a long sigh. 'What a contemptuous fool,' he swallowed a few even more unsavoury words. 'Thank the Lord that's over.' They made their way to the vestry. The room was lit by cold fluorescent strip lights whose casings had become coffins for an assortment of insects. Dusty, velvet curtains hung against one wall next to a workman's bench. A pungent smell was a combination of coffee and glue. In expectation of their arrival, a plate of sandwiches and iced buns were already set out on the edge of a workbench.

'Ah, there you are,' Duke, sweat shining on his forehead, divested himself of his vestments as he entered. Seeing him close to, Reggie noticed he had dark penumbras smudges beneath bloodshot eyes and thin vermilion blood vessels snaking across his cheekbones and nose. 'I apologise for the mess. Workmen have started on the roof. Would you like a cup of tea?'

'That would be nice,' Sylvia politely responded. 'How about you Reggie?'

'Tea?' Even though his mouth was dry with holy dust, he declined the offer. 'But maybe something a little more on the, should I say, prurience side?' He had spotted an item of interest on a shelf above the bench. Pointing to it, he said, 'Is that bottle just going to sit there or are you going to turn it into a lamp?'

Sylvia cringed; Reggie's foot was never far from his mouth.

'Oh, I see,' Duke gave a small, dry laugh, not noticeably offended by Reggie's discourtesy. 'Could I entice you to partake in a glass of whisky?'

Reggie raised his hand in benediction. 'You can indeed, Padre.'

Stretching on tiptoes, Duke's hand shook as he took the half-empty bottle down from the shelf. Unfortunately, the exertion triggered off an explosive sneeze, instantly followed by a loud hic – like half a hiccup. Reggie struggled to keep a straight face. 'May Jupiter bless you.'

'Oh, thank you,' FitzPeter took out a large handkerchief and wiped his nose. 'I damaged my trigemtval nerve many years ago playing rugby, and this allergy developed from that.

I seem to be allergic to almost everything these days. Hence the constant sneezing. There's no cure ... or so I'm told.'

'That's too bad,' Reggie sympathised. 'In the Talmud, a sneeze is considered a favourable omen.'

FitzPeter smiled. 'I should probably change my religion then.' Taking two glasses out of a drawer, Duke trembled as he tipped a measure into the smaller glass, passing it to Reggie. He then half-spilled a larger glass which he despatched in one draught without even blinking.

Against his natural habit, Reggie felt it appropriate to demonstrate a more refined way, by first inhaling the liqueur, then a small sip to swirl it around the mouth, before swallowing to appreciate the flavours. This approach failed as he grimaced at the inferior taste. Glancing at the label, he saw it was a bottle of *Jock McDongle's Bonnie Mist*.

'I asked you to stay behind as the police have been to see me a couple of times.' He tilted back in his chair to contemplate the smoke detector in the ceiling above his desk, which generated another stentorian paroxysmal. 'I apologise for that,' Duke said. 'It gets worse when I'm worried.'

'And what, pray, are you worried about?'

'It's the police. D I Farthing informed me that Miss Smythe's death, God rest her soul, was suspicious.'

Leaving the remainder of the *Jock McDongle* untouched, Reggie said, 'Are you a suspect in her suspicious death?'

'Oh no,' was Duke's instant response. 'Farthing just wondered if I could cast a light on anything or, indeed, anybody who might hold a grudge against the dear lady.'

'Why would he think that?'

'Well, you see, I knew Miss Smythe quite well, calling on her once a month, in my parochial duties of course. We prayed together.'

'Did you.'

'Yes, but Farthing thought she may have revealed something in confession, but we don't go in for that sort of thing. He told me he was a Catholic.'

'Ah, that explains it.' Reggie had a mischievous look on his face. 'The Catholic Church is just for sinners whereas respectable people feel the Anglican Church will do.'

FitzPeter gave a nervous laugh.

'And did she?' Reggie pressed.

'Did she what?'

'Did she put the knockers on some villainous blackguard who could be a suspect?'

'Not at all. She never spoke ill of anyone.'

'That is ruddy nonsense, Duke, and well you know it. Cressida Smythe spoke ill of virtually everybody.'

He attempted a smile that didn't quite reach his eyes. 'Anyway, it seems that dear Cressida Smythe, God rest her soul, remembered the church in her will. As you're her closest relative, and no doubt *au fait* with her wishes, I was hoping you could provide some clarification on what the church might expect, and when.'

'Really.'

'Is that a problem?' he stuttered.

'I'm wondering why you are asking me. I was never *au fait,* as you put it, with her wishes. I'm assuming you've been in contact with her solicitor, Edgar Ormrod, as you seemed to be well acquainted with each other.'

'Yes, he's been most helpful. It's just that the church will receive a part of her estate once probate has been granted, but it is delayed because of police enquiries. Do you know when this will take place, so we can carry on with the repairs?'

'No, I've no idea. I take it you know the value of her estate?'

This made the Duke hesitate. 'Edgar did hint that it was several million pounds, or so.'

'And did he tell you what portion of her estate would come to the church?' Reggie's question, delivered vigorously, was not threatening in any way, but, for some reason, Duke was getting more nervous, and his trembling increased.

'Edgar said something around ten percent, which might be five hundred thousand pounds, which would go a long way to fix the roof.'

Curious as to why Duke was getting more jittery, coupled with the fact that he developed a dislike to the man, Reggie was interested to see his reaction to his next statement. 'As two of the original beneficiaries have recently died under suspicious circumstances, you, meaning the church, could receive around seven hundred and fifty thousand pounds. Now, if the body in the morgue is Gertrude Dogberry, and therefore eliminated from the will, you and Edgar would each get three million.'

FitzPeter put his face in his hands. His jaw trembled making it difficult to breathe. 'Oh, my Lord.'

'And if, by some unforeseen tragic event,' Reggie enjoyed seeing the disagreeable man on the verge of apoplexy, 'that Edgar Ormrod got his comeuppance before probate is granted, you would get the whole bonanza – over six million quid.'

The Duke's lips moved but no sound emerged. Wiping a torrent of sweat from his brow, he seemed to physically deflate before their eyes, sinking into a chair, but not before he sneezed so loud, it echoed around the vestry, causing his whisky glass to fall out of his hand, smashing into tiny pieces on the floor.

Bidding a hasty retreat, Sylvia took Reggie's arm. 'That was strange, wasn't it? He's weird.'

'Indeed,' Reggie gave her a smile. 'That was as much fun as a tea party in Berchesgarten,'

CHAPTER FORTY-FOUR

By the time they left the church, it was nearing midday. The sun, striking vertically down through what had been a thin haze, was already hot. Still attired in their finery, they strolled regally from the Market Square into the High Street, ignoring stares and murmured asides from people who parted like waves before them as they did for Moses. Much to her own surprise, Sylvia was enjoying it. 'I feel like I'm out walking with a Union Jack.'

Reggie smiled. 'And why not, indeed. The High Street has hardly changed, except, of course, there are far more cars.'

A smell of curry drifted from one of the nearby restaurants. 'There was no foreign food forty years ago, it was mainly fish and chips or burgers and bangers ... but that's not a bad thing.'

Although it was Sunday, people spent time at the several shops that were open, especially those providing refreshments. Tourists in summer attire sauntered up and down; men in shorts and ladies with streaked fake tan on their fleshy bits.

'If you feel up to it, Reggie, we could continue from here along Christchurch Road to Greyfriars.'

'Do I know Greyfriars? Not another place of worship, I hope.'

'No, it's Ringwood's Community Centre and it recently celebrated its 60th anniversary, so it was going well before you left town. The library is next to it, you'll remember that.'

'Vaguely I do. It was a dreary place if I remember correctly. I think they were waiting for the Doomsday book to come out in paperback, or something like that.'

'Now you're being silly. Anyhow, it's not dreary any longer. It is quite lively and modern, but it's closed today. The Art Society's annual exhibition is on in Greyfriars now and it is open on Sunday afternoons. I've been a member for many years.'

'Have you really? Am I to see you in a new light?'

'Well, all the paintings in the living room are mine.'

'And why, pray, didn't you tell me that before. I must have seen them without realising you were the creator. In my limited experience, however, most amateur scribblers offend the discerning *penetralis mentis*.'

'Huh, whatever that means,' Sylvia frowned. 'You may be in for a pleasant surprise.'

'Ah yes, I do remember this building,' Reggie said when they arrived at Greyfriars.

'Freddie used to come here regularly,' Sylvia said. 'His was a serious philatelist.'

'Really?'

'Yes, he collected mainly British stamps, all the way from the first penny black right through to George V.' She gave a pensive smile, 'He won his one and only penny black in a raffle at their annual stamp fair, Ringpex – it was worth over one hundred pounds, unlike the rest of his collection.'

'Good for Freddie.'

'It's a very active club, and he enjoyed the monthly meetings with speakers showing their priceless collections. One year, he won The Traditional Class trophy – The John Cup.'

'Jolly good show. I used to collect stamps myself.'

'Did you? When was that?'

'We had a club at school, but when I left I gave my collection away – and, you know, I can't remember why.'

'Well, whoever got it is now probably relaxing in the South of France on the proceeds.'

He laughed. 'I don't think so. Maybe a couple of days in a Blackpool B and B.'

'Well, you'll never know.' Sylvia chuckled. 'And Freddie was also a member of the Writers Circle. He wrote short stories and a couple of novels.'

'He was a busy chap. Was he any good?'

'He was, but sadly, his attempts to get his stories published never got off the ground. His sole compensation was the satisfaction of having been rude to some of the most famous publishers in London.'

'Jolly good for Freddie. I can't compete on that front, I'm afraid.'

The entrance door soundlessly slid open, and they walked across the central courtyard towards the Exhibition. A heavy old woman with her hair in a bun sat on a bench and squinted at them as they passed.

'One of your friends?'

'Not a friend, no,' Sylvia said. 'Sally Crosbie, poor thing. Well past her sell-by date, I'm afraid. Decayed by drink and falling off horses I believe.'

the entrance, they were greeted by a handsome

d rangy with high cheek bones, and taut, smooth

lvia.' She wore casual but expensive clothes, her

t leather tassels, showed good taste. 'My, Sylvia,

rather smart today.'

ie. Yes, we've just been to church. Let me

my friend. Reggie. This is Lizzie Prendergast,

rd today.'

noon, Chief Prendergast. Are you by any

the Prendergast's of Esher? A friend from

of course ...'

ughed, 'I'm from the Prendergast's of

cashire, but we don't talk about that very

a definite northern inflection in her voice.

instant liking to her. 'I'm sure Ramsbottom

n,' he laughed, 'but it might puzzle a few

en they ask where you come from.'

peace, where have you been hiding Reggie?

'

d for Sylvia. 'Yes, we're hot, passionate

)on't embarrass me.'

u,' Lizzie laughed. 'It's been a while since

Reggie and I are actually old friends. We knew each other forty years ago.'

'Oh, I see,' Lizzie replied, even though she didn't see at all. She would no doubt find out later. 'Welcome to our highly-rated exhibition, Reggie.' She gave Sylvia a broad wink.

'Thank you so much, Lizzie Prendergast,' Reggie tipped his hat. 'I'll look forward to inspecting your entry.' He paused. 'I'll re-phrase that, I'm looking forward to seeing your artwork.'

Sylvia grabbed Reggie's arm and pulled him into the Ann Rose Room before he could embarrass her any further. Due to his attire - Panama hat, monocle and silver-topped cane, to say nothing of his booming, cultured voice, he became the centre of attention. Adjusting his monocle, he moved closer to examine a painting of a pride of lions with a snow-capped mountain in the background. 'Oh, I like the look of this one, with Kilimanjaro in the distance, it would go very well in our Kingston flat. I think I'll buy it.'

'Reggie dearest, it's the most expensive painting in the exhibition at £950. Are you sure?'

'Absolutely positive. It is a first-class piece, very professional. I love it.'

'But you've not seen the rest yet.'

'Well let us do just that.'

After spending a full hour viewing the exhibits, Reggie's purchases amounted to four paintings totalling two-thousand, one hundred and twenty pounds.

'I trust you will accept a debit card for these,' he asked a lady steward wearing jeans and a sweater printed with cartoon characters.

Putting down the magazine, she stared at him. 'Oh yes, of course, sir.'

'It's not "sir" Margaret,' Sylvia laughed. 'It's Reggie.'

'Oh, hello Sylvia, I didn't see you there,' Margaret smiled. 'Wherever you got Reggie from, would you kindly go and find another one. This is the best sale we've had.'

Leaving Greyfriars with their new artwork, Reggie and Sylvia arrived back in Shady Grove just after three o'clock. Across the road the horse chestnuts, heavy with blossom, stood in the sun - it was a golden summer day. Then, a rude awakening. Sylvia's over-familiar neighbour, Grace Pluck, supporting herself against the door frame, stood holding a glass of wine in her hand. Wasps buzzed around an empty wine bottle at her feet. She was enfolded in what appeared to be a dazzling bright yellow attire resembling a carpet of oilseed rape. She was talking intently to Edgar Ormrod.

'Hello, you lovebirds,' she slurred. A self-conscious Edgar turned, and gave a wave.

Reggie whispered. 'I don't trust the bounder at all, let's interrogate him.'

After briefly greeting Grace, Sylvia invited Edgar into the house.

'Can I come too?' Grace emptied her glass and threw it on the lawn. Knocking over the empty bottle, she stumbled across the garden towards their house.

'No Grace,' Edgar firmly gestured. 'I'll see you later. Go inside and make yourself some extra-strong coffee.'

With a distraught look, she did as she was told. Edgar clearly had authority over her, even in that state.

The three of them went into the house and through to the kitchen. 'I'll put the kettle on,' Sylvia said. 'Tea or coffee, Edgar?'

'Er, I think I'd prefer ... '

'We'll have whisky, thank you, my dearest,' Reggie took an unopened bottle and two glasses out of the cupboard. 'Now then, Edgar, you are up to your scrawny neck in the murder and suspicious deaths of several people, including your own son. Why you're not behind bars is a bloody mystery to me. You have perverted the course of duty by lying to D S Clapp, you have evaded questions from D I Farthing, and you identified a body in the morgue as Gertrude Dogberry which is another bloody lie. What in God's name are you up to?'

Trembling under Reggie's barrage, he replied weekly, 'No, I never lie.'

This made Reggie even angrier. 'You told Clapp and me that you'd never heard of Gertrude Dogberry. Was that a lie?'

'Oh yes, I did do that, didn't I?'

'You withheld information about Jacob and Stella Pinch, knowing full well they had brought up Gertrude Dogberry from birth.'

'Oh, I did that as well, didn't I?'

'You answered questions from D I Farthing by saying "no comment", and you identified the body in the morgue as Gertrude. Well, is it her?'

'I'm not sure, it could be ... er,' he shook his head.' Probably not.'

'Now Edgar, when Cressida gave birth in Norfolk, did she have twins?'

Reaching for his glass, he found it empty. 'Yes,' he mumbled. Holding out his glass for a refill, he whimpered, 'I'm out of my depth, Reggie. And I'm frightened.'

'What do you mean, frightened? Frightened of who or what for God's sake.'

He took another large drink. 'Someone's trying to kill me. It's to do with the money.'

'Money! You mean Cressida's will money.'

He nodded. 'I should tell you everything but swear to me you'll keep it secret.'

'No, I bloody well won't keep your pathetic secrets, especially if it'll stop all the killings and deceit. You should tell this to the police, not me.'

'I know. You see, Reggie, being a solicitor, I am used to keeping secrets, client confidentiality and all that. But some secrets are hard to keep and end up harming people.'

'I can understand that, but people are dying including your son, flattened by Tiffany steamroller. Was that murder or an accident? And don't tell me the police are making enquiries.'

'I have no proof but I'm sure Redknapp was murdered. He was due to get ten percent of the will.'

'Yes, I know. And what about Dorothy Smerdal, impaled on the Bournemouth pier zip wire, was she murdered?'

'I'm sure she was. She was also left ten percent. It's the money again, you see.'

'And then there's the death of Jacob Pinch who wrote Cressida's will. He was killed by a run-away Mr Whippy ice cream van – allegedly carrying a bag of sausage rolls at the time.'

'I know nothing about that.'

'But why did Jacob Pinch write Cressida's will and not you? You were her solicitor.'

'I couldn't do it as I'm a beneficiary. Before they left Ringwood to go and live in Seaton, Jacob and Stella were close friends of Cressida's, and as you know, they brought up Gertrude as their own, from birth.'

'I know, and they only told her the truth about her biological mother on her twenty-first birthday which shattered her life.'

Edgar looked puzzled. 'How do you know?'

'She told me.'

'Who, how, when? I don't understand.'

'Gertrude Dogberry contacted me two days ago in Kingston. Sylvia and I met her. She is also very frightened. Her friend, a lady called Portia Barton was mistakenly killed in Gertrude's car by a combine harvester. Stella Pinch was poisoned by drinking from Gertrude's whisky bottle, which was laced with cyanide. What do you know about that?'

'Nothing, I promise, I was as shocked as anyone.'

'So, after our meeting with Gertrude, we know it wasn't her body in the morgue, although, I must admit, they look alike.'

'It's Gertrude's twin. The police might eventually trace her, but I know who she is. Her name was Felicity Fringe.' Tears streamed down his face, 'What a mess.'

'And who killed Felicity Fringe?'

'Again, I do not know, but it will be the same person who killed everyone else and is after me. If Gertrude and I die, he will get the lot, the whole six million, except, of course, the ten percent for the church. I don't think whoever it could murder a church, do you?'

'Apart from blowing it up, no. But who is this mysterious murderer, and how can that person get the money if they're not listed as a beneficiary? There are only three left: Gertrude, the church and you.'

Edgar had had enough and helped himself to another whisky.

Standing behind Reggie, Sylvia had listened to all that had been said. 'Tell me Edgar,' she spoke softly. 'There is one key question that may throw a light on the whole saga. Do you know who the father was? The father of Cressida's twins.'

'Yes.'

'Was it you?'

'Oh, good heavens no. Not me.'

'Then who was it?'

'You've asked me a question I can't answer. Client confidentially.'

Stimulated by his intake of whisky, Reggie went over and grabbed Edgar by the shoulders, and began to aggressively shake him. 'You can stuff your bloody solicitor's creed or whatever mumbo-jumbo you get up to, tell us now, who is the father, or I'll inflict some serious damage to your nether regions?'

Sylvia had never seen Reggie like this before. She decided not to intervene.

'I can't tell you,' Edgar pleaded. 'Client confidentiality is respected by the courts.'

'Well, you snivelling piece of excrement, I'm not the bloody court or the bloody police, I've become the people's enforcer and I won't stand by while other people get killed.' Reggie continued his assault. 'You've lost your only son, you're a liar and charlatan, and you've deliberately deceived the people who could have prevented some of these deaths.' Reggie put his head close to Edgar's and yelled at the top of his voice. 'Who is the father?'

Edgar's eyes almost popped out of his head as Reggie grabbed him by the throat. 'Alright, I'll tell you,' he croaked, 'don't hurt me. It's the Reverend Marmaduke FitzPeter, he's the father.'

CHAPTER FORTY-FIVE

Sylvia took the empty whisky bottle and glasses to the sink. 'I find it difficult to believe Edgar's a solicitor. He doesn't look or even speak like one. He's too – I don't know, too anaemic.'

'I know what you mean, he's not what one would call a whirling dervish of wit and charisma. It's like having a conversation with Alan Bennett on Valium.'

This made Sylvia laugh. 'But do you think he was telling the truth just now? He was a bit squiffy after quickly downing half of your bottle of whisky.'

Reggie laughed. 'You mean was he telling the truth about Duke being Cressida's impregnator?'

'Yes, he must have been a teenager at that time,' Sylvia said. 'Hard to believe, though. Is Edgar trying to shift suspicion on to Duke?'

'The answer, m'dear, is I don't know. Edgar has certainly lied in the past so this could be yet another one. I also believe he's withholding useful information. One thing though, he certainly gave the impression of being anxious, thinking some evil-doer is after him, or was it just an act?'

'He's hard to fathom. Now Reggie, it is almost five o'clock and we've not eaten anything since breakfast, except for those token bites in the vestry, what do you fancy?'

'How about a large steak with chips,' Reggie said without hesitation. 'Aida makes wonderful chips.'

'Unfortunately, I cannot compete with Aida on the chip scene, but luckily, I bought steaks from Sainsburys and …' She was interrupted by the doorbell. 'Damn,'

'Oh God,' Reggie sighed. 'If that's *Mrs next door*, get rid of her. Tell her we've run out of booze.'

It wasn't Grace Pluck but Detective Inspector Farthing. 'I'm very sorry to disturb you on a Sunday afternoon, Mrs Makepeace, but may I come in - just for a moment.'

'Well actually Inspector, we were just about to have dinner but …'

'I'll be very quick. It's because Mr Ormrod has just left your house.'

'And?' Sylvia questioned.

'And I er, want to know if he may have revealed something to you, you know.'

Reggie called from the kitchen. 'Kindly let the Inspector in, m'dear.'

Reluctantly, Sylvia led him through to the kitchen.

'I think, Sylvia, my angel,' Reggie gave her a smile, 'we should delay our dinner for a little while. We have a lot to discuss with the Inspector. Can I get you a drink, Farthing? I'm about to open a new bottle of Scotch and Sylvia is well into her Sauvignon Blanc.'

'No thank you, sir. On duty er, well no, I'm not, am I? Maybe a small one with a dash of water.'

'Of course. Do I take it you were following Edgar Ormrod?'

Farthing hesitated before replying. 'In a manner of speaking, yes.'

'God almighty, man,' Reggie retorted. 'Don't be so wet. Were you following him or not?'

Emptying his glass in one gulp, he nodded his head. 'I'm clutching at straws here, and if you wouldn't mind, I'd like this to be off the record. I'm getting hell from my Chief Constable, and he is having a hard time from his counterpart in the Devonshire Constabulary. Too many suspicious deaths, three in Devon and four here.'

'There you go again,' Reggie retorted. 'There's nothing ruddy well suspicious about them, they are all murders. Face the facts, won't you. Your problem is you don't know who the killer is and following Ormrod's movements is sheer desperation on your part. If you want suspects followed, get your bloody staff to do it.'

Almost cowering under Reggie's verbal onslaught, he squirmed in his seat, examining his empty glass.

'Don't you have any other suspects?'

'No, not really. Along with the Devonshire police, we've interviewed everyone directly and indirectly involved in all those deaths, and we've come up with nothing. But I am sure Ormrod knows more than he's saying. Tell me, why was he here?'

'More or less the same reason as you, except in his case, he's frightened for his own life, or at least he says he is.' Reggie refilled both their glasses.

'My team are working on the possible motives for killing Miss Smythe, which seems to be the catalyst for all the other deaths,' Farthing took a sip from his glass. 'Once we know the motive, we have a chance of catching the killer.'

'And pray, what motive has your team of peelers come up with?'

'Only one thing, one motive - Cressida Smythe's estate of close to seven million pounds.'

'Seven million?' questioned Sylvia. 'I thought it was nearer six.'

'Yes, but the finance chaps found another on-line betting account in Miss Smythe's name with over three hundred thousand.'

'My God.'

'In that case,' Reggie said, 'your only suspects are Edgar Ormrod, Gertrude Dogberry and the church, as they are the only beneficiaries left. Two other potential inheritors have already bitten the dust.'

Farthing emptied his second glass and weakly nodded his head. 'Yes,' he whispered. 'Although not the church ... of course. Mr Grosvenor Smythe, you told me on the phone that you met Gertrude Dogberry in Kingston and she was supposed to be hiding from the killer. Did you believe her?'

'I am not a student of the criminal mind, Inspector, so whilst she seemed honest enough, neither Mrs Makepeace nor I can be certain. But she went to extraordinary lengths to make sure we were who we said we were. In addition, purely based on her appearance – a good likeness of Cressida - I did not see nor ask for her identification. However, at that time, I did not know, and she did not inform me, that she was one of twins. The body in the morgue looked very much like her. So, who is who?'

Farthing vigorously rubbed his brow. 'If the woman you met in Kingston lied, and was the twin, the body in the morgue would be Gertrude Dogberry, and then that would leave only two to inherit. Do you know how I can contact this woman?'

Sylvia had Gertrude's mobile contact number but had promised to keep it secret. 'No Inspector, we have no way of contacting her.'

'If she does contact you again – well, I need to speak to her. She and Ormrod must hold the key.'

'She's too frightened to reveal her whereabouts. But we have some information which you may not be aware of.'

'And that is?'

'According to Ormrod, the Reverend Marmaduke FitzPeter is the father of Cressida Smythe's twins. Whether FitzPeter is aware that he is the father, or not, Ormrod didn't know.'

CHAPTER FORTY-SIX

Reggie woke with a dry mouth and a pounding head. He groaned, 'I must have over indulged.' Lifting his aching head, found he was speaking to an empty bedroom. 'Oh!'

Staggering into the living room, he found Sylvia watching the early morning news on television.

'I think, my *fragolina,* I need a double infusion of extraordinarily strong coffee.'

She gave him a reproachful look. 'It probably serves you right, Reggie. In my calculation, you consumed a bottle and a half of whisky. You drank to my health but spoilt your own ... oh dear, am I beginning to sound like a nagging wife?'

Reggie was wise enough not to answer that leading question.

She stood up slowly. 'In that case, my liege, as I'm a kept woman, I guess you would like me to get coffee for you.'

'That would, indeed, be most kind of you, my angel. Your Brownie points are growing by the day.'

She headed to the kitchen. 'And what, sire, will I get when I decide to cash them all in?'

'Ha, I'd prefer to answer that once my head has cleared - but I can assure you it will at least match the treasures of King Solomon's mine.'

'I can't wait. But returning to your painful head, you once told me that those who do not remember the past, are condemned to repeat it.'

'Did I say that? Yes, I probably did. But no doubt relating to more ancient history. However, a point well made.'

He downed two cups of coffee and brightened up a little. 'Now, what's on our agenda for today?'

'After breakfast, Mr Lee and Mrs Kim are calling to collect the pictures you bought and take them to Kingston. After that, I have grocery shopping and then Chester is coming round later this morning. I never know whether he's staying here or at his flat.'

Feeling much better after breakfast, Reggie answered the door to greet the Korean lovers.

'*Hewo, Weggie*, Mrs Kim and me go now Kingston with *wented* van, but massage parlour not give Mrs Kim everything. We *weturn Wingwood* on *Fwiday*. But now we take your pictures.'

'Thank you, Mr Lee. Please give them to Aida.'

'But when you *weturn, Weggie*?'

'There are several complications to overcome regarding my late Aunt's death, but we hope to return in a week or two but ... we aren't sure.'

'You not sure? That bad. We have saying in my *countwy*. We say, 'when *guest-es* come to *cwimb wice* mountain, children *cwy* if *guest-es* put *wice* in sacks to *cawwy* away. You have same saying in your *countwy*?'

'I don't believe we do, Mr Lee. In England, we say, "one day's delay is another day without action".'

'Oooh, that good saying, *Weggie*. I *wike* it.'

After seeing Mr Lee drive off in the hired van, Sylvia went shopping and Reggie settled down to read the morning paper. There was an article about yet another ship being named after the Queen. 'Oh, poor lady, she must be beginning to think there is some resemblance.' Other news was all about the endless vistas of conflict operating in every corner of the world. 'Twas ever thus.' He quickly reached the centre page when he heard the front door open, and Chester came in.

'Morning greetings to you Ches. Your mother is out shopping at the moment. Can I get you anything?'

'No thanks, Reggie.' He sat in the chair opposite. 'So, is there any progress in Cressida Smythe's murder?'

'We had the police here yesterday, but the answer to your question is "no". Interesting, isn't it?' Reggie continued, 'The legacy of Cressida Smythe's time in the world lingers on, throbbing like an unjust hangover afflicting all of us, the living and the dead. It's remarkable what has happened since she died.'

'And it's very worrying,' Chester said. 'Once the whole story gets out, all hell will break loose with the world's media.'

'And when that happens, we should be sure to be away from here,' Reggie said. 'I'm pretty certain that all the deaths were deliberate. There is a serial killer out there and the police have no idea who it is. And as Cressida's seven million quid is the only motive, the main suspects are still Edgar Ormrod and Gertrude Dogberry, both of whom claim to be scared stiff they will be the next. Although the church is also a beneficiary, it is not thought it is involved, even though I find the Reverend Marmaduke FitzPeter, to be an unpleasant character in the extreme.'

Chester nodded. 'When the young FitzPeter was in Ringwood as a curate, he had the reputation as a womanizer.'

'Did he now? Interesting.'

'After several complaints to the diocese, he was quickly removed, only to return four years ago.'

'That fits in because Edgar Ormrod reckons Marmaduke FitzPeter was the father of Cressida's twins. Was FitzPeter here around the time Cressida got pregnant.'

'I think so. FitzPeter could be involved after all.'

They were interrupted as Sylvia came in loaded with shopping. She looked highly animated. 'I have some news for you both. There was a lot of excitement in the Market Square with an ambulance and two police cars. I saw D I Farthing and spoke to him. It seems there was an accident during bell ringing practice.'

'Bell ringing, hey,' Reggie smirked. 'That does sound exciting.'

Ignoring Reggie's sarcasm, she added, 'The larger bell lost its clapper. It fell and knocked out one of the bell ringers who's unconscious and in Bournemouth hospital.'

Reggie sympathised. 'Someone you know?'

'Edgar Ormrod. He's critically ill but not on the danger list.'

There was a stunned silence for a few seconds before Reggie found his voice. 'By the Lord Harry, was it the killer who got to him with a loose clapper?'

Shaking his head, Chester added, 'You've got to hand it to him, whoever it is has got an impressive imagination.'

'That's if it was a, 'he' Sylvia said.

'Yes of course,' Reggie acknowledged, 'If Gertrude is in the frame for this one, then it's a "she". I guess the question is, was it an accident. Was the church largest bell's metal clapper deliberately loosened in an attempt to eliminate Edgar Ormrod from getting his mitts on Cressida's bounteous wealth? Luckily, the death by clapper,' he paused for a moment's thought, rubbing his chin. 'You know something, I like the sound of that – could be a new Hercule Poirot mystery - *Death By Clapper* by Agatha Crispie. What a wonderful title – but this time, the clapper plan failed.'

'I think it's you with the imagination, Reggie,' Chester laughed. 'Although I take your point. In fact, there could be a whole series of murder mysteries with intriguing titles, all linked to Cressida's death: *Death in a barrel of Dorset Best Bitter*, or *Death by Steamroller*.'

'What about *Death by Mr Whippy*,' Sylvia laughed, 'With a strap line *"Whilst carrying a bag of sausage rolls"*. Or even *Death on Bournemouth Pier's Zip Wire*.'

'I guess *Death by Cyanide* would be too boring,' Reggie added. 'The only one we've missed is *Death by a Runaway Combine Harvester*. No matter how sad and tragic all these deaths are, the killer is certainly full of ideas. But we really shouldn't laugh; it's not funny for poor old Edgar Ormrod who'll suffer from a Herculean headache once he's conscious.'

'I'm sure he will,' Chester agreed, 'But no doubt the intrepid D I Farthing will be looking into the loose clapper as we speak. Did he say anything else to you, Mum?'

'Only that he'll keep us posted. Well, in actual fact it's you Reggie, he wants to keep in the picture, because you can look into things that he, a police officer, can't … if that makes sense.'

Chester gave Reggie a broad wink. 'I think he likes using you as a sort of adjutant – a *fidus a chates*.'

'Oh, not you too, Ches,' Sylvia sighed. 'I have enough trouble understanding Reggie without you chiming in showing off your Latin credentials.'

Reggie returned Chester's gesture. 'Actually Ches, I'm not sure that's a role I want to play. During the past two weeks, Farthing has morphed from a belligerent, confident investigating officer into a lost soul. When he took over from poor old Clapp, he arrogantly thought he'd have this case wrapped up in no time. I'd say he still hasn't a clue about who he's up against.'

'Whether you're right about Farthing or not,' Chester said, 'I want to know who killed Cressida Smythe. Although I didn't know it at the time, she was my closest relation, apart from you two, of course.'

'I'm with you on that score, Ches, my boy.'

'Not a good time for me, is it?' Chester said. 'One month ago, the only relation I had was my mother – nobody else. I knew Freddie Makepeace wasn't my biological father from the start, but he brought me up very well. But since then, I've learnt for the first time who my real father is. I think I'm a candidate for counselling, don't you?'

Sylvia put her arms around him, kissing him on the cheek. 'I'm sorry, Ches, of course I knew who your father was, but as he'd sowed his seed and buggered off before you were born, I thought – what was the point? It might have upset you even more. And what was the point of telling you that Cressida Smythe was your Great Aunt. We all disliked her.'

Reggie followed Sylvia by putting his arm around Chester's shoulders, but didn't kiss him - that was too continental. 'And as you know, son, I didn't know about you either. But now that we have met ... well, I'm thrilled to bits. I have a son. A grown-up son of whom I'm immensely proud.'

Chester sat and smiled at them both. 'I think I'll save the counselling for later.'

'If anyone needs counselling it's me,' Reggie said. 'Looking back now, I have much to regret. Just because I did not hear a word from my Foxy, I should have tried later.' Holding Sylvia's hand, he said, 'You were my love – you were especially important to me and I missed you dreadfully.'

'Oh Reggie,' Sylvia sighed, 'I was as much to blame as you. With hindsight, I could have tried harder to contact you.'

'Well, we are where we are,' Reggie gave a gentle smile. 'Whilst it is only inadequate compensation, I did acquire significant personal wealth over my working life and would be delighted, Ches, if you would accept a father to son gift, making up for missing your childhood and youth. How about say one million pounds, and it's entirely up to you what you do with it.'

Chester stayed seated for a moment, contemplating the table. 'Are you serious – one million pounds?'

'Absolutely serious, you can have more if you want. I'm presently worth over six million.'

'Oh my God, you didn't tell me you were so filthy rich,' Sylvia said, 'although I knew from your penthouse in Kingston that you were worth a few bob.'

'I've often wondered how people feel when they win a million on the lottery,' Chester laughed. 'Bloody hell.'

'After that bombshell,' Sylvia said, 'it's time for lunch and some liquid refreshment to accompany it.'

'Foxy, m'dear, may I enquire as to what tantalising dish you have prepared for the two millionaire men in your life?'

'Ham sandwiches. After trawling around Sainsbury's whilst you were both in your armchair putting the world to rights, you can get them yourselves - I'm pooped.'

'Oh gosh.' Reggie and Chester, duly reprimanded, raised their eyes in unison and went through to the kitchen. Reggie first went to the cupboard to retrieve his usual tipple, whilst Chester sliced the loaf. Between them, they made a plate full of sandwiches and took them through to Sylvia. 'Well done, boys. Now I'll have that drink – champagne I think.'

Feeling on top of the world, Reggie hurried to carry out her instructions.

'I've had better,' Sylvia voiced her opinion after the sandwiches had been eaten, although the champers helped it down. She was about to say something when Chester's mobile phone rang.

'It's for you, Reggie, it's Gertrude Dogberry.'

'Gertrude,' Reggie asked in disbelief, 'how on earth did you get Chester's number?'

'Never mind about that,' she said. 'Is it true that Edgar Ormrod has been attacked? Is he dead?'

'It is true, but he's not dead. He is in Bournemouth hospital, severely injured but expected to live. How did you hear?'

'Never mind.'

'Where are you? Are you still in Kingston or down here?'

'For the third time of saying, Reggie, never mind. All you need to know is that I am in hiding until whoever is killing us has been caught. Only then will I be prepared to meet the police.' The phone went dead.

'Damn the woman, I wish she wouldn't do that.'

Chapter Forty-Six

No sooner had she hung up than Reggie's mobile rang. It was D I Farthing.

'I've just been with Ormrod – he's just come to.'

'And how is the poor chap?'

'Sedated. The doctor said he'll be under observation for at least a week – head injuries are difficult to fathom. Even though groggy, he asked for you to go and see him.'

'Why would he want to see me?'

'He said he doesn't trust me or my men, only you. He's scared stiff and wants your help. Can you go this evening, at 7 o'clock?'

'I don't like the sound of this, Farthing. He is not my friend; in fact, I have no connection with him at all. If he has problems, then you are the man to talk to.'

'He's adamant, he wants you.'

'Okay, I'll go. By the way, Farthing, I trust you have put an officer in his room. The failure to kill him with the clapper means that whoever it was will try again.'

There was a moment's silence. 'Er, yes it's er ... been arranged.'

CHAPTER FORTY-SEVEN

Without the chauffeuring of his Korean friend, Reggie reluctantly drove the Rolls to Bournemouth Hospital. Leaving Poulner, he headed into Ringwood town and then took the A31 South, turning onto the dual carriageway A338 at the Ashley Heath roundabout. Luckily, traffic was light and within fifteen minutes, he took the slip road to the hospital. Only then were his worst fears confirmed as the neon-lit parking notice showed all car parks full. Damn, he should have insisted on Farthing providing a police car.

Nearing the main entrance was an empty parking space marked Hospital Manager. 'That'll do nicely,' he murmured - he was on official police business after all.

Impressively dressed as always, he marched purposefully through the entrance hall straight to the Reception Desk, avoiding eye contact with anyone on the way. In his experience, he knew that taking this sort of action created an impression of authority, and usually worked.

Two harassed-looking receptionists were at the desk, one busily working on a computer, whilst the other attended to a long queue of people.

'Good evening to you, ladies,' Reggie boomed in his most commanding, cultured voice, 'My name is Reginald Grosvenor Smythe OBE and I'm here on official business.'

Both ladies, seeing the daunting, monocled presence of Reggie, carrying a silver-topped cane like a general's swagger stick, looked stunned, as were the rest of the people in that area, who stopped whatever they were doing to stare.

'Can er ... can I help, sir?' one stuttered leaving her computer, doing her best to stand to a form of attention. The name on the badge fastened to her chest was Rachel Hannah. She wasn't sure if this man – this gentleman with the air of an aristocratic patrician, was an NHS Inspector who'd randomly called for an unannounced inspection, or even a Government Minister. Whoever he was, he clearly expected to be obeyed.

'Indeed, you can, madam,' he replied loudly. 'There is a patient in this edifice for the ailing and sick named Edgar Ormrod, that's O R M R O D. Kindly lead me to this gentleman as a matter of urgency.'

'Yes, I er ... I'll will check to see ... er,' she tapped away on her keyboard.

'As quickly as you can, Rachel Hannah,' Reggie feigned impatience.

Looking up from her computer, she said, 'I've found him, Mr Edgar Ormrod is in Ward 23E, sir.'

'Splendid. I'd be obliged, Rachel Hannah, if you will kindly escort me there straight away.'

'I'll have call for an order...'

'No Rachel Hannah, you can do it,' Reggie responded at full volume.

The poor woman had no choice. Her companion used her phone to warn management of their visitor.

Rachel Hannah led the way up a flight of stairs and along a corridor, passing groups of people who, seeing the formidable presence of Reggie striding decisively down the corridor, immediately parted to each side.

Arriving at ward 23E, Rachel Hannah knocked on the door, opened by a rather untidy looking policeman, his uniform appearing to be too tight. Reggie wondered where Farthing had dug this chap up: probably a reservist.

'Thank you for your kind help, Rachel Hannah,' Reggie beamed and shook her hand. 'You have performed your duties admirably; I'll be alright from here on in.'

Turning to the policeman, Reggie said. 'Good evening to you Constable No 479. Kindly tell me your name.'

'Eh?'

'Your name, my man,' Reggie's voice reflected his impatience.

'It's er ...' He looked anxiously down the corridor as though needing help.

'Surely that is one piece of information which should be familiar to you.'

Still looking anxious, he said, 'What's it to you?'

'I need that piece of information so that my report to Detective Inspector Farthing, on your duty this evening, will be complete. Now then,' Reggie increased the volume of his voice, 'what is your name?' Reggie couldn't understand why such a simple request made the constable nervous. Was something wrong here?

'Oh yeh, it's Walter Plinge, sir.' His high-pitched voice was not dissimilar to that of Kenneth Williams in the Carry-On films.

Reggie took a step back to get a better look at him. He was not impressed. 'Is Mr Ormrod awake?'

Plinge looked blank. 'Who? Oh, you mean the chap in 'ere. Yeh, 'e okay. 'E opened his eyes when I went in a few minutes ago, but when 'e saw I was a policeman, 'e closed 'em again.'

'Thank you, Constable Plinge. Now, wait outside whilst I check on the patient.'

Reggie entered the room and saw Edgar Ormrod's prone body lying in bed. He knew immediately what he was looking at. It was unmistakeable. It is not just the colour- the face literally empties. He was dead.

'And then there were two.' A weary Reggie entered Sylvia's house.

'What do you mean?'

'And then there were two – two beneficiaries left to inherit seven million quid.'

She gasped. 'Oh no, does that mean Edgar Ormrod is dead?'

'Regrettably, yes it does.'

'Oh poor chap. And all along, we thought Edgar was behind the killings.'

'Yes, we got it wrong, didn't we? Poor old Edgar, he was a modest chap who actually had a good deal to be modest about,' Reggie mused, 'But I'm going to miss all the merriment and his infectious laugher.'

'Reggie, that's not nice. You shouldn't speak ill of the dead.'

'You're quite right, my angel, I take it all back, and will issue him with my posthumous apologies.'

'Good. Now tell me what happened. You've been at Bournemouth Hospital for over two hours.'

'I left as soon as I could, but I'm rather way-worn and footsore at the moment. After I had found the Angel of Death had inflicted her final judgment on Edgar, I immediately raised the alarm. But it took over half an hour before two uniformed police officers appeared.' Wearily, he shook his head. 'We live, m'dear, in an age when an order for a pizza gets to you before the police.'

'And what did the policemen do?'

'Well, I alerted them to the fact that an imposter, dressed as one of them, going by the name of Constable number 479, Walter Plinge, had been in Edgar Ormrod's room just before I entered. Unfortunately, their searches and questioning of staff failed to find any trace of him.'

'Not surprising, is it?' Sylvia sympathised. 'This Plinge guy had time to get away.'

'Indeed, he did. I refused to make a statement until Farthing turned up, but it was another fifteen minutes before he materialized, looking harassed and depressed. The officer he'd assigned to protect Edgar was still on his way.'

'That is bad,' Sylvia said. 'One would have thought his man would have been in situ well before that. Me thinks Farthing's Chief Constable will not be well pleased. Anyway, what did he do?'

'There wasn't much he could do except bring in a forensic team and take statements from virtually all the hospital staff, as well as several patients and visitors. It seems the CCTV camera on that corridor was out of order.'

'Typical. Do they know how Edgar died?' Sylvia asked.

'Not until the post-mortem, but Farthing mentioned some tinted marks around his throat which indicated he was probably strangled.'

'Do you think this man, Walter Plinge, did him in then?'

'Well, yes of course, he was there. It must have happened just before my arrival, but when I realised Edgar was a gonner, Plinge had done a runner.'

'Didn't you think at the time that Plinge looked odd - you said he was untidy and his uniform too tight. Wasn't that a clue he was a phony?'

'I'm sorry to report, my cherub, that my 20 x 20 hindsight failed me. However, on thinking about it, he did have the look of a fugitive – one who had just heard bloodhounds in the distance. I'm afraid my little grey cells let me down – I'm not in the same league as the infallible Inspector Clouseau.'

'Not Clouseau, Reggie – I've told you before, you mean Agatha Christie's Belgian sleuth, Hercule Poirot.'

'Do I? Oh yes, of course.'

'Oh, Reggie,' Sylvia sighed, 'If the police are right in believing the only motive for these deaths is Cressida Smythe's riches, then the killer must be either Gertrude Dogberry or the church ... well no, that's silly, not the church as such, but someone from the church who will gain in some way. Could it possibly be the venomous Reverend Marmaduke FitzPeter? At least seven million pounds would get his roof fixed.'

Reggie poured himself a measure of malt and sat in the armchair, removed his shoes, flexed his toes a couple of times, then gingerly placed his stockinged feet on a footstool.

'I didn't realise you had such big feet,' Sylvia laughed. 'You know what they say about men with big feet?'

'No, but I'm sure you're going to tell me.'

'Big feet ... big shoes.'

'Oh, very droll,' Reggie smiled. 'Let's us return to the murder mystery. I can't believe either of the two remaining beneficiaries could possibly be involved, and the police have got the motive wrong. Maybe it is nothing to do with the inheritance. In my calculation, there have now been eight suspicious deaths in the last month, with Cressida's being the first. The police haven't officially admitted that any of these deaths are murders. But some investigative reporter will latch onto it very soon and then the place will be swarming with television cameras and all their entourage.'

'Yes, I agree.' Sylvia poured herself a glass of wine. 'Maybe there is a different motive because I also can't believe FitzPeter is a mass murderer. And Gertrude's fear of being next on the list seemed real to me.'

'Oh, I forgot to tell you. Farthing told me FitzPeter was in Chichester at a seminar all the time, from when the clapper felled Edgar to his subsequent death, which rules him out.'

Their conversation was interrupted by a commotion outside the house, followed by the front doorbell. When Sylvia opened it, a flushed and out of breath Gertrude Dogberry pushed her way in, slamming the door behind her. 'I'm being followed,' she cried. 'They're after me. Please Reggie, will you go out and stop them.'

Seeing the state Gertrude was in, Reggie eased himself out of the chair. 'Who's after you? Man, woman or beast, alone or in groups?'

'A man – there may be two, followed me from the bus stop. Quick Reggie, do something.'

Taking a deep breath, Reggie gently pulled the door open, and stepped out onto the drive. It was a dark evening, with a full moon peeping through light cloud. Shady Grove had very few streetlights, so the chances of seeing any villain were slim. Looking in both directions, he couldn't see anyone.

Next door, Grace Pluck opened her door and walked down her drive. 'What's happening, what's all the noise?' She was wearing an exceptionally large white tent-like nightdress, reminding Reggie of the Jungfrau in moonlight.

'Nothing to concern you, Mrs Pluck, why don't you ...'

The first shot thundered in the still evening air, alongside a flash from the opposite side of the road. A long, silent moment of shock followed, then a frantic high-pitched scream. The second shot silenced the scream.

The normally quiet Shady Grove neighbourhood rapidly became a scene of chaos. Flashing blue lights coupled with shrill sirens echoed down the street and into every house, bringing inquisitive residents out in their droves, in many cases, not before recording *Strictly Come Dancing*. They were joined by the first flush of newspaper reporters, as though they had been stationed at the end of the road waiting for something to happen. Official blue and white tape cordoned off houses on both sides of the road.

A tent had been erected over the prone body of Mrs Grace Pluck. The police photographer, a gnarled, grey-haired Scotsman, wearing a tartan kilt, received raucous wolf-whistles from some of his colleagues – he was not amused. He'd been ordered away from a clan reunion. His flashing camera added to the sense of disorder. Other officers, looking like aliens in their forensic suits, grew in number by the minute, like bees buzzing between the tent and the house.

Other officers were going from door-to-door on both sides of Shady Grove, in the hope that someone had information on the incident.

One resident, Mr Norman Holehouse from number 16, known locally as Norman the moron, thought he was witnessing a TV police drama. Still wearing slippers, he excitedly went round, thrusting a pen and paper into the faces of those he thought were actors, asking for autographs.

Reggie and Sylvia sat in the kitchen of number 28 with a uniformed D I Farthing, accompanied by a note-taking Constable Gladys Slocock, an attractive young woman with soft blonde curls around her elfin face. Sylvia, Farthing and Slocock held mugs of tea, whilst Reggie had a glass of whisky. Earlier, at the first sound of gunfire, a frightened Gertrude Dogberry had rushed upstairs locking herself in the back bedroom. As the police hadn't asked to search the house, Reggie and Sylvia did not reveal her presence.

'I'll go over it once again, sir,' Farthing drummed his fingers on the table. 'You heard a disturbance in the street at about 20.50 hours this evening.'

'That is correct, Inspector.'

'And this disturbance, indistinct as it was, sounded like at least two people arguing or possibly squabbling, but you were unable to distinguish whether the voices were male or female.'

Reggie nodded his agreement, before quenching his thirst from his glass.

Farthing continued. 'Thus alerted, you then opened the front door and walked a few yards down the drive, at which point all was quiet. You did not see anybody in the street.' As he was speaking, Constable Slocock busily took notes in her notebook.

'You are entirely spot on, Inspector.'

After taking a sip from his mug, Farthing continued. 'You say that within a few seconds of leaving these premises, the next-door neighbour, one Mrs Grace Pluck, came out demanding to know what the commotion was about. Have I got it right, sir?'

'You have indeed, Inspector, that is exactly as it happened.'

He gave a slight cough to clear his throat. 'As Mrs Pluck finished speaking to you, the first gunshot came from the other side of the road ... you believed from the front garden of number 33. You saw a flash from there. It was then that Mrs Pluck gave, in your words, sir, a loud ululation, which translated by Constable Slocock means a loud scream. Is that correct, sir?'

'Well done Constable Slocock,' Reggie smiled. 'You are a credit to the English education system. And yes, Inspector, that is correct.'

Slocock was about to acknowledge Reggie's compliment when she gave a startled cry, looked at her watch and cried. 'Oh shit, I left a chicken in the oven.'

Farthing gave her a withering scowl. 'That is not police business, Constable. Kindly return to your notes.'

'But it'll set fire to the house,' she argued. 'I only live three streets away.'

'Then I'll alert the fire brigade, won't I? Now kindly resume your duties.'

A chastised Constable huffed and did as she was told.

Farthing turned back to face Reggie. 'Now sir, where were we? Ah yes. Mrs Pluck's loud scream was quickly followed by a second gunshot from the same direction, which had the effect of silencing the lady. Now sir, is there anything else you want to add?'

'What do you mean?'

'I mean have you left any details out – maybe something slipped your mind.'

'My dear Inspector, let me assure you, absolutely nothing has slipped my mind.'

'Er ... well, thank you, sir. Now, what did you do after the second shot?'

'I immediately went to see if I could be of help to Mrs Pluck.'

'What, even though a gunman was on the loose, firing shots in your direction. Didn't you think of taking cover.'

Reggie bristled. 'No, I did not. A lady had been shot so I ran to give what assistance I could – that is what the English do, Inspector. The care and welfare of our fellow man, or in this case, woman, has always been attributed to the peoples of these islands, and recognised as such around the world. Therefore, my own safety was of no matter.'

Farthing rolled his eyes and sighed.

'Anything else, Inspector,' Reggie asked.

'And did you?'

'Did I what?'

'Did you attend to the lady? See if she was still alive.'

'There was nothing I could do as half her head was missing.'

'Oh, yes of course. And that's when you called 999.'

Sylvia butted in. 'No Inspector, I did that as soon as I heard the first shot.'

'I see. Thank you for that, Mrs Makepeace. Would you, or Mr Grosvenor Smythe know of a reason why anybody would want to kill Mrs Pluck? She is your neighbour after all.'

'But, as you know,' Reggie said, 'she was the personal secretary of Edgar Ormrod who was murdered only yesterday. I would hazard a guess that there may be a link.'

'We've already thought of that, sir,' Farthing gave the impression that he was ahead of events. 'Mr Ormrod's house and office are currently being searched, and our forensic officers are searching Mrs Pluck's house. Now then, Mrs Makepeace, would you mind if my officers checked your house and garden to see if there is any trace of the killer – it's just a formality of course.'

Sylvia gave Reggie a nervous look. Before she could answer, a constable entered through the open front door. 'Excuse me Guv, but I thought you should know that TV cameras have arrived and they're asking for a statement.'

'Damn their bloody hides,' Farthing cursed. 'This'll open a can of worms.' Placing his Inspector's hat on, he said, 'Okay Constable, I'm coming now.'

'Well now,' Sylvia said as the door closed. 'You know what that means, don't you?'

'Go on,' Reggie nodded.

'It definitely rules Gertrude out of the frame. She was cowering upstairs when Grace was murdered. It's not her. That only leaves the church.'

'Unlikely, m'dear. There must be another explanation. I need a drink.'

Pouring a generous measure into his glass, they heard a fire engine racing to a nearby fire.

CHAPTER FORTY-EIGHT

It was well after midnight before the police left Shady Grove, leaving just one officer stationed outside Grace Pluck's house. Before the exodus, Farthing had told them that he and the team would be back in the morning to continue searching Grace's house and also the nearby gardens. For the next two to three days, the area around their house would remain cordoned off but residents would have access as usual. Reggie's Rolls Royce could remain parked on Sylvia's driveway.

Gertrude Dogberry only ventured downstairs when they'd all gone. 'Would you mind if I stay the night? I'm sorry to be a burden but ... well, I dare not go out now. The police officer may spot me and, well ... bloody hell, the killer may still be out there.'

'Yes, of course you can stay,' there was a noticeable catch in Sylvia's throat. 'Poor Grace, I've known her for over twenty years and being shot like that is terrible.' She wiped a few tears from her face.

Reggie hurried to her side and held her close. 'It's incredibly sad, m'dear. Grace Pluck, and all the others. You've stood up remarkably well the past few weeks with so many of the people you know having been terminated.'

'Thank you, Reggie, – you're my rock.'

Feeling drained, it was mutually agreed that they would wait until morning to talk anymore of the day's events.

After a restless night, Reggie and Sylvia rose at seven o'clock to get tea and breakfast. Within a few minutes of bacon frying, a weary-looking Gertrude appeared.

'Could I have some of that, I'm starving? I haven't eaten since yesterday morning.'

Sylvia assured her there was plenty, and all three breakfasted together. After putting the dishes and pans in the dishwasher, they went through to the living room.

'For reasons I'm not too happy about,' Reggie spoke in a low voice, 'I failed to tell the authorities about your arrival yesterday, or that you were being followed by one of two men. This, I will have to rectify within the next hour, otherwise slings and arrows, whips and scorns et al, will be hurled in my direction. You do understand that don't you?'

She laughed. 'Me thinks, sir, you misquote and missed out the *outrageous fortune* bit.'

'Ah,' Reggie beamed. 'Your knowledge of Hamlet is to be applauded. Misquotation is, in fact, the pride and privilege of the learned. A widely-read man never quotes accurately for the obvious reason that others will assume he has read too widely.'

Gertrude frowned and Sylvia sighed deeply. 'I think you may have lost me there, Reggie.

Of course you must inform the police,' Gertrude gently placed her hand on his arm. Looking at Sylvia, she added, 'And thank you both once again. If it's alright with you, I'll wait here until D I Farthing arrives.'

'A cautionary note if I may?' Reggie said. 'I have my doubts about Farthing's abilities and what to tell him. It is best policy, therefore, to speak the truth – unless, of course, you are an exceptionally good liar.'

Gertrude shook her head. 'I'll bear that in mind. I'm still frightened and cannot help thinking that I was the target last night, not Grace Pluck. One thing that's certain is that Edgar Ormrod was directly involved with everything that happened – that's from when Cressida first got pregnant up to the present. And throughout all that time, Grace Pluck was his secretary, so she would probably have known the lot. But why, oh why, was she killed?'

'Why indeed?' Reggie had a moody expression on his face. 'By the way, out of curiosity, where were you going when you got off the bus in Ringwood? Were you planning to come here?'

'Yes, I just wanted confirmation on how and why Edgar was killed. All along, I have thought he held most of the answers and I was hoping he'd passed them onto you. With regards to being chased, I didn't actually see the men's faces - just shapes and shadows. I wasn't sure at first if they were following me, but when I picked up the pace and started to run, they ran as well.'

'That's pretty conclusive,' Reggie said. 'But going back to Edgar, the first time I went to see him in the hospital, he did reveal a few things of which you may be unaware. He was going to tell me much more on my next visit, but, of course, he was strangled by a police imposter before he could do so. Even from the grave, Edgar is still with us – in a way.'

'Yes, he is,' Gertrude agreed. 'So, what can you tell me that's new?'

Reggie stroked his chin in thought, uncertain in what order to divulge his information. 'I'll start with this. A few days ago, the dead body of a woman was found semi-immersed in a barrel of Dorset Best Bitter. Edgar identified the body and told the police it was you. Did you know about that?'

'What,' she shouted. 'In a barrel of beer! Who on earth was it then, and why would Edgar lie?'

'Oh dear,' Sylvia went and put her arm around Gertrude's shoulder. 'Don't you know?'

'What are you on about – know what?'

'The body in the morgue was your twin.' Sylvia was expecting a startled reaction, but all Gertrude said was, 'So I had a sister.'

'You were born at about five o'clock in the afternoon on a Friday,' Sylvia said. 'It wasn't until almost a day later, the midwife realised another baby was on its way. It seems these things can happen. It was a girl. Remember, because of the subterfuge in pretending Stella was the mother, they did not use the services of a doctor or hospital at any time, only using Fran Fringe, the midwife.'

Speechless, Gertrude buried her face in her hands, rubbed it hard and looked up.

Reggie tried to comfort her. 'By the time the second baby was born, Stella and Jacob had already left with you. They didn't know Cressida hadn't finished. And as far as Edgar knew, Stella was never told about the second baby.'

'Oh my God,' Gertrude sank back in the chair. 'So, who is ... er was my twin? She must have been murdered by someone who thought she was me.'

'I think you're right. However, according to Edgar, because no doctor was involved, and neither the midwife nor Cressida knew quite what was happening, the second baby was delivered deprived of oxygen. She was handicapped. Fran Fringe felt all the guilt, thinking it was her fault. She kept the baby and looked after her all her life. Being handicapped, she never went to school or mixed with other children. Fran Fringe died two years ago.'

'But how's that possible?'

'Edgar wasn't sure. His only contact with Miss Fringe was the occasional letter. Now whether that is true or not we'll never know. Just what Cressida knew about the second baby was never discussed. He thinks she deliberately forgot about her.'

'So, all my life, I had a twin sister, oh – my – God.'

Awaiting the arrival of D I Farthing and the team of the forensic experts, Sylvia tried her best to ease Gertrude's stress.

'And she died in such a horrible way,' Gertrude sobbed. 'Who would kill a woman in such a barbaric manner, and a handicapped woman at that?'

Words seemed to elude Reggie, which was rare. 'Who indeed?' he eventually replied. 'I'm afraid the advancement of civilization means that evil perpetrators are continuing to find new ways of killing mortal souls like ourselves.'

Whether Gertrude listened to Reggie's homily was unclear. 'It's obvious Edgar Ormrod knew and, of course, Cressida. It's strange though.'

'What is?'

'As a child, like many children, I had an invisible friend. I called her Sadie. We played pretend games with dolls and one day - I was eighteen at the time, there was a fair in Lyndhurst, and I saw a clairvoyant's booth, Madam Rose. I went in, for a bit of a laugh, if I'm honest. As I placed my hands in hers, Madam Rose closed her eyes, and gave this beautiful smile – I can see it now. Then nodding a couple of times, she said I had a twin sister. I told her she was wrong, but she wouldn't have it. Still smiling, she told me that when the time was right, I should ask my mother about my twin sister.'

'Good heavens,' Sylvia said.

'But Madam Rose was right, wasn't she?' She took a deep breath. 'But it's too late now. The bastard thought it was me; to get his hands on the seven million pounds?'

'That, my dear, we can only guess,' Reggie said. 'Once the killer is caught and interrogated, the police may be able to find an answer to that question, as well as solving all the other deaths.'

'Solving them or not,' Gertrude said. 'I'm frightened that I'll be next. Someone out there wants me dead. I feel like hiding. I might even change my name again.'

'Oh come, come now, chin up old girl,' said Reggie, not pandering to defeatism. 'You must be resolute. Remember my dear, you have Grosvenor Smythe blood flowing vigorously through your veins. Over the centuries, we British have evolved a world class system of tradition and virtues of our own, which have seen us through difficult times in our past and will provide the best route to better times in the future. And the future, as they say, lasts for an awfully long time.'

'I'll do my best,' she murmured. The space between the two cousins trembled slightly, but not enough for an embrace.

'Jolly good show,' Reggie beamed. 'However, investigative journalists, aka the scum of the earth, will have a field day over Grace's horrific death. If any of us is cornered by them, we say absolutely nothing. Because if you do say anything at all, it will be twisted to make a sensational headline.'

'You're right, Reggie,' Gertrude said. 'But I'm hoping they, the media that is, won't know who I am or why I'm here.'

'Let's hope not,' Sylvia looked at her watch. 'It's almost nine o'clock. I thought Farthing would have been here by now.'

'Yes, so did I,' Reggie said. 'He has all the virtues I dislike and none of the vices I admire, and he'll be under severe pressure to get a quick result, or he'll be replaced.'

The front doorbell rang. 'Ah, that'll be him,' Sylvia hurried to let him in.'

'Ah, *hewwo Sywvia*.' It was Mr Lee. 'You *vewy popuwar wady* so many person here.' He pointed to the throng who were obediently standing behind the police cordon tape. 'I come see *Weggie*.' A dozen cameras flashed, and a television camera focused on Mr Lee, who waved at them, grinning from ear to ear.

'But how did you get here – to the door?' Sylvia asked.

'Oo, it *vewy* easy,' he squeaked. 'I just *wift bwue* and white tape, walk under, and I here. *Vewy* easy. Is *Weggie* in?'

'But you're not supposed to ... it's a police cordon. Oh, it doesn't matter.'

'It nice see again, *Sywvia*,' Mr Lee followed her into the living room.

'*Hewo Weggie*,' Mr Lee gave a big smile. '*Sywvia a vewy popuwar wady*.'

'Indeed, she is, Mr Lee,' he smiled as they shook hands. 'Mr Lee, I'd like you to meet my cousin, Miss Gertrude Dogberry.'

'Oooo,' Lee gave his usual oriental cry, followed by a deep bow. 'I not know you have cousin. *Hewo Weggie*-cousin. My name *Ee su won*,' he piped and bowed again. 'I *fwiend Weggie*.'

Gertrude stood open-mouthed as the tiny Asian man straightened up, only coming up to her chest. 'Hello Mr Lee,' was all she managed.

'*Weggie and Sywvia*, I come ... and I go.'

'Er right,' Reggie responded. 'I didn't know you were back in Ringwood. But now you say you are going again.'

'Ah, yes. We go now. Mrs Kim had big *quawel* with massage *pawlour*. They keep her money. So we come back to *cowwect*. An eagle does not catch *fwies*.'

After a long silence, Reggie asked, 'Have you got all her money.'

He grinned. 'Oh yes, we *cowwect* it all. We have saying in my *countwy*.'

Reggie sighed. 'And I can't wait to hear it,' he mumbled sarcastically.

'We say: if bad *peoples'ses* take not belong them, we call *spiwit dwagon* and snake *bwood* power. It make bad *peoples'ses* vomit money and jewels to good *peoples'ses*. You have same saying in this *countwy*?'

Shaking his head, Reggie replied. 'No, not quite, Lee. We say, "revenge is sweet".'

Mr Lee frowned. 'Oo, that *vewy* small saying.' Thinking for a second, he put on a smile and added, 'But a *vewy* good saying – *wevenge* is sweet like sugar – it good.'

Their verbal nonsense was interrupted by the front doorbell. 'Ah,' Mr Lee said, 'it Mrs Kim for me. We go now.'

It was not Mrs Kim but D I Farthing and Constable Slocock. Mr Lee bowed deeply. 'Ah Inspector Farting, we meet again.'

'It's not er ... It's F a r t h i n g, he spelt it out slowly, with a belligerent look in his eye.'

'That's what I say,' Mr Lee said, taking umbrage. 'Farting.'

Irritably, the Inspector turned to Reggie. 'Is there a room we could use? There's a couple of things I want to tell you ... in private.'

'Yes, of course Inspector. But first I'd like to introduce you to this lady,' he nodded in Gertrude's direction. 'Inspector Farthing, I'd like you to meet Miss Gertrude Dogberry.'

'Good heavens!' Farthing stared disbelievingly at her. 'You're Gertrude Dogberry.' A piqued Farthing turned his back on Reggie. 'My colleagues in the Devonshire Constabulary are actively trying to find you, Miss Dogberry. You're listed as a missing person. What are you doing here?'

'I came to see you, Inspector, especially after the death of Edgar Ormrod.'

'I see, and why Edgar Ormrod specifically?'

'Because he was privy to all matters relating to Cressida Smythe and ...' she was interrupted by the front doorbell. Farthing frowned at yet another disruption.

'Ah, it Mrs Kim for me.' Mr Lee, standing amongst them unobserved, had only half-understood the exchanges that had taken place, but this did not stop him piping in. 'Inspector *Farting* when you catch *kiwwer of peoples-es?* Too many *peoples-es* die.'

Glaring down at him, Farthing's fists involuntarily clenched. Oh, how he would love to indulge in a bit of good old police brutality on this annoying little man.

'Okay, you no answer.' Mr Lee quipped. Then, one by one, he gave a series of bows to the others. 'I *sowwy* but I go now. Be *cwever powiceman Farting*, and catch *kiwwer*.' With a half-cheeky smile, he turned to face Sylvia. 'See you *water, Weggie and Sywvia*.'

'Goodbye Mr Lee and thank you for passing by.' For Farthing's benefit, Reggie kept a straight face. 'We hope to be in Kingston next week and we'll see you then.' And with that, the tiny man gave a final bow and left unmolested.

'Now, where were we?' Farthing exhaled deeply; his concentration interrupted. 'Ah yes, Miss Dogberry,' dragging his wayward brain back to the reason he was there. 'Yes, Miss Dogberry, let me explain something. Because of Mr Grosvenor Smythe,' he almost spat out the name, 'and his relationship with the late Cressida Smythe, he has been made aware of the many unfortunate deaths that have occurred over the past month and, in this regard, I have held confidential discussions with him and Mrs Makepeace. And, because of your connection with the late lady, I think we could include you in these discussions. Can you assure me that nothing whatsoever will be revealed outside these four walls?'

'Yes, of course, Inspector.'

'Good, and especially to the media,' Farthing nodded sagely. 'We live in a shameless age when people readily reveal information to the media, even intimate secrets, in the hope of getting their faces in the press or on television. Let us start then. Now, tell me again, Miss Dogberry, why did you come here?'

Gertrude gave her version of the previous evening's events. The story came out pat which made Farthing think it was just a little bit too well rehearsed. 'I think those shots were meant for me,' she whimpered.

'Really. And where were you last night when the police arrived?'

'I hid upstairs, here. I was traumatised – uncontrollable,' she exaggerated, hoping he'd believe her. 'I begged Reggie and Sylvia not to tell anyone where I was.' She did her best to appear a poor, timid victim.

Whether Farthing was taken in by her performance was unclear, but he saved his stern rebuke for Reggie. 'I'm holding you responsible here, Grosvenor Smythe, you should have informed me last night – we've lost twelve hours of investigation.'

Reggie nodded solemnly. 'You're quite right, Inspector. I humbly apologise.'

'Oh!' An apology was the last thing Farthing expected. 'Now Miss Dogberry, why did you think those shots were meant for you?'

'Because of the inheritance. I'm due to get the bulk of Cressida Smythe's estate.'

'Inspector,' Sylvia said. 'Even in the dark, it would be hard to mistake Grace Pluck for Gertrude. She was such a, you know, a large lady.'

'Indeed, but it's quite possible that Mrs Pluck actually was the target. Please don't repeat any of this, but going through some files in her house, and others in Ormrod's office, it's becoming clear that they were in cahoots together. Without beating about the bush, they were blackmailing someone.'

'My God. Who?'

'We aren't sure.'

'But surely that person must somehow be linked with all these deaths and the inheritance,' Reggie said.

'For the time being, it's no comment,' Farthing replied. 'But I do have some other information for you. You know Reverend FitzPeter was a curate here thirty years ago, only returning here three years ago.'

'Yes, we know that,' Sylvia said.

'We've now discovered that during his long absence, he acted as Chaplain at the Frankland High Security Prison in Durham. It housed many hardened criminals as well as political deviants.'

'All that time?' Reggie questioned. 'But does that have any bearing on what's happened here for the past month?'

Farthing remained tight lipped. 'The other piece of news is that the lady you saw last week in the morgue has been identified as Felicity Fringe, who used to live in Norfolk. It appears she was handicapped and was looked after by her mother until she died two years ago. Since then, she has been in the care of Social Services. We are currently trying to ascertain how she came to meet her unfortunate end here in Ringwood.'

Gertrude sighed, staring at her hands and spoke very quietly. 'I have to tell you, Inspector, that I've just been informed that Felicity Fringe was my twin sister.'

'Oh my God.' D I Farthing raised his eyebrows as if he could scarcely believe of yet another twist in the tale.

CHAPTER FORTY-NINE

Sylvia had just finished preparing breakfast when there was a knock on the door. A uniformed constable informed her that the police cordon was to be removed forthwith, and that Mrs Pluck's house had been sealed off until further notice. Touching his helmet in the form of a salute, he apologised for any inconvenience over the past two days.

As soon as he'd gone , Gertrude came downstairs and entered the kitchen. 'When the coast is clear, I'll be on my way.' She'd covered her normally brown hair with a blonde, shoulder-length wig, and wore a short, green dress, blue tinted tights and white trainers.

'You've certainly done a good job with your disguise, I hardly recognised you.' Reggie thought she looked a bit tarty but refrained from saying so. 'But I'm sure Sylvia won't mind if you want to stay longer.'

'That's kind of you both but I need to disappear again.' She peeked through the front window without disturbing the curtains. 'The killer knows I'm here. He'll try again, I'm sure of it.'

'But where will you go that's safe?'

She smiled. 'I have a good friend, single lady, who lives in a secure house in the New Forest not too far from here. It is so remote that she's installed every conceivable hi-tech security device known to man – not because of me, of course, but for herself as it's remote. I've stayed with her on several occasions.'

'But didn't you promise Farthing you'll be at Lyndhurst Police Station this afternoon to make a statement.'

'I lied. It would be crazy to leave myself open to the killer if I did.'

'Before you go,' Reggie said, 'who do you think Edgar Ormrod and Mrs Pluck were blackmailing?'

Gertrude shook her head. 'I've no idea, but it adds another dimension to the whole sorry business, doesn't it? But if the blackmail was to do with the inheritance, well, except for me, all the other beneficiaries are dead.'

'But there is still one more beneficiary, the church,' Sylvia reminded her.

'Yes, I know, but it's difficult to take that seriously. I'll leave this mobile phone with you,' she took one out of her bag. 'It's all set up. Only use it to call me for anything really important. Otherwise, I'll contact you.'

Sylvia gave a short laugh. 'How many phones do you have? We have had at least four from you. You must be the shareholders' best friend.'

'I probably am,' she acknowledged, 'But they're cheap and the best way of communicating without being traced.'

Sylvia nodded. 'Now, if you want to leave without being seen, use the back door. There is a gate in the left-hand corner of the garden which leads to a narrow pathway coming out at the end of North Poulner Road. There's a bus stop there.' She checked her watch. 'If you leave now, you won't have to wait long. Anyway, dressed like that I don't think anyone would recognise you.'

'I hope you're right.'

The phone rang.

Gertrude stiffened. 'If it's to do with me ...' she gestured with her hands not to give her away.

'No, it's okay,' Sylvia reassured her, 'It's Chester, his name is on *caller display*.' She picked up the receiver.

Giving them both a wave, Gertrude left by the back door.

'Hello Ches, everything alright?' She listened to his reply, nodding her head a couple of times. 'Erm, no, that'll be fine. We'll see you in half an hour and I'll have tea ready.' Replacing the phone, she looked at Reggie. 'Ches is coming round with Pandora, he has some news for us. Should we be alarmed?'

Chester looked at them quizzically as he and Pandora let themselves in. 'We hear poor Grace Pluck was shot dead last night. My God, the whole of Ringwood is all of a buzz. We've just come from Greyfriars and it's the only topic of conversation at the moment. A bit scary, though, isn't it?'

'Yes Ches, it certainly is, especially as Gertrude Dogberry was here at the time. She believes the gunman was after her and not Grace.'

'My godfathers!' Chester exclaimed. 'When will all this end?'

Sylvia sighed. 'Surely it must be soon. All the people due to inherit Cressida's bounteous wealth – the suspects – are rapidly being bumped off. There's only Gertrude left, and we can vouch she did not kill Grace.'

An apprehensive Pandora looked as if she had lost even more weight since they last saw her. They sat at the kitchen table drinking tea and munching hobnobs. Sylvia recounted the whole saga from the moment an out-of-breath Gertrude arrived, right up to when she had left to go into hiding again, still in fear of her life.

'Poor Gertrude. The police can't seem to stop these killings and arrest the evil-doer.'

'Apparently not,' Reggie said. 'And as you can imagine, your friend Farthing is getting rather desperate. But Ches, my boy, all that can wait for the time being - you told your mother you had some news for her ... am I included in this?'

'Of course you are; you are my father, after all. The news is actually about Pandora – she's moving to Edinburgh. She's finished a series of operations and got the all clear.'

'Oh, er ... 'Sylvia faltered. 'You hadn't told me about the operations. But if you have got the all clear, Pandora, then that's particularly good news.'

Reggie joined in. 'And from what I can see, young lady, you need building up – put some flesh on your bones. And Edinburgh's the place for some jolly good porridge coupled with a generous measure of the spirit of Bonnie Scotland. So, what laid you low in the first place?'

Pandora looked at Chester to reply for her.

'It's a long story, Father, but I'll leave the details for now, other than the fact that the corrective surgery is over, and Pandora is now officially female.'

There was a moment's awkward silence. Sylvia frantically mimed *sealed lips* to Reggie and held her breath.

Her efforts came to nought as Reggie exclaimed, 'Officially female? By the Lord Harry, what on earth were you *officially* before?'

'Reggie!' A furious stare came back at him from Sylvia. 'Don't be so intrusive. What happened to Pandora is a private matter and I'm happy for her.'

Duly reprimanded, Reggie gave a humble apology. 'It's just that I ...' he started to say before Sylvia yelled, 'Reggie, not another word.' This time, banging her fist on the table.

Chester gave a wry smile. 'That didn't go down well, I'm afraid, Father - you're in the doghouse.'

'Indeed, I am, my boy and no doubt, my punishment awaits.'

Chester laughed, 'But apart from this *contretemps* – which I'll pass over for the moment. Are you going to live in Kingston or stay here?'

'It will probably be Kingston,' Sylvia replied, 'But not just yet. It's difficult to leave before Cressida's death is resolved – and all the other related killings.'

'Of course, I understand. I only ask because ...' he stopped speaking as two loud bangs came from around the front window. 'Hang on,' Chester said, 'What the hell is that? I'll go and check.'

Opening the front door, he rushed out and yelled, 'Hey you, what are you doing?' Inside, they could hear a muttered exchange. Then they heard Chester say, 'Oh, I'm sorry, you're a police officer.'

Reggie was on his feet in a flash. He'd been fooled once before and was not going to let the same thing to happen again. Storming out, he recognised the imposter immediately, it was the same Walter Plinge. He even wore the same ill-fitting uniform. On seeing Reggie, an alarmed Plinge pulled a gun out of his pocket, holding it out threateningly. A trickle of sweat ran like an ant from his brow down towards his frayed collar. 'Send Gertrude Dogberry out or I'll use this.' Concentrating on Reggie, he turned his back on Chester. Big mistake. Chester, jaw trembling with rage, picked up a hefty rockery stone from the edge of the path, bringing it down with all his might onto the gunman's head. Plinge's eyes glazed over as he sank to the ground, dropping the gun as he did so.

Reggie immediately picked it up. 'Oh, jolly good show, Ches my boy. Bloody marvellous.'

Sylvia came to the door. 'I've called the police, they're on their way.'

'Thank you m'dear,' Reggie calmly replied, knowing that he and Chester had the upper hand.

Groaning, Plinge slowly picked himself up, gingerly rubbing his head. 'Ow, me fuckin' 'ead.'

As if she was used to events like this, Sylvia returned carrying a role of gaffer tape and, with Chester's help, bound an unresisting Plinge's hands behind his back.

'So, Mr Walter Plinge, I assume you were sent here to kill Gertrude Dogberry.'

The man looked around for a way of escape. 'Oh fuck,' he muttered.

'Tell us who sent you, or we'll invoke the Hammer of Thor on you.'

He stared blankly at Reggie but said nothing.

'Well then, Mr Plinge, let me explain something to you so you'll be crystal clear on what's going to happen now.' Reggie gave the impression that he was enjoying himself. 'Unencumbered as I am, unlike our loyal guardians in the police service, I'll take the opportunity to quickly use my

SAS-trained torture skills to elicit the name of the person who sent you to kill Miss Dogberry.'

'Eh?'

'Sylvia, my dear, kindly go and get a hammer and pliers – bolt cutters if you have any, and with Chester's assistance, I will start removing Plinge's fingers, one by one, before starting on his genitals. During my training, I mastered the art of inflicting maximum pain, and this method always works. You hear that, Plinge? It always works.'

'Er, 'ang about guv, you can't do that.'

Reggie gave a smile. 'Not only can I do it, Plinge, but it will give me huge enjoyment at the same time. Now, as the transphalangeal amputations may result in getting a spot or two of blood on my best suit - and we wouldn't want that now, would we? I would like you to tell me the name of the person who sent you. It's your last chance.'

A rather worried looking Sylvia arrived with a selection of tools, including a large pair of wire cutters. 'You're not going to use them, are you Reggie?' she whispered.

'Oh yes I am, m'dear, but you may want to step inside as the sight of what I'm about to do may trouble you. Now then, Ches, hold his right arm firmly and I'll start.' Reggie opened the cutters and placed them around Plinge's little finger. 'Here we go now, this little piggy ...'

'Don't, don't, Plinge screamed and struggled, genuine fear in his eyes. 'I'll tell you.'

'Oh dear, and I was just about to enjoy myself, Plinge. But go on, who sent you?'

'It were Jessie – you know, Jessica.'

'You pathetic creature - Jessica indeed.' Reggie tightened the grip on the pliers.

'Honest guv, as God's me witness,' he cringed and wet his trousers. 'It were Jessica.' Turning pale, he gasped, then hacked and choked like a cat trying to cough up a Brillo pad. He then fainted, dead eyes staring into space.

Just then, with a blaze of sirens and twirling blue lights, a police car came screaming to a halt outside the house.

CHAPTER FIFTY

'You've certainly brought heaps of excitement to Ringwood,' Chester gave Reggie a wicked grin. 'And Poulner in particular. Can it only be six weeks since you entered our lives, and a mass murderer began killing all and sundry?'

'It does seem a long time, doesn't it?' Reggie stood poised with a half empty bottle of *Ancestor* in his hand. 'Can I top you up, son ... and how about you, Pandora; you look as though a wee dram will bring some colour to your cheeks.'

'No thank you, Reggie,' Chester replied for them both. 'We must be on our way. It's all been very interesting though. When Farthing took Walter Plinge away, I thought he was on the point of smiling until, I guess, he realised that it was *we* who caught him and not the police. That obviously bugged him.'

'It did, but he jolly well should be pleased, catching old Plinge should be the major breakthrough he's painstakingly been waiting for since he came on the case.'

'Oh, now then, Reggie,' Sylvia chucked, 'You and the SAS - what was all that nonsense about using your SAS-torture techniques on Plinge. That wasn't true, was it?'

'Ah, you're right, it wasn't,' he acknowledged, 'I got a little confused. It was not the SAS but ... wait a minute, yes,

I remember, it was the SCS. That is right, the SCS – the Specials Croquet Society. And a vicious bunch they were – have your guts for garters at the drop of a hat.'

Rolling their eyes, Sylvia and Chester laughed in unison. 'Well, you had Plinge fooled. And who do you think this Jessie or Jessica is? At first, I thought he was joking, a bit of bravado on his part, but he wasn't joking – he thought you were serious about cutting his fingers off. So, when he said he'd been sent by Jessica, he meant it. So, who the hell is she?'

'I have no idea,' Reggie replied. 'Do you know anyone called Jessica?'

Even Pandora joined them in shaking her head.

Reggie puckered his brow. 'D I Farthing will no doubt be grilling Plinge about this but whether he'll give the game away i.e. become a stoolpigeon, is very unlikely. Unfortunately, the police can't use the SAS or even the SCS torture techniques - pity. Hardened criminals know they can get a lawyer and then "no comment" will be all he'll say.'

Helping Pandora rise from her chair, Chester said, 'We're going now, but be sure to let me know if you hear anything.'

'Of course we will, my love,' Sylvia kissed him on his cheek and then did the same to Pandora, who went rigid as she did so. Reggie shook Chester's hand and gave Pandora his version of a friendly wave.

'Now, what's the story on Pandora?'

'I think she's had a sex change, but I'll have to get confirmation from Ches. It's quite common these days.'

Reggie shook his head. 'Is that so? But what is Ches's relationship with the ... er, woman? Surely it can't be a sexual one.'

'I'm sure it isn't.'

'Now then, what do you suggest we do for the rest of the day?'

'Well, we did promise the Duke we'd let him know of any developments. We could go and see him and then I'll pop into Sainsbury's. Our bare cupboard needs re-stocking.'

CHAPTER FIFTY-ONE

Reggie parked the Rolls in a reserved space outside the church, placing the crested pennant on the front wing. 'You know, m'dear,' he mused as they approached the church, 'I always feel more religious on a sunshiny day.'

'I've never thought about it that way before, but yes,' she nodded, 'I take your point.'

Inside, the church was quiet, not a soul to be seen, until the noise of the Duke's unmistakeable sneeze came from near the pulpit. He came over carrying an empty collection plate. 'Ah, greetings to you both.' the Duke smiled. 'And to what do I owe the pleasure of your visit today?'

Reggie beamed, 'We have come, Padre, to bring you tidings of great joy which shall be to all residents. The police have, this morning, arrested the killer ... or to put it correctly, the alleged killer of Miss Grace Pluck and Mr Edgar Ormrod, and maybe one or two more poor souls.'

The Duke let out an audible gasp. 'Oh ... well, that's er ... wonderful news.'

'His name, that's if he was telling the truth of course, is Walter Plinge, who decked himself out in a fake policeman's outfit. He was looking for Gertrude Dogberry with the malicious intent to bump her off.'

'Oh dear, that's dreadful,' FitzPeter said solemnly. 'And did he actually erm ... as you put it, bump her off?'

'No, he didn't.'

'Oh,' the Duke's voice fell to a whisper. 'So does that mean this man – the killer, is now in police custody.'

'That's correct, but the other interesting thing was that he said that he'd been sent by a lady called Jessie or Jessica – a female mastermind, we assume.'

'Oh my God,' FitzPeter gasped, putting a hand to his mouth.

Reggie had never seen anyone change colour so fast.

With shaking hands, FitzPeter ran fingers through his hair, then hid his face behind his hands as though it was a bad dream.

Looking concerned, Sylvia asked, 'Are you alright, vicar? You look er ... upset.'

'Yes er ... no.' The muscles around his eyes began to twitch.

Sylvia tried her best to comfort him. 'There have been so many deaths in the past few weeks, and a lot of them suspicious. Anyway, we thought we'd let you know about the arrest.'

Looking stricken, FitzPeter glared wildly about, not appearing to focus on anything in particular. His total demeanour had changed, taking on a haunted look; sweat formed on his brow. A trademark sneeze followed. Mumbling something incoherent, he used a handkerchief to cover his nose and headed for the vestry. Shocked at the Duke's bizarre behaviour, Reggie took Sylvia by the hand and followed.

Wondering whether FitzPeter knew either Walter Plinge or the Jessica woman, he asked. 'Is there something you want to tell us, vicar?'

But FitzPeter had gone into a stupor. He fell to his knees, looked heavenward and prayed, his voice crackling with passion. 'Forgive me Father, for I know not what I've done.'

'And what, in God's name, have you done?' Reggie roared. 'Are you involved in these murders?'

Seemingly oblivious to their presence, FitzPeter's world had stopped turning on its axis - he stood paralysed. 'I'm Jessica,' he rambled, 'yes, Jessica, it's plan B now … plan B.' Frantically, he began to open desk drawers and cupboards, picking up various items and shoving them into a black leather briefcase. Inside one cupboard was a safe. With fumbling fingers, he managed to open it and took out three large wads of cash as well as what looked like two passports and a travel agent's ticket wallet. 'Plan B, yes,' he mumbled again.

'What in the blue-blazes are you doing?' Reggie demanded. 'For God's sake, get a grip on yourself.'

As though coming out of a trance, he looked up, surprised to see Reggie and Sylvia. His nostril flared and eyes bulged from their sockets. 'It'll be alright,' his breathing laboured. 'Yes, plan B.' Looking at them, he said, 'Why are you? … you have to stay here.' Picking up a bunch of keys, he picked up the briefcase and another bag from behind his desk, and ran to the vestry door, closing it behind him with a loud bang. They heard the lock being turned.

Taken by surprise, Reggie yelled, *Great balls of fire,* and with adrenaline pumping, ran to the door - it was well and truly locked. 'FitzPeter,' he bellowed, 'Open the ruddy door, don't be a bloody fool.' There was no reply.

'Can you break it down,' Sylvia cried. But seeing it was well constructed out of solid wood, realised it would be difficult.

Reggie shook his head. 'No, I need to phone the police – quickly. FitzPeter must be as guilty as sin and now wants to escape.' Patting his pockets for his phone he swore, 'Damn and blast, it's in your house. I left it on charge. Is yours working?'

'I didn't bring it. What shall we do?'

'I don't know. There's no point yelling – the church is empty and any sound we make wouldn't reach the street.'

Sylvia pointed to the desk. 'Look – the landline.'

'Of course,' Reggie grimaced. 'What's Farthing's number?'

CHAPTER FIFTY-TWO

It took more than fifteen frustrating minutes of being passed from one officer to another before Reggie was able to speak to a sergeant who actually listened. Briefly explaining what had happened, he demanded that D I Farthing be informed immediately. A further twelve minutes slipped by before a uniformed police constable forced open the vestry door.

On seeing the aristocratic appearance of a fuming Reggie and a distressed Sylvia, he saluted. 'Are you alright, sir and madam?'

'Constable,' Reggie answered through gritted teeth, 'Mrs Makepeace and I have been illegally incarcerated here for half an hour and no, we are not alright. Now then, Constable 404, have you caught the Reverend FitzPeter? He was trying to escape?'

Constable 404 looked blank. 'I don't know, sir. All I was told was to let you out of the vestry.'

'Give me your name, constable,'

'It's P C Trumble, sir.'

'So, Constable Trumble, get me D I Farthing on your radio ... now.'

'I erm ... am not authorised,' was as far as he got before Reggie exploded.

'Look here, Trumble, the Commissioner of Police has given me full authority over police matters regarding a multiple murder case, so do as I tell you. Understand?'

Believing Reggie's tale to be correct, Trumble only hesitated a moment before accepting Reggie's authority. Getting on his radio, it only took a few seconds before Reggie heard Farthing's voice. He snatched it from Trumble.

'Farthing, it's me, Grosvenor Smythe. Have you been told what's going on?'

'Only that you were locked in Ringwood church, and something about the vicar.'

'Right, then listen carefully. The Reverend FitzPeter is Jessica and behind the murders of Edgar Ormrod and Mrs Pluck. Now he's trying to escape.' Reggie knew this was not strictly correct, but he had to motivate Farthing somehow. 'That's why he locked Mrs Makepeace and me in the vestry. He's taken a couple of bags with him, a load of cash and two passports. He also had a travel agent's wallet. He's fleeing the country.'

'My God,' Farthing gasped. 'Are you sure about this ... the Reverend FitzPeter?'

'Of course, I'm damned sure.' He wanted to add some additional *in terrorem* but decided now was not the time. 'Put out a search for him now – top alert, and put-up roadblocks, and notify airports and coastguards or whatever you do. And do it now. Is that clear?'

'Now look here, Grosvenor Smythe, I don't take orders ... '

'Don't be a pathetic Pizzle, 'Reggie bellowed, 'It's FitzPeter – he's the murderer and trying to escape, so get cracking,' He immediately switched Trumble's radio off before Farthing could dither any further. Turning to Sylvia, 'What do you think? Where will FitzPeter go?'

'Aren't you going to leave it to Farthing? He should be in charge now.'

He shook his head. 'I don't see Farthing mobilising anything quickly enough. FitzPeter will be out of the country as quick as an eagle-winged rocket. We must take the initiative.'

'Well, if you're sure. The obvious place to start would be Bournemouth airport.'

'Yes, I think you're right. P C Trumble, you heard the inspector,' he bluffed, 'take us immediately to Bournemouth airport.'

The poor chap looked bamboozled. 'I don't think ...'

'You don't have to think, Trumble. I am giving you a clear order. Take Mrs Makepeace and myself to Bournemouth airport now and put your ruddy foot down. Got it?'

Wavering for a moment, he really wanted D I Farthing to confirm this, but one look at the defiant Grosvenor Smythe convinced him otherwise. The three of them got in the car. 'Now go, put your bloody siren on full blast and go like the wind. It's vital – utterly vital we get there quickly.'

Trumble, a frustrated racing enthusiast, threw caution to the wind and willingly accepted the challenge. With sirens blaring, he set off screeching around corners, weaving in and out of other traffic, pell-mell out of Ringwood onto the A31, then the A338 at the Ashley Heath roundabout. Encouraged to go even faster, he aggressively forced traffic out of the way, reaching the turn off for the airport in Hurn in less than five minutes, then another three minutes before screeching to a halt outside the departure terminal.

'Well done, officer, now quickly follow us inside and find the head of security. And by the way, from now on call me "Minister". I have full authority from the Commissioner of Police,' Reggie racked up even more lies. 'Now bring the security chappie to the departure desks.'

Trumble didn't know what to do. 'I could get in big trouble if ...'

'Nonsense,' Reggie bellowed. 'Fear is a reaction; courage is a decision. Now take courage and you will have my full support.' Reggie felt the hand of history on his shoulders and couldn't help putting on his Churchillian voice, *"We shall not fail or falter, Trumble, nor shall we weaken or tire"*. Now off you go.'

As Trumble scurried off, Reggie took Sylvia's arm and, staring straight ahead, magisterially marched through into the terminal, ignoring protesting people as they went. There were two check-in desks open; one of which was about to close. The other had a long queue waiting to be checked in. 'Foxy m'dear, you go to that desk – the one just closing. See if FitzPeter went through there, and officer Trumble and I will check this one. Now Trumble, do not look apprehensive, man, you're now a senior officer.'

'Yes sir, er Minister.'

Looking closely at everyone in the queue, it was clear that FitzPeter was not there. Marching to the front, Reggie tapped the desk with his cane and, in his most authoritative voice, spoke to the two check-in assistants, 'We have an emergency alert here, looking for an escaped prisoner who's trying to flee the country. I am Grosvenor Smythe, OBE, Minister of Police. Has a man called FitzPeter checked in at this desk?'

Reggie's presence was such that the people in the process of being checked willingly moved aside, and the check-in staff paused, unsure of what to make of this order. One of them said, 'I'm sorry, Minister, but I'll need authority ...'

'Stuff and nonsense. Out of the way.' Reggie, followed by Trumble, climbed over the scales and roughly took the passenger check-in data and looked down the list. There was no FitzPeter.

'Excuse me Minister. My name is Jones, Chief of Security. What's going on?'

'Excellent Chief Jones. An escaped murderer is trying to leave the country as we speak. Kindly use your powers to stop any flights leaving, until a full search has taken place. A further contingent of police, headed by Detective Inspector Farthing, is on their way but we must act now.'

'Yes sir, I'll get my men and we'll start here.'

'The escapee's name is FitzPeter. Medium height with black hair aged about fifty-five.'

Amongst the hullabaloo caused by a very eager Jones, Reggie suddenly heard Sylvia calling from the other desk – she was frantically waving at him. 'Over here, Reggie.'

'Come with me, Chief, my assistant may have something.' They went to join Sylvia.

'This is Claire Comfort,' Sylvia indicated the uniformed check-in assistant behind the desk. 'I asked if anyone had booked at the last minute – someone who paid cash for a ticket, and she said yes. A lady had done just that on the flight leaving now for Turkey.'

'But why tell me that? We want FitzPeter and not a woman.'

'Yes, I know, but Claire ... tell the Minister what she did.'

'Well, as she left the desk, she gave a strange sneeze – a sneeze with a bit extra on the end, like a hiccup.'

'Could it be? Of course, it must be him in disguise. What name was on his passport?'

'It was Miss Jessica Frankland.'

'Ha that's definitely him, Jessica and Frankland Jail. Where is he or she now?'

'He's already boarded - the gate's closed and it's just started to taxi to the runway.'

'What's his seat number?'

Clair Comfort admitted that the system had gone down. 'As there were thirty-two empty seats on the flight, we told him he could find his own seat.'

'Chief, radio the pilot to stop the plane and we will go and inspect the passengers. Our man, disguised as a woman, is onboard.'

'It'll be the control tower actually,' Chief Jones said. Suddenly feeling unsure, he asked, 'What authority do I have to stop and board a plane?'

'You have the Minister of Police's authority, quoting section 473 of the Home Security Act.' Reggie amazed himself sometimes, at how easy the lies flowed.

Nodding his acceptance, the Chief used his radio to order the control tower to stop flight 7040 to Turkey, and to be ready for steps to be placed by the plane's front entrance.

'Sylvia, my angel, you wait here for Farthing, and tell him what's happening.'

Reggie knew he had the rouse his troops, Chief Jones and P C Trumble. It was now or never. Taking a deep breath, he struck a pose and articulated clearly in his well-practised

Churchillian tone, 'Now then, you chaps, there is a tide in the affairs of men which, taken at the flood, leads to take the bull by the tail and to seize the day.'

Jones and Trumble knew they were in the presence of a true commander-in-chief and would follow him all the way.

'We blessed few have the opportunity to stop a mass murderer escaping. If we fail to act and he escapes to Turkey – and there is no extradition treaty with Turkey – then the shame will be ours, heads will roll, and we will forever be accursed. But if we catch him – and we will - the glory will be yours.'

Chest out and eyes glistening, Chief Jones marched them out onto the apron. The steps were being rolled out to the stationary plane.

The pilot met them at the door. 'I hope you know what you're doing,' he angrily shouted as Chief Jones led them up the steps.

'Of course we do,' he shouted back, waving his badge in the pilot's face, and forcibly led the way inside. He was enjoying himself. Power had gone to his head. 'Come Minister, show me the person to be removed.'

The pilot, muttering angrily under his breath led them slowly down the aisle. Reggie examined each face, men and women - the others followed behind. Reaching the back of the plane, there was no sign of FitzPeter.

'Where is the man?' the pilot asked belligerently.

Reggie was dumbstruck, and silently swore under his breath. Had he made a mistake - a monumental mistake? FitzPeter was nowhere to be seen. 'Ah, what about the lavatories?'

'I've checked - all empty,' a steward said.

The enormity of what he had done hit Reggie like a poleaxe. His lie upon lie was about to bite him on his backside. Nothing now could stop him being charged with such a multitude of offences, he would be behind bars for the rest of his life.

'Well then,' the pilot demanded, 'Where is he?'

Reggie was about to crumple when there was a loud sneeze followed by a hic, coming from a seat two rows from where they were standing. It was like music to Reggie's ears. Hiding under a long blonde wig, dressed as a woman and wearing lipstick was FitzPeter.

With Chief Jones holding one arm and P C Trumble the other, they marched FitzPeter into the terminal just as D I Farthing and two uniformed police officers came rushing in. Feeling on top of the world, Reggie gave a brief bow. 'He's all yours, Inspector. The murderer of Edgar Ormrod and Mrs Pluck.' Ignoring protests from Farthing and the assembled officers, Reggie was definitely not going to get involved in the fallout, and no-one was going to stop him. Taking Sylvia's arm, they went straight to the taxi rank. Just as the door was about to close, a gigantic sneeze followed by a hic was all they heard.

CHAPTER FIFTY-THREE

Mid-October - a change of season. It had started to feel like autumn and under a threatening sky, strong winds blew the first leaves off trees, sending them scurrying down the road and pathways. Reggie and Sylvia hurried back to the flat following a brief shopping expedition. The streets and those who walked them, looked grey and dreary. 'It's that time of year of gloom,' Sylvia said, unzipping the hood of her coat.

'Cheer up, old gal.' Standing in the foyer, Reggie helped her out of her heavy overcoat. 'Just think what awaits us upstairs in our sanctuary.'

She laughed. 'I know what awaits you, but for me, it'll be a nice cup of tea.'

'I wonder what Aida has prepared for lunch today?' Reggie gave her a kiss in the lift as they ascended to their penthouse.

'Well, my lover, I can tell you it's fish. Fish of all types from shell and line, from which Aida is presently creating another of her Asian masterpieces.'

'I hope she's making her special chips again, they're top-notch.'

'And with Aida at the helm, that's what you get every day. Have you ever cooked anything yourself?'

'Only when I had to, and then the results were not the best. However, my proudest culinary memory was cooking a dish of animal testicles on a Baby Belling in N'Zerokori.'

She grimaced.

'I thank the Lord my imagination can't conjure up that image.'

As they entered the flat, Aida was there to take their coats. 'You like tea, madam?'

'Perfect, thank you Aida.'

'There phone call for you, sir, at quarter past the hour of eleven o'clock. It a man called Farting. He say he call back in few minutes.'

'Thank you, Aida, I wonder what he wants?'

'Not trouble, I hope.'

Reggie was about to reply when the phone rang. He listened for a few minutes. 'That will be fine Inspector, see you then.' He turned to Sylvia, 'That was the man himself. He's been attending a meeting at Scotland Yard and wondered if it would be convenient to call round on his way home, to bring us up to date on the investigation. He'll be here at around two o'clock.'

Reggie showed Farthing into the living room. 'You are most welcome, Inspector. Can I entice you to partake in some refreshments – we finished our midday meal, but I know Aida had some left over. And it was particularly good, by the way; Philippine cocotte, lightly spiced, followed by homemade rhubarb crumble and crème Anglais. Unbeatable.'

'Thank you, sir, but no. I ate at the Yard before coming here.'

'A drink then.'

'Coffee would be nice.'

'Are you sure I can't tempt you to have a Scotch?'

Farthing shook his head. 'My workload, sir, is enormous at the moment so keeping a clear head is vital.'

'Ah yes,' Reggie said, 'Work is the curse of the drinking classes.'

Sylvia glared at him. 'On a more serious note, Inspector, I hope you have news on the case. It was reported that you'd arrested Reverend FitzPeter, and that Walter Plinge escaped from police custody.'

'You are right on both counts, Mrs Makepeace. It was most unfortunate about Plinge - the ensuing enquiry resulted in D S Clapp being summarily demoted – he's since taken early retirement. But returning to the case, it was, as we expected, Mr Grosvenor Smythe's aunt's murder that triggered off all the other deaths. It only proper that you are brought up to date with our investigation.'

'Thank you, Inspector,' Reggie reached for the whisky bottle.

Farthing took a tentative sip of coffee. 'First of all, I put my neck out on a limb for you, Grosvenor Smythe. I had to persuade the Chief Constable and the Home Secretary that what you did, using false credentials and lying left, right and centre, was justified in catching FitzPeter.'

'Very kind of you, old chap. But we got the job done, didn't we?'

'Indeed. Moving on, have you heard from, or do you know, the whereabouts of Miss Dogberry?'

'Not a damn word.'

Farthing thought for a moment. 'It's because we wonder if she knows that her biological father is almost certainly FitzPeter.

We conducted DNA tests on him and the late Felicity Fringe, Miss Dogberry's twin sister. These confirmed that they are father and daughter, and we assume Miss Dogberry's DNA will confirm the same relationship. FitzPeter himself, had no idea he'd impregnated Cressida Smythe, and was utterly devastated when informed that she'd given birth to twin girls – his twins; Felicity Fringe and Gertrude Dogberry.'

'Was he involved in all the murders?'

'Yes, all of them.'

'My God,' Reggie sighed.

'We believe it was he, himself, who murdered Miss Smythe. He's reluctant to actually admit that one. From the police point of view, it matters little.'

'So, he did the dirty-deed on Aunt Cressy - and he almost got away with it – only Walter Plinge let him down, and he is now on the loose.'

'Yes, that's right, sir, that and the post-mortem. FitzPeter used ex-inmates of Frankland Jail to carry out these evil deeds. He has given us the names of these individuals – some are already in jail after being convicted of other crimes. One is dead, and two are believed to be in hiding in Spain.'

'My God, so many. But why did he do it?'

Farthing frowned. 'Once he knew the size of Miss Smythe's estate, and that there were five beneficiaries named in her will, one of which was the church, he decided he wanted the lot. His plan to add a spire to rival Salisbury Cathedral, and extend the church premises for the benefit of the people of Ringwood. I've seen the plans.'

Sylvia looked puzzled, 'To the best of my knowledge, Salisbury Cathedral Spire is the tallest in the UK.'

'You are right, Mrs Makepeace, Salisbury is 404 feet tall, but FitzPeter's plan is for a 444 foot spire made from modern ultra-light materials and completely covered in solar panels. The electricity generated would illuminate half of Ringwood.'

Reggie rolled his eyes. 'Incredible.'

Farthing nodded. 'He justified the murders by pointing out that only nine people had died, compared to the numbers who died in the construction of all the major Cathedrals in the country. It seems hundreds died when St Pauls, Westminster Abbey, Salisbury Cathedral and others were built. It was pointed out that those that had died were not murdered – unlike in his case.'

'And what was his reaction to that?'

'Utter disdain. He thought that once completed, the result would bring truth, joy and justice to the peoples of Ringwood.'

'He's obviously mad,' Reggie said. 'But his delusion has nothing to do with justice. If it did, Jesus would have died of old age in his bed.'

Farthing wasn't sure what he meant. 'Anyway, sir, one thing of interest – in fact quite puzzling, was he expressed regret that suggested he was as disappointed as everyone else.'

'What in the blue-blazes does that mean?'

Farthing paused and checked his notes. 'When interviewed ... and these were his exact words, he said, *"I was deeply saddened that I ordered the deaths of nine people. I don't know what the world's coming to."*

'Oh my God,' Reggie laughed. 'Make of that what you will,'

'Indeed, sir. He also kept repeating *"The end justifies the means"* and what he would build would be to the glory of God.'

Sylvia shook her head. 'I believe Adolf Hitler used the same slogan, the end justifies the means, when he murdered millions of Jews,'

'Yes, you're right, Mrs Makepeace. So FitzPeter will be charged at Southampton Magistrate's Court on Monday 4th November. I assume he is in no doubt aware of *vigilantibus et non dormientibus jura subveniunt.*'

'Why, of course Inspector, In Ringwood they speak of little else.'

Farthing blinked with irritation. 'Yes, well. Both the counsels for the prosecution and defence think it will be unnecessary for either of you to give evidence. When presented with the facts, FitzPeter pleaded guilty to every charge. He believes in telling the truth, and nothing but … you get my meaning.'

After a long silence absorbing the unbelievable facts of FitzPeter's murderous campaign – his greed for money, Reggie said, 'Someone once said *"that only those who will risk going too far can possibly find out how far one can go"*.

Feeling more relaxed, Farthing continued. 'The church authorities have refused to accept any funds from Miss Smythe's will – for obvious reasons I believe. So Gertrude Dogberry will inherit the lot. Probate has been granted and all Ormrod and Ormrod's business, including Cressida Smythe's files, have been passed solicitors Whacket and Grubb in Fordingbridge. The fortune is ready for her to collect, subject naturally to proof of identity.'

'She is going to be one very wealthy young woman,' Reggie said. 'Now then, Inspector, we still don't know how FitzPeter's scheme – his plans that is, how it all unravelled.'

Chapter Fifty-Three

'Ah yes, the breakthrough was Jessica.'

'Who was she then?'

'Not a 'she' sir. As I said earlier, FitzPeter was Chaplain at Frankland High Security Jail in Durham.'

'Yes,' Sylvia confirmed. 'Before that, he'd been curate in Ringwood over thirty years ago, and had left under a cloud – womanising or even coveting,' she smiled using the biblical term. 'He obviously coveted Cressida which she kept very quiet about. FitzPeter only returned to Ringwood three years ago.'

'That's correct. According to the prison governor, FitzPeter was extremely popular with some of the inmates, even hardened criminals, and put a word in for them at parole hearings. In the jail, and due to popular demand, there was a series of cult films, shown time and time again called *The Spawn Universe*. Ever heard of it, sir?'

'Can't say that I have. Have you, darling?'

'No, never.'

'Well, the main character and principal killer, admired by the prisoners, was one Jessica Priest.'

'Ah.' Sylvia laughed, 'I understand. The killer in the film was called Jessica Priest and FitzPeter was a priest – hence giving him the nickname of Jessica.'

'Correct, Mrs Makepeace. So, when Walter Plinge, himself an ex-inmate of Frankland, said that Jessica had sent him to kill Miss Dogberry, he actually meant FitzPeter had sent him.'

'By my sainted aunt,' Sylvia exclaimed, 'Just to get his hands on all the money?'

'Yes. He was obsessed with getting the church roof renewed and also the spire and new church hall. A real obsession. The police doctor had him examined by a team of psychiatrists and, in their considered opinion, FitzPeter is the classic psychopath.'

'Really! A real-life Jekyll and Hyde. On the hairy edge between glory and madness.'

'Something like that, sir.' Farthing nodded. 'It seems that during a pastoral visit to Miss Smythe, she had told him in confidence about her windfall from the lottery. He was in desperate need of money to repair the church roof and the rest. But Miss Smythe's will stated the church would receive only ten percent of the estate, around seven hundred thousand. A substantial amount, but not enough to cover his ambitious plans. Hence his idea to kill off Miss Smythe and the other beneficiaries.'

'That's hard to believe.' Reggie poured himself another whisky.

'But Inspector,' Sylvia said, 'you told us earlier that Edgar Ormrod and Miss Pluck were blackmailing someone. What was that all about?'

Farthing nodded. 'That's right. Somehow or other, and I'm not sure how, Ormrod discovered FitzPeter's plan, and demanded half of the estate to keep his mouth shut.'

'So that's why Ormrod was killed. FitzPeter got rid of the blackmailer and Ormrod's ten percent went to increase the pot.'

'Yes, and he found out that Mrs Pluck was in on it to, so she had to be killed off.' Farthing rose to leave. 'I have a car outside to take me to Lyndhurst.'

Sylvia said, 'Thank you for giving us the information. It will take a bit of time to absorb it all, but at least there will be no more suspicious deaths.'

Reggie murmured to himself, 'Can we be certain of that?'

CHAPTER FIFTY-FOUR

'Good afternoon, madam, my name is Reginald Grosvenor Smythe and, in the company of the charming Mrs Makepeace, have a meeting scheduled with Mr Whacket for two thirty this afternoon.' Julia Totton was on the nameplate in front of her. Lowering his voice as if making a confession, Reggie added, 'You will note, Miss Totton, that we are fifteen minutes late due to there being far too many damn vehicles on the roads. We trust, however, that our late arrival hasn't inconvenienced Mr Whacket too greatly.'

'No, of course not,' she smiled. She used her phone to inform Mr Whacket of their arrival and then took them through to his office.

Alexander Whacket was a burly, medium-sized man, quite bald, except for a few traces of brown hair around his ears. He was smart, in a tailored navy pinstripe three-piece suit, and greeted them with firm handshakes.

'First of all, I would like to thank you both for coming today. We are talking about a considerable sum of money, and as I've not met the lady before, your presence as witnesses will give me much needed reassurance. Miss Gertrude Dogberry phoned earlier to say she would be here at three, so that would be ...' he looked at his watch, 'in around fifteen minutes.'

'We'll help where we can,' Reggie said, 'but neither of us knows her very well. She has been under a great deal of stress and in hiding since Cressida Smythe was murdered. You will, no doubt, have heard of Reverend Marmaduke FitzPeter and the numerous murders he organised with a group of villains.'

'Yes Indeed,' Whacket shook his head. 'One of the most shocking cases I've ever heard of, and the fact that Miss Smythe was killed for her inheritance – well, it's hard to believe. I also read the files kept by Edward Ormrod and, my-oh-my, what a devious web of lies, mis-directions and even blackmail he was involved in. If he hadn't been killed by that gangster, Walter Plinge, I'm sure he would have been charged with a multitude of crimes.'

'We thought as much,' Reggie said. 'D I Farthing gave us a condensed version of the sorry saga a little while ago.'

'And now, Miss Dogberry has made what is tantamount to the strangest request.'

Reggie and Sylvia looked puzzled. 'And what might that be?'

'Ah, you obviously don't know. She wants the full amount in cash.'

'In cash,' Reggie cried in disbelief. 'What, the whole seven million quid?'

'Oh, it's not that much. The accountants had a fair old tussle with HMRC, and the result is that she receives net of taxes, four million, one hundred and twenty-four pounds – the rest goes in inheritance tax; just over three million.'

'Great Gods of Albion,' Reggie gasped. 'I'd forgotten all about the ruddy tax man. Over three million in death duties – that's ridiculous.'

'It's the law, Reggie,' Sylvia said. 'But nevertheless, it's a lot of money. So, Gertrude only gets four million. Oh dear, how will the poor girl cope – does she know that?'

'Oh yes,' Whacket confirmed. 'She knew it would happen.'

'But you say she wants it in cash,' Reggie said. 'Why? She'll probably have the lot snatched the minute she leaves here.'

'My thoughts exactly,' Whacket nodded. 'I strongly advised her against it, but she insists and legally I'm obliged to do as she instructs. She says she's bringing an armed bodyguard with her – an expert with police training.'

'Really,' Sylvia raised her eyebrows. 'So, she must be expecting trouble.'

'Do you have the cash here?' Reggie asked.

'Yes, it's all in there.' He pointed to a large steel safe behind his desk. 'I even had to take out extra insurance.'

The phone rang. Whacket listened for a second. 'Send them in please, Julia.'

Gertrude Dogberry entered, stopping short when she saw Reggie and Sylvia. She scowled, 'What are you doing here?'

'They're here because I asked them to come,' Whacket said curtly. 'They know you and I don't. It was for my reassurance as well as yours.'

A man, chewing gum, followed Gertrude into the room.

'By the Saints of Hengis,' Reggie exclaimed. 'D S Clapp, what on earth are you doing here?'

Smirking, he used his thick rubbery lips to manoeuvre gum around his mouth. 'It's plain Mr Clapp if you must know. I resigned from the police service and I'm here to protect Gertrude.'

Reggie turned to Whacket. 'I wasn't expecting this. You see this fellow Clapp here, he was the detective sergeant initially in charge of investigating the murder of Miss Smythe. I'm guessing Clapp, that you found Gertrude early in the investigation without revealing it to anyone, including your inspector.'

Clapp's smirk grew bigger. 'I'm saying nothing, mate,' and took Gertrude's hand. They smiled at each other.

Gertrude laughed. 'How do you think I knew what was going on all the time? Dorian kept me informed of everything that was happening while keeping me safe.'

Sylvia looked outraged. 'But you pretended not to know who was involved.'

Gertrude laughed again. 'Pretend, pretend, blah blah. I had you two fooled from the start.'

'But you may have broken the law.'

'How have we?' Gertrude said with a malicious glare.

'Because we haven't done any such thing,' Clapp added. 'I should know. We have been very careful not to infringe the law.'

'So, there you are,' Gertrude said bluntly. 'Now, Mr Whacket, can we get a move on? Dorian and I have a plane to catch. Where's the money?'

'I have it all here in the safe, but there are papers to sign and witness.'

Reggie and Sylvia were fuming, after all they had done for her. Clapp stood close behind Gertrude as they completed the documentation. Whacket took his time to double check that the papers she had brought confirmed her identity and that all the paperwork was correct to safely hand over the money.

'Everything seems to be in order,' Whacket sighed, as though he was hoping for errors. 'Now Miss Dogberry, it is my duty to ask you once again to reconsider your demand for your inheritance to be in cash.'

'No, I want it all in notes, and the reason why is none of your business, is it Dorian?'

'No, it's not,' Clapp hissed. 'Hand the cash over now.'

Shrugging his shoulders in despair, Whacket went to the safe and entered the combination code. Pulling the handle, the massive door opened with a whoosh. At that moment Gertrude pressed two digits on her mobile phone.

The moment's silence was suddenly broken by a startled cry coming from reception, and what sounded like a cupboard crashing to the floor. The door burst open. A man, holding Miss Totton with an arm around her neck, held a gun to her head.

Everyone in the room stood transfixed. 'What the ... how dare ...' Whacket spluttered, 'What are you doing?'

'My God,' Reggie bellowed, 'It's Walter Plinge – the murderer, Walter Plinge. What in the blue blazes are you doing? Release Miss Totton immediately.'

It seemed everyone shouted at once until Plinge yelled at the top of his voice, 'Shut up all of you.'

Clapp gave the broadest of smiles. 'Perfect timing, Walter. The lolly's ready for taking.'

Open mouthed, Gertrude glared at Clapp. 'What do you mean? You're working for me – I'm paying you.'

'You silly bitch,' Clapp sneered. 'Did you really believe you could pay me off with a measly hundred thou? Walter and I will share the lot between us – two million each. Why do you think I helped him escape in the first place?'

'So you planned this,' Reggie was almost speechless. 'You utter bounder, joining forces with a murderer.'

'I'm not so dumb after all, am I, Mr Grosvenor bloody Smythe and your soddin' OBE?' Clapp gave a wicked grin. 'Who's the fool now then?'

Still holding Julia Totton round the neck, Plinge ordered Whacket to take the case containing the money and give it to Clapp.

Whacket took a deep breath. 'This is armed robbery.'

'Oh, clever you.' Plinge still had a gun at Julia Totton's head. 'I'll count to three – pass the money over or she gets a hole in her head.'

Whacket wisely decided not to take any chances. 'Let Julia go, and I'll do as you say.'

Remaining quiet, Reggie was trying to think what he could do. When Plinge roughly pushed the sobbing Julia Totton away, Whacket and Sylvia rushed to her aid. Reggie, his dander well and truly at boiling point, took the opportunity to gradually sidle in the gunman's direction, trying not to be noticed..

Gertrude noted Reggie's movement and knew a distraction could help. She plucked up courage, glaring at Plinge. 'You're not getting my money, and you're not going to use that gun – it probably isn't even loaded.'

'Don't mess me around, Dearie. It's a fuckin' gun and it's fuckin' loaded. Remember, I'm a fuckin' killer, so I'm happy to bump a few more off, especially the bastard, Grosvenor Smythe – I've got a bloody big bone to pick with that fucker.'

'Don't be silly,' Sylvia shouted, as she also guessed what Reggie was up to. 'You won't shoot that thing.'

'Oh really,' Plinge grinned. 'I'll show you.' Looking round, he said, 'I'll check out the toughness of the safe – a bit of target practice,' he grinned. Aiming the gun at the safe, he pulled the trigger.

The noise deafened all of them. The air inside the room seemed to expand and left them feeling as if their ears had been plugged by cotton wool. They all stood stock-still, blinking as several years of dust was released. Everyone, that is, except Reggie. He quickly sprang a couple of yards, bringing his silver-topped cane down with a whack on Plinge's gun hand, followed immediately by crashing it on his head. The gun dropped to the floor.

Clapp, showing his true colours as a wimp, didn't move.

Plinge groaned. 'You broke me fuckin' wrist.'

Reggie picked up the gun. 'Sylvia, go with Miss Totton and bring me some tape, and we'll bind these two cretins until the police arrive.' Keeping the gun pointing at Plinge and Clapp, he asked, 'Is everyone else all alright?'

They all said they were, save one. The one who remained silent was Gertrude Dogberry, who, with a groan, slowly slipped to the floor, blood pouring from the front of her blouse. The bullet fired by Plinge, had ricocheted off the safe door hitting her full in the chest.

Sylvia rushed to help but it was too late. Gertrude Dogberry was dead.

EPILOGUE

It was several months before the dust finally settled following the events in Whacket and Grubb's offices in Fordingbridge. Both Ringwood and Fordingbridge were overrun by local, national and international media organisations describing it as the crime of the century.

At separate trials, FitzPeter was sentenced to life imprisonment, with a minimum tariff of 30 years before possible parole, Walter Plinge was sentenced to life imprisonment, with a minimum tariff of 20 years before possible parole. The lesser sentence for Plinge took in the fact that (a) he had been manipulated by FitzPeter in carrying out the killings, and (b) he had a mental age of sixteen. Mr Dorian Clapp, a retired police detective sergeant, was found guilty of aiding and abetting a known murderer and was sentenced to five years in custody.

Gertrude Dogberry had died intestate, and Reggie requested Alexander Whacket to obtain probate under the Intestacy Rules from the Registry for the Grant of Administration. Advertisements were duly placed in the appropriate journals asking for any relation of Gertrude Dogberry to register an interest, but none was forthcoming. As her only known relation, the total value of Gertrude Dogberry's estate amounting to four million, one hundred and ten pounds was transferred into Reggie's bank account.

Reggie, not wanting personally to benefit from this inheritance, paid for the repair of the Ringwood Church roof to be completed, as well as improving the building's insulation and installing a new, efficient heating system. He also paid for a suitably worded plaque to be mounted on the church wall adjacent to the pew where Miss Cressida Smythe regularly sat, honouring her devotion to the church and her posthumous funding of all the work carried out. The money left over was given to charities.

Two months after the work was completed, Reginald Grosvenor Smythe married Sylvia Alexis Makepeace at Ham Parish Church near Kingston upon Thames. Amongst the guests were Chester Makepeace and his new lady friend, Ringaile Nauseda, Mr Lee su wan and Mrs fal Kim, the Moores of Bray with Joe Cardiff, the newly promoted Chief Inspector Farthing, Pam and friend from Sainsbury's and representatives from Greyfriars Community Centre of Ringwood.

All's well that ends well.

THE END.

Milton Keynes UK
Ingram Content Group UK Ltd.
UKHW010625121023
430452UK00001B/6